D1265760

THE SCOTTISH INVENTION OF
ENGLISH LITERATURE

The Scottish invention of English Literature explores the origins of the teaching of English Literature in the academy. An international team of contributors demonstrate how the subject began in eighteenth-century Scottish universities before being exported to America, Canada, India, Australia, New Zealand and, indeed, England. The emergence of English as an institutionalized university subject was linked to the search for distinctive cultural identities throughout the English-speaking world. This book explores the role the discipline played in administering restraints on the expression of indigenous literary forms, and shows how the growing professionalization of English as a subject offered a breeding ground for academics and writers with an interest in native identity and cultural nationalism. *The Scottish invention of English Literature* is a comprehensive account of the historical origins of the university subject of English Literature and provides a wealth of new material on its particular Scottish provenance.

Robert Crawford is Professor of Modern Scottish Literature at St Andrews University.

THE SCOTTISH
INVENTION OF ENGLISH
LITERATURE

EDITED BY

ROBERT CRAWFORD

CAMBRIDGE
UNIVERSITY PRESS

PUBLISHED BY THE PRESS SYNDICATE OF THE UNIVERSITY OF CAMBRIDGE
The Pitt Building, Trumpington Street, Cambridge CB2 1RP, United Kingdom

CAMBRIDGE UNIVERSITY PRESS
The Edinburgh Building, Cambridge CB2 2RU, United Kingdom
40 West 20th Street, New York, NY 10011–4211, USA
10 Stamford Road, Oakleigh, Melbourne 3166, Australia

© Cambridge University Press 1998

This book is in copyright. Subject to statutory exception and to the provisions
of relevant collective licensing agreements, no reproduction of any part may
take place without the written permission of Cambridge University Press.

First published 1998

Printed in the United Kingdom at the University Press, Cambridge

Typeset in Baskerville (MT) 11/12½pt in QuarkXPress™   [GC]

A catalogue record for this book is available from the British Library

Library of Congress cataloguing in publication data

The Scottish invention of English Literature / editor, Robert Crawford.
p.   cm.
Includes index.
ISBN 0 521 59038 8 (hardback)
1. English literature – Study and teaching (Higher) – Scotland –
History.   2. English literature – Study and teaching (Higher) –
English-speaking countries – History.   3. English literature –
History and criticism – Theory, etc.   4. Education, Higher –
Scotland – History.   5. Scotland – Intellectual life.   6. Literary
form.   I. Crawford, Robert, 1959– .
PR51.S36S36 1998
820'. 71'1411 – dc21   97-27464   CIP

ISBN 0 521 59038 8 hardback

PR
51
.S36
S36
1998

in memory of
Robert Alexander Nelson Crawford
1914–1997
with gratitude

Contents

Notes on contributors

PAUL G. BATOR's articles on eighteenth-century rhetoric have appeared in *Eighteenth-Century Studies, Rhetorica*, and other journals. He is Lecturer in English at Stanford University, California.

FRANKLIN E. COURT is author of *Institutionalizing English Literature* (Stanford University Press, 1992). He is Professor of English at Northern Illinois University.

ROBERT CRAWFORD's books include *Devolving English Literature* (Clarendon Press, 1992). His most recent collection of poems is *Masculinity* (Cape, 1996). He is Professor of Modern Scottish Literature at the University of St Andrews.

RAJIT S. DOSANJH, a graduate of Stanford University, is a British Marshall Scholar at Edinburgh University completing a doctoral thesis which compares depictions of religious extremism in nineteenth-century Scottish fiction with discussions of justice in Enlightenment moral philosophy.

IAN DUNCAN is author of *Modern Romance and Transformations of the Novel: The Gothic, Scott, Dickens* (Cambridge University Press, 1992). He is Barbara and Carlisle Moore Professor of English at the University of Oregon.

LINDA FERREIRA-BUCKLEY is author of *On the Origins of English Studies: The Influence of Rhetoric in Victorian England* (forthcoming from University of Pittsburgh Press). She is Associate Professor of English at the University of Texas at Austin.

ANDREW HOOK's books include *Scotland and America: A Study of Cultural Relations 1750–1835* (Blackie, 1975) and he is co-editor with Richard B. Sher of *The Glasgow Enlightenment* (Tuckwell Press, 1995). He is Bradley Professor of English Literature at the University of Glasgow.

MARTIN MOONIE is a Pirie-Reid Scholar at Somerville College, Oxford, completing a thesis on print culture in the Scottish Enlightenment. He is writing a biography of Alexander Donaldson for the History of the Book in Scotland project, and is one of the organisers of the History of the Book at Oxford website.

JOAN H. PITTOCK is author of *The Ascendancy of Taste* (Routledge and Kegan Paul, 1973), and founder editor of the *Journal of the British Society for Eighteenth-Century Studies*. She is an Honorary Research Fellow in English, University of Aberdeen.

NEIL RHODES is author of *Elizabethan Grotesque* (Routledge and Kegan Paul, 1980) and *The Power of Eloquence and English Renaissance Literature* (Harvester, 1992). He is Reader in English Renaissance Literature at the University of St Andrews.

FIONA STAFFORD is author of *The Sublime Savage: James Macpherson and the Poems of Ossian* (Edinburgh University Press, 1988) and of *The Last of the Race: The Growth of a Myth from Milton to Darwin* (Clarendon Press, 1994). She is Fellow and Tutor in English at Somerville College, Oxford.

CHRIS WORTH is co-editor of *Postmodern Conditions* (Berg, 1990), and author of articles on Scott. He is a Senior Lecturer in English at Monash University, Melbourne, where he also directs the Centre for Comparative Literature and Cultural Studies.

Acknowledgements

As editor, I wish to thank the School of English, University of St Andrews, St Leonard's College (University of St Andrews), and the Folger Institute, Washington, for supporting the 1995 St Andrews symposium on 'The Scottish Invention of English Literature' which allowed many of the contributors to this volume to meet and discuss their ideas. At Cambridge University Press Mr Ray Ryan, who commissioned the book, has been a staunch supporter of the project. In St Andrews Professor Douglas Dunn and my other colleagues in the School of English, both academic and secretarial, have provided valuable continuing support. Also in St Andrews Professor John Guy deserves thanks for making possible contact with the Folger Institute through St Andrews becoming the first European member of the Folger universities consortium; in Washington Dr Lena Orlin and Ms Amy Adler were trusting, helpful and generous. As the project grew, it gained immeasurably from the willingness of other scholars to share their thoughts and material. I wish to thank in particular Professor Thomas Miller of the University of Arizona for making available a copy of the typescript of his forthcoming book *The Formation of College English*. Librarians in the manuscript and special collections departments at the libraries of the universities of St Andrews, Glasgow, Aberdeen and Edinburgh, as well as at the National Library of Scotland, the Bodleian Library, Oxford, the universities of Texas at Austin, Northern Illinois, Yale, Oregon and Wisconsin, Monash and Melbourne were unfailingly helpful. Without them, the book would not exist. For help with footnotes, I wish to thank Martin Moonie; for the index, I am in the debt of Valerie A. Elliston; and for copy-editing, I would like to thank Kay McKechnie of Cambridge University Press.

I am one of many, many students who owe a debt to Professor John C. Bryce of the University of Glasgow, not only for his edition of Adam Smith's *Lectures on Rhetoric and Belles Lettres*, but also for the way he would wander far from his script to speak about the professors whose portraits hung round the walls of the Glasgow lecture theatre. I hope he enjoys this book.

Ultimately, my greatest debt is to my wife, Alice, who brought our daughter into the world during the period of this book's composition, and whose love and courage did not fail. Thank you.

RC, St Andrews

Introduction

Robert Crawford

This book is about the early emergence of English literary study in
the universities, and about the consequences of its growth there. Such
history and consequences matter to present and future debates about
the global subject of 'English'. The book offers not an exhaustive history
or geography, but widely resonant examples. A close initial focus on the
university development of the subject in eighteenth-century Scotland
makes possible a more detailed and provocative primary examination of
university 'Rhetoric and Belles Lettres' than exists to date. It also avoids
repeating available work on such areas as the Dissenting academies and
other non-university institutions. Readers more familiar with the culture
of England may be struck by linguistic and other parallels between the
Scots and the 'provincials' of the English regions. Yet Scotland has a
national history and national institutions in such areas as church, law
and education which give it a distinctive inflection that is more than
regional. This means, for instance, that in the eighteenth century in
the area of Rhetorical teaching the practice in the ancient universities
north of the border was significantly different from that in the ancient
universities of England. In England the teaching of English literary
texts develops most fully in institutions which are 'dissenting' or otherwise alternatives to the universities, whereas in Scotland such teaching
is from its origins part of the university mainstream. So it is that English
Literature as a university subject is a Scottish invention. Attentive to
the nuances of Scottish culture, this book's contributors demonstrate
such a proposition and develop its implications. Later chapters on the
impact made by this Scottish-developed university subject as it was
exported and renamed 'English' offer the fullest available treatment of
the international spread of a discipline whose impact has conditioned
the writing and reading of literature throughout the world.

The best-known accounts of the development of university English, such as those by Baldick, Eagleton and Graff, downplay or ignore

eighteenth-century Scotland and assume that the middle or concluding years of the nineteenth century in England and America witnessed the subject's birth.[1] This book contests, complicates and in important ways overthrows that assumption. It is attuned to, and builds on, such works as the present editor's *Devolving English Literature* (1992), Franklin Court's *Institutionalizing English Literature* (1992), Winifred Bryan Horner's *Nineteenth-Century Scottish Rhetoric: The American Connection* (1993) and Thomas Miller's *The Formation of College English* (1997), but surpasses these volumes in range and detail.[2] Not least, it indicates how crucial to the origins of the university discipline were issues of perceived marginality in space, gender and genre. So, as well as examining the development of university English in Scotland, America, England and Australasia, this book presents such surprising topics as the nineteenth-century Scottish invention of American Studies; as well as involving the genre of poetry, this volume identifies the emergence of that new and marginal genre, the novel, as a subject within university English; attending not only to the Glasgow of Adam Smith and the Edinburgh of Hugh Blair, chapters rediscover the marginalized sexuality of William Greenfield, and the prominence of the northern 'fringe' universities of Aberdeen and St Andrews as launch sites of the new discipline. Previous studies have realized neither the early date at which this subject appears on the academic horizon in the Scottish universities, nor the extent to which it grows in those often considered as being on the cultural margins. A spirit of empowering marginality presides over much of this book, informing not least the investigations and argument of its Introduction.

In November 1720 the University of St Andrews in Fife on the beautiful North Sea coast of Scotland drew up regulations for the first university Chair of Eloquence in the English-speaking world. St Andrews, founded in 1411, is the oldest of Scotland's medieval universities. Though a major northern European site of medieval pilgrimage and learning, as well as a key location of the Protestant Reformation, St Andrews by the eighteenth century was an isolated country town with a shrinking university. It was also having to come to terms with its marginality in a Scotland whose major urban centres lay to the south and whose parliamentary government had shifted to Westminster with the controversial Act of Union in 1707. The proposed Chair of Eloquence should be viewed in this context. Discussions about the chair's regulations continued throughout November and December 1720, with senior members of the university making various amendments to the draft drawn up by an internal committee.[3] The title of this 'Profession of Eloquence' would appear to have been based on French precedents. In Paris Charles Rollin was at the time 'Professeur d'Eloquence au Collège Roial, et associe à l'Académie Roiale des Inscriptions et Belles-Lettres'.[4] It was while he was a professor of Eloquence that Rollin wrote his lectures on the study of the belles lettres. The terms 'eloquence' and 'belles lettres' have been seen by Adam Potkay as significantly at variance, but for Rollin they went together, and in the context of eighteenth-century Scotland they were linked by the fact both might be applied to work in modern English.[5] Recent investigations by Richard Terry suggest that the conceptual space we now denote by the word 'literature' was being marked out by the phrase 'belles lettres' from its invention by René Rapin in the late seventeenth century.[6] Terry's work reinforces this book's evidence for the fact that when we talk about eighteenth-century Scottish universities' 'Rhetoric and Belles Lettres' and nineteenth-century university classes in 'English Literature' we are talking about one evolving subject.

Certainly in early eighteenth-century Scotland the title 'Professor of the Belles Lettres' was not unfamiliar. In 1708 the author of the first full-scale biographical account of Scottish authors, George MacKenzie, in the 1708 volume of his ambitious *Lives and Characters of the Most Eminent Writers of the Scots Nation* (1708–22) uses it of more than a dozen Scots of the fifteenth, sixteenth and seventeenth centuries.[7] MacKenzie deploys the title 'Professor of the Belles Lettres' loosely, to include schoolteachers, advocates and literary intellectuals based in Britain and continental Europe. None of these figures, however, held that title at a British university. The proposal for the St Andrews chair marks an important institutional milestone. For this is the first time in an English-speaking university that we encounter mention of a chair in the subject that will become English Literature.

The chair was to be funded by a wealthy patron of the arts and Fellow of the Royal Society, James Brydges, Duke of Chandos, but it appears that it was his son's tutor, Dr Charles Stuart, who was particularly keen to see a Chair of Eloquence established at St Andrews. A Fellow of Gresham College (a London foundation for public lectures which elected its thirteenth Professor of Rhetoric in 1720), Stuart was a Scot in his mid thirties who had studied medicine at Leyden, travelled in Europe as tutor to a Scottish aristocrat (in 1717 he was at Padua with the son of the Earl of Galloway), and become a Fellow of the Royal Society in 1719. More immediately, he had been in St Andrews in the

summer of 1720 when the university had given him an honorary degree.
Stuart was accompanying the sons of Lord Chandos, one of whom
had got into trouble and been handsomely treated by the university
with whose Professor of Greek, Francis Pringle, Stuart was on friendly
terms.[8] Stuart appears to have advised the Duke of Chandos about an
appropriate subject for a professorship at St Andrews, and it was Stuart
who wrote in late 1720 to inform the university that the Duke wished
to endow a Chair of Eloquence there.

When the university requested a Chair of Medicine rather than
Eloquence, it was Stuart, not the Duke, who showed annoyance. The
debate among the university's senior members led to Francis Pringle
and one of his colleagues, James Duncan, taking the unusual step of
recording formal objections to the carrying of a motion to send the
Duke not the Chair of Eloquence proposals, but only those for Medicine.
The university suggested that none of their number seemed suited to
fill a Chair of Eloquence, and that 'where to meet with a lucky stranger
we yet know not'.[9] Stuart replied, claiming to be impartial, but making
it clear that the subject of Eloquence had been carefully selected, and
going so far as to suggest that the chair be filled by his friend Pringle
or by the distinguished grammarian, Thomas Ruddiman, author of the
Rudiments of the Latin Tongue (1714), and at that time Under-keeper of the
Library of the Faculty of Advocates in Edinburgh. Stuart's letter is
worth quoting in particular for its implication that in helping establish
a Chair of Eloquence at St Andrews he will be doing Scotland a
special service. After detailing arguments against establishing a Chair
of Medicine or of Civil History, he continues:

... these reasons determined the choice in favours of Eloquence, as to which
I must beg leave to say that the reason you give against it, namly the difficulty
of finding a person qualify'd for it, seems to me rather to be a good argument
for the necessity of such a Profession at this time in our country than a solid
reason against it; but I hope it is not quite so bad with us as you imagine. I'm
sure I know one in your own University very capable of it, nor do I see how
it is inconsistent with the Profession he already holds, or if he shou'd not care
to accept of it I'll take upon me to name another who in my opinion wou'd
be an ornament to any University in Europe, for I know he is reckon'd by
very good judges to be one of the best Grammarians now alive, the person
I mean is Mr. Rudiment, keeper of the Advocats' Library ...

Stuart contends that his letter is prompted by 'the earnest desire to see
useful learning flourish in my country'.[10] His tone is not simply pet-
ulant. It shows how strongly he thought that in this period so soon after

the Union of 1707, when the Scots were under considerable pressure to accommodate themselves to, or at least engage with, English cultural and linguistic norms, the establishment of a Chair of Eloquence would be a service to 'our country'. Such a conviction again informs a letter from Stuart to Pringle in which he attacks the university's decision not to press ahead with the Chair of Eloquence and complains that the university is throwing away the Duke's money, 'and this is not my opinion only, but the opinion of every one I have convers'd with in this country on the subject, whither English or Scots'.[11]

In suggesting that the Chair of Eloquence might be filled either by Ruddiman or by 'one in your own University very capable of it', Stuart appears to have in mind his friend Pringle, a man interested not only in classical culture but also in Scottish literature; Pringle was one of the early subscribers to MacKenzie's *Writers of the Scots Nation*, for instance, though he was also very committed to the ideal of British union, and anxious to further it.[12] A clear indication of this, and of the awkward position of many eighteenth-century Scots towards their cultural heritage, is his caution that though the Scottish history by George Buchanan is 'preferible to some of the Romans themselves . . . in Stile, yet I would not advise to put him in the hands of Our Scotch Youth, while at School, now there is an union between the two Kingdoms, for fear of awakening the Old Natural grudge, that should now be . . . industriously forgotten'.[13] Pringle's literary teaching was governed by the political considerations of British unionism. For a chair of Eloquence Thomas Ruddiman was an even more interesting choice. As well as having authored a work on Latin grammar which Pringle considered 'the compleatest of [its] kind', by 1720 'the Learned Thomas Ruddiman' had distinguished himself by his work on editions of older Scottish writers, including the St Andrews graduates George Buchanan and Gavin Douglas, first translator of the *Aeneid* into a European vernacular, for whose epic translation Ruddiman produced the first 'Dictionary of the old Scottish Language'. Ruddiman's work as editor and later as publisher reinforced the prestige of Scottish Latinists and encouraged a younger generation of writers in Scots such as Allan Ramsay (whose *Poems* he published in 1721), though Ruddiman's own writings were not in Scots but in English and he had a pronounced passion for 'correctness'.[14] This combination of interests, not least his commitment to correctness and to English as the language of modern educated discourse in Scotland, made Ruddiman a suitable candidate for Dr Stuart to propose for the St Andrews Chair of Eloquence.

Stuart was clearly anxious about the state of 'eloquence' in Scotland. The subject, as taught by Rollin, whose *De la manière d'enseigner et d'étudier les belles-lettres* was published in Paris in 1726–8, was one including both public speaking and literary composition. The title page of the 1734 English translation of this work made clear its usefulness as 'An Introduction to Languages, Poetry, Rhetoric, History, Moral Philosophy, Physics, etc., with Reflections on Taste, and Instructions with regard to the Eloquence of the Pulpit, the Bar, and the Stage, the Whole Illustrated with Passages from the most famous Poets and Orators, ancient and modern, with Critical Remarks on them, Designed more particularly for Students in the Universities'. Written in the correct modern French vernacular, and including examples from modern writers, Rollin's work on eloquence was very different from the *Praelectiones Poeticae* delivered by Joseph Trapp, who became Oxford's first Professor of Poetry in 1708, lecturing in Latin largely on classical subjects. Rollin's work offered a guide for aspiring students whose future professional careers would require public speaking and literary composition. This was the modern subject of Eloquence which Stuart sought to develop in Scotland. It might be connected to the familiar Latin study of Rhetoric, which presumably led to the St Andrews academics considering the putative chair as one of 'Rhetoric & Eloquence', but its French antecedents had ensured a strong connection with modern, educated vernacular discourse, both spoken and written.[15]

If St Andrews academics of the early 1720s voted down a Chair of Eloquence, there is strong evidence that their students were eager for instruction in the subject. Library records from the succeeding decades show constant heavy borrowing of the *Spectator*, the text which would be so often recommended as a model of good English style by university teachers of Belles Lettres in the mid century.[16] We can see interest too from the 1730s in such works as Wagstaff's *Polite Conversation*, and when the second (1737) edition of the English translation of Rollin's *Method of Teaching and Studying the Belles Lettres* entered the St Andrews University library it was borrowed repeatedly, with a hundred recorded borrowings of volumes of the work in the decade 1741–50. Borrowings increased substantially towards the end of this period, when the academic population of the university was small, with between five and twenty students matriculating each year.[17] Probably the high level of borrowing was prompted not only by students' desire for 'improvement' but also because students were directed to Rollin by their teachers, men such as Henry Rymer, from 1709 a professor of Philosophy at St Andrews, and from 1747–56 the first person to hold the title of Professor of Logic, Rhetoric and Metaphysics there. Some students borrowed only one or two volumes of Rollin's *Belles Lettres*; others borrowed all four volumes one by one. Among these in the 1740s was Robert Watson, who would be appointed in the next decade to the professorship of Logic, Rhetoric and Metaphysics at the university, becoming one of the first university teachers of the new Rhetoric in English. As a regular reader of Pope, Addison and the *Spectator*, as well as a reader of Rollin and a sampler of the university library's selection of novels (he borrowed *Moll Flanders* in 1745), Watson was fairly typical in his borrowings; he was formed by the St Andrews academic culture of the 1740s, though only in the following decade did he become a university teacher of Belles Lettres.

While St Andrews was the first university to consider having a Chair of Eloquence, and was one of the universities in which the critical study of modern English-language texts developed, what happened there should be seen in terms of a much wider Scottish ambition to engage with metropolitan England on its own cultural ground. This encouraged pro-Union Scots such as Adam Smith at Glasgow University, Robert Watson at St Andrews, Hugh Blair at Edinburgh and many others beyond academia to design courses promoting the writing and speaking of 'correct' metropolitan-oriented English rather than Scots or 'impure' Scoticized English.[18] For these Scots a fully British ethos would be developed only if many of the cultural and linguistic differences between England and Scotland were abolished; though they were often proudly Scottish, they saw future Scottish prosperity as British in nature. To make Britain work the Scots needed to develop access to the markets of England's colonies; they wanted to speak persuasively in the British Houses of Parliament; to be taken seriously many Scots aimed to rid themselves of linguistic markers of cultural difference (not least the notorious 'Scotticisms') which identified them as coarse outsiders, and to refine their language, assimilating it to polite, Anglocentric, *Spectator*-like metropolitan norms. One might argue (as Fiona Stafford does in the present volume) that such assimilation was a matter less of internal colonialism than of the Scots gaining clarity in their communications, yet it is hard to deny that issues of cultural politics were involved. If, today, English writers were made to use American spelling and diction for the sake of global clarity, then many in England might feel a heightened sense of cultural imperialism.

To improve commercial, professional and cultural exchange what was needed was mastery of the medium of communication used at the centre of British power. Earnestly recorded by his Scottish biographer, Doctor Johnson famously quipped that 'the noblest prospect which a Scotchman ever sees, is the high road that leads him to England!'[19] For many Scots like Boswell the linguistic and literary equivalent of that high road was a university course in the new Rhetoric and Belles Lettres. In England, where there were still only two universities, the subject was given formal institutional recognition in the Dissenting academies which, as their name suggests, were alternatives to the Oxford and Cambridge university mainstream.[20] In Scotland, though, where there were universities in St Andrews, Glasgow, Aberdeen and Edinburgh, the new subject was installed at the very heart of the mainstream university culture as part of a project that may be seen in part at least as a kind of internal colonialism in which Scots schooled other Scots to conform to an Anglocentric norm in order to advance in Britain and the British Empire. They did so from patriotic motives, believing that Scotland's future lay with a Britain and an empire whose language of educated discourse had to be not Scots, not Latin, and certainly not Gaelic, but correct, metropolitan English.

If the London of the court and parliament, and the English universities of Oxford and Cambridge were the centres of correct, metropolitan English, then the Scots, like the members of the English Dissenting academies and like the Irish were in important ways distanced from the centre of cultural authority. This distancing was not simply a matter of physical geography; it was also a matter of cultural and, particularly, linguistic space. In an age preoccupied with ideas of correctness and regularity Scotticisms were seen as consigning their users to the margins. Those who needed to make the most effort to educate themselves in 'correct' English usage through the study of texts in which such usage was displayed were the people on the fringe of the geography of power – whether margins of class, province or nationality. That is why the university subject of English Literature has its origins in sites far from London, Oxford and Cambridge.

Scottish universities were both central and peripheral. Aberdeen and St Andrews were at a remove from the growing urban areas of Glasgow and Edinburgh, yet all were central to the educational and cultural mainstream of their nation: Scotland; equally, after 1707 all were peripheral in terms of their state: Britain. Nevertheless, being part of an independent educational system in some ways more developed than that of England, allowed the Scots to nurture in their universities the new subject of Rhetoric and Belles Lettres, and to export it – first of all to other margins of the English-speaking world, such as America and India; then, later, as the education of those marginalized within England itself became more of a political and academic issue, the subject was exported to English universities, particularly University College London, where, along with the influence of Dissenting academies, it shaped English literary studies. Recently Thomas Miller has made clear the part played by Trinity College, Dublin, while contending that 'the Scots were the first to introduce formal studies of English literature into the university curriculum'.[21] Individual chapters of this book examine the stages of this process first of all within the Scottish universities themselves, and later within universities beyond Scotland. Frequently the subject was bound up with colonial expansion and the 'taming', controlling, or 'refining' of people on those margins, as well as with the championing not only of Anglocentric literary correctness but also, in some cases, of works of local origin which were seen as fit to hold their own alongside works from the assumed English cultural centre. The chapters which follow examine new aspects of the material treated. Cumulatively they supply a comprehensive new narrative for understanding the origins and development of the university study of English.

Among the opening chapters are detailed considerations of the increasingly well known courses on Rhetoric and Belles Lettres delivered by Adam Smith and Hugh Blair at Glasgow and Edinburgh universities. Yet here I concentrate on St Andrews University for three reasons: firstly, because the debates over the establishment of the St Andrews Chair of Eloquence provide an appropriate starting point for the study of the development of the new subject in Scottish universities; secondly, because the developments in St Andrews have been all but totally ignored by modern commentators; and thirdly, because the empowering marginality of St Andrews and the links between the teaching of English literary texts there and the process of colonization make it a striking example of what this book is about.

After Adam Smith took up his Glasgow University Chair of Logic in 1751 he gave up his 'improving' public lectures on Rhetoric in the Scottish capital, which were taken over by Robert Watson.[22] Yet, though Watson may have spent some time in both Edinburgh and Glasgow, his signed records of borrowings from St Andrews University library show that he was frequently in St Andrews and its university throughout the late 1740s and 1750s. Watson was then training to be a Church of Scotland minister, and reading many theological works. Though scholars have tended to assume that we cannot be certain exactly when between 1751 and 1756 he was delivering his Edinburgh public lectures, an entry in *The Scots Magazine* records that these were given by Watson in the winter of 1755–56 (immediately before Watson accepted his chair at St Andrews) and met with 'great approbation'.[23] Throughout this period Watson was reading intensively in the areas of literature and criticism as well.

In May and June 1750, for instance, Watson was borrowing Pope's *Essay on Criticism*, Quintilian's *De Institutione Oratoria*, and Rollin on the Belles Lettres. Rollin, Aristotle, Locke, Addison, Cicero's *De Oratore* and Shaftesbury's *Characteristics* he borrowed more than once in the early 1750s. All these works underpin his lectures. Though theology dominates his St Andrews borrowings in the early 1750s, from the start of 1754 until 1757 his borrowings indicate that he worked intensively on developing the Rhetoric lectures, reading and rereading Tacitus, Demosthenes, Euripides, Pindar (in West's translation), Aristotle, Terence and Aristophanes among classical authors. Among modern works Watson borrowed in this period were writings by Addison, Shaftesbury's *Characteristics*, Molière, Locke (including the *Essay concerning Human Understanding*), Pope (including the *Dunciad Variorum*), Gay's *Fables* and Allan Ramsay's poetry. These were supplemented by modern critical and philosophical works. Among Watson's borrowings in this modern area there was a perceptible emphasis on early Scottish Enlightenment literary intellectuals. So Watson borrowed and reborrowed alongside Rollin between 1754 and 1757 such works as James Geddes's *Essay on the Composition of the Ancients* (1748), Thomas Blackwell's first (1753) volume of *Memoirs of the Court of Augustus* and Francis Hutcheson's *Essay on the Nature and Conduct of the Passions and Affections* (1726). Readers of Paul Bator's detailed study of Watson's Rhetoric lectures will see how thoroughly this reading underpinned what he told students when he was appointed Professor of Logic, Rhetoric, and Metaphysics at St Andrews in 1756. My aim here is not to repeat what Bator has written elsewhere, but to supplement his work in a way that makes it clear how much Watson was an emanation from the academic climate of earlier eighteenth-century St Andrews, and how much he remained part of that academic community throughout the period between his graduation in 1748 and the commencement of his St Andrews professorship eight years later. Adam Smith had become Professor of Logic and Rhetoric at Glasgow University in 1751. When in 1756 Watson became the second professor of the new art of 'polite letters' at a British university to hold a chair whose title contained the term 'Rhetoric', he appears to have learned not only from Adam Smith and from Hugh Blair (to whom Watson was probably related and who acquired the title Professor of Rhetoric and Belles Lettres at Edinburgh University in 1762), but also from his constant reading in St Andrews and his continuing contact with the professors there. Though the precise nature of those contacts is uncertain, we know from library records that they were regular. Watson appears to have been particularly close to James Murison, Principal of St Mary's College, and to Andrew Shaw, Professor of Divinity and Biblical Criticism.[24] A qualified minister, Watson became, like Hugh Blair, a member of the Moderate party in the Church of Scotland, for whom cultivation of polite letters was closely linked to ethical and moral improvement.

Because the introduction to Adam Smith's lectures has not survived, Watson's is the first extant preface to the university teaching of the new subject. Though the expanded text of his lectures is missing, we have several sets of students' notes. This means that Watson's lectures seem much more meagre than the later lectures of Hugh Blair, published by the author in their expanded form. Watson's introductory definition of Rhetoric makes it clear that older writers on Rhetoric are to be censured 'for confining their Praecepts to one particular Sort of Discourse viz; Publick Orations', and that in fact 'many of the Rules of this Art . . . ought to be deliver'd as general.' Watson goes on to declare that 'an Acquaintance with the Rules of History, and Poetry, is at least of Equal Consequence to the Improvement of Taste, as an Acquaintance with the Rules of Orations'.[25] His foregrounding of poetry sets him decidedly aside from Adam Smith, whose lectures show comparatively little interest in poetry compared with prose, and aligns him much more closely with the later lectures of Blair. Watson's Rhetoric makes it clear also that what he is teaching is a subject geared not only to literary criticism but also to literary composition. The 'Rules of Rhetorick' matter not just from the critical point of view 'Because they are a Standard by which particular Passages may be try'd', but also from a creative point of view 'Because they exercise or employ Taste which is manifestly the best Way of improving it' so we may 'write with great Justness, Eloquence & Politeness'. Watson maintains that 'the Improvement of Taste is nearly connected with Improvement in Virtue'.[26]

Clearly Watson's students are being taught to write as well as to read, and they are not only being directed to English writers but also

alerted to the existence of successful Scottish writers who might be
emulated. So, in a discussion of the use of compound words, the students are told that 'No Author in the English Tongue has oftener
practis'd with Success this Method of Compounding Words, than our
Country-man Mr Thomson.'[27] In apparently ignoring much Scottish
writing, Watson's lectures, like those of Adam Smith and Hugh Blair,
devalue the native literary currency, choosing to compliment it only
when it accords with Anglocentric rules of propriety. This act of cultural self-censorship is one which will be repeated in Scotland many
times, and which will be exported abroad. While one might expect
the 'provincial' origins of the university teaching of English to have
valorized works produced in distinctively non-metropolitan modes, in
fact anxiety about provincialism ensures that the reverse is the norm.
Only works which can be seen as matching metropolitan standards of
language can be viewed with unqualified approval. Other works are
usually ignored.

The Scots poet Robert Fergusson almost certainly attended Watson's
lectures as a St Andrews student in the 1760s. Certainly Watson is
among those attacked in Fergusson's acute and energetic poem 'To
the Principal and Professors of the University of St Andrews, on their
Superb Treat to Dr Samuel Johnson' in which Fergusson deploys
Scots vernacular in ways which anticipate Burns, and mocks the syco-
phantic treatment afforded to the Scotophobic Johnson by anxious St
Andrews academics.[28] Fergusson invokes the Scots-English/Dog Latin
tour de force 'Polemo-Middinia' by William Drummond of Hawthornden,
but such a figure gets no mention in Watson's lectures, where the
increasingly powerful and long-lived native strain of Scots poetry which
Fergusson represents is ignored. We know that Watson borrowed
Fergusson's poetry from the St Andrews University Library in 1778,
just as he had borrowed the poems of Allan Ramsay in 1757, but we
have no comment by Watson on these authors or others like them.
They were part of the native culture which he, like the other teachers
of the new Rhetoric in Scottish universities, were consigning to the
past in their wish to create an Anglocentrically correct linguistic and
literary future.

Watson's Logic lectures ended with a section on 'Means of
Improvement' which, under the heading 'Of Reading' made it clear
that 'Till one has made a considerable progress in Study it would seem
a wise resolution never to read any books without having heard the
opinion of some person of taste and judgement concerning them since

by reason of the great number of bad books the chance is much greater that if left to himself, a young man will make a wrong choice rather than a right one.'[29] This may be seen as an attempt to police students' reading habits, a project of intellectual colonization which complements Watson's immense interest in the great Spanish imperialists Philip II and Philip III of whom he wrote large-scale historical studies. On the other hand, we may take a more charitable line, perceiving that Watson wanted to do all he could to help his students get on in the developing British imperial state, and saw Rhetoric as a key to personal and national 'improvement'.

That interests in colonization, improvement and rhetoric went together is nowhere more strongly illustrated than in the career of Watson's successor at St Andrews, William Barron. Born in 1735, Barron, like Watson and Blair, qualified as a Church of Scotland minister, and was a Moderate in his sympathies, displaying 'manly eloquence' in his preaching.[30] Being a rural minister did not content Barron, who complains in his later lectures that a minister may aspire 'to the eminence of pulpit eloquence' in 'some humble and remote station' where there is much 'hypocrisy, and whining, and nonsense, carrying away the approbation of the vulgar' but 'To keep alive the fire of genius, to preserve application, or to attempt eloquence, in situations not only not encouraging, but depressing and dejecting, is beyond the power of all the exertions of human industry.'[31] One may sympathize, though it was in similar communities that the vernacular strain of which Robert Burns is the most striking example was nourished. Barron appears to have little sympathy with such culture, and even preferment in the Church is seen by him as insufficient since 'however this preferment may gratify a generous mind, animated with the most exalted sentiments which can influence a human breast, it will not, at least in the church of Scotland, much flatter that ambition which prompts the most illustrious exertions of genius, namely, to acquire influence over the minds of men, a capacity of being useful to himself, and to those with whom he is connected.'[32] Of poor parents, Barron was a Scotsman on the make, and polite literature was his route to social preferment.

Such a strategy and a concern for 'improvement' underlie his early *Essay on the Mechanical Principles of the Plough* (1774), a work which makes Barron one of a number of Scottish writers (including Lord Kames, William Wilkie and Robert Burns) whose careers linked agriculture to literary culture. Barron suggests that the increasingly cultivated Scottish soil may benefit from an improved plough, and nudges readers with the statement that 'If the Author is successful in this attempt, there can be no question that he will render an important service to his country.'[33] In 1777 there followed his *History of the Colonization of the Free States of Antiquity, Applied to the Present Contest between Great Britain and her American Colonies*, a work clearly aimed to attract parliamentary attention as it relates the contemporary American rebellion to classical colonial precedents, making some play of its author's scholarship and learning. Barron flatteringly disagrees with Adam Smith's view of colonization and views the conduct of Great Britain as exemplary: 'No colonies were ever so prosperous and so happy. Great Britain has not hitherto oppressed them. What will tempt her to do so in future?'[34] Interestingly, he is aware of the strong argument linking the position of the American colonies' claims for representation in the British parliament with the position of Scotland after 1707. He is sympathetic to the process of colonization, viewing it as a progressive development. Around the same time, while still a clergyman, Barron worked on his *History of the Political Connection between England and Ireland from the Reign of Henry II to the present time*, published in 1780. This is again aimed at the influential. Barron hymns Britain's constitution and presents colonization as a narrative of improvement:

One remark, however, will occur to every reader, that the policy of England, with regard to Ireland, for the last hundred years, has gradually become more liberal, as commercial and political knowledge have been advanced and extended; but that all the examples of national generosity, which this period can exhibit, disappear, when compared with the magnitude of late acts and resolutions, which are to extend to Ireland the advantages of a free trade. One step only remains, perhaps, to secure the future prosperity and happiness of the two kingdoms, to extend the benefits of the British constitution over the British Isles.[35]

By the time he published these words Barron had been two years as Professor of Logic, Rhetoric, and Metaphysics at St Andrews, having attracted the interest and support of Lord Suffolk, one of the Secretaries of State, who recommended him to the University. At St Andrews Barron developed what can be seen as Watson's intellectual colonization of the Scottish intelligentsia, emphasizing in his lectures on 'Polite Literature, or Belles Lettres' that the way to succeed was to conform to the Anglocentric linguistic norms of the modern texts on which he lectured. His overall purpose and its local relevance are evident early in his lectures:

If, then, any young and rising genius is ambitious of obtaining the most flattering distinction competent to human nature, namely, the acquisition of well-founded merit and fame, attended with its natural influence on public opinion; to sound and enlarged views of knowledge, let him add the ornament of a graceful and elegant manner, and his power will be irresistible . . . The beneficial influence of assiduous culture is not restricted to individuals; even communities partake something of the same distinction . . . Here also, as in the case of individuals, [industry] surmounts the defects of nature, and the inconveniences of climate and situation.[36]

Barron makes it clear that his audience's ears must be attuned not to the 'rude' and 'harsh ' sounds of Gaelic or the 'uncouth' older Saxon language or modern provincial dialects (in which, of course, much of the work of Ramsay, Fergusson and Burns was written). Rather they must learn from

the superior refinement of the English ear, to that of the other nations who employ languages descended from the same source. Scotland presents a striking and pleasant illustration. The use of the harsh combinations of consonants, and of the guttural sounds, though still very general, manifestly begins to disappear. Her intercourse with England, now so common and easy, the introduction of many of the arts with which that rich and industrious country abounds, the refinement of manners and taste, the extension of science and literature, all have concurred to cultivate the public ear, and to polish her language and her pronunciation.[37]

It is in this spirit of internal colonialism that Barron's lectures develop. He delights that a day is dawning when, despite her history and situation, 'Scotland, by proper culture, is qualified to furnish English compositions, not less pure and correct, perhaps, than England herself.'[38] Though it lapsed through lack of support from his academic colleagues, a class which Barron instituted in his early years at St Andrews concentrated entirely on students' compositions and orations as a practical continuation of the Rhetoric lectures. Barron aimed to convince students that 'Persons may write well a language they cannot speak' until they so improved that they could 'write the language of the purest authors of their age. There is, therefore, nothing in the nature of the thing that should hinder the language of England from being written well in India or America.'[39]

This last reflection prepares us for the impact made by the subject of Rhetoric and Belles Lettres when it was exported to these other continents where, as in Scotland, it operated in conflict with native cultures. At St Andrews Barron's lectures continued to be read by students well into the nineteenth century, when the spirit of the eighteenth-century inventors of Rhetoric and Belles Lettres continued.[40] Among the first acts of Barron's immediate successor, James Hunter, was the borrowing of Addison's works and the four volumes of Rollin on the Belles Lettres from the university library along with other Scottish Enlightenment writers on taste and rhetoric such as James Beattie. Hunter was also interested in Blair's work and in Alexander Gerard's essay on taste.[41] By this time the linguistic and literary attitudes of the teachers of Rhetoric and Belles Lettres in the Scottish universities were being exported to America, India, and elsewhere. When Gauri Viswanathan writes of early English Studies in India and of 'the irony that English literature appeared as a subject in the colonies long before it was institutionalized in the home country' she appears quite unaware of the developments in literary teaching in the Scottish universities. So, for example, the Indian educator and St Andrews professor, Alexander Duff, whose impact on English education in India Viswanathan describes as 'staggering', was a student in James Hunter's St Andrews where he encountered the works of Beattie and Addison as well as developing his literary tastes through reading of Shakespeare and such modern poets as Scott, Southey, Byron and Wordsworth.[42] Duff's Free Church Institution (later incorporated into the University of Calcutta) prescribed Schlegel's *History of Literature* as a course book for English Literature; this was among the books which Duff had borrowed as a student at St Andrews where he had also developed the taste for Romantic poetry apparent in the Calcutta reading list.[43] The impact of English literary teaching in the colonies (and the argument that formed round it about native versus Anglocentric models) is a clear development of the position in the Scottish universities. This accounts, for instance, for the way Duff in his *New Era of the English Language and English Literature in India* (1837) compares the position of native Indian literary studies with the study of the traditional literature of Scotland as collected by Scott and Macpherson.[44]

A similar mapping occurred when St Andrews became the first British university to teach American Literature.[45] William Spalding, Professor of Logic, Rhetoric and Metaphysics from 1845 to 1859, and working on his *History of English Literature* (1853) right at the midpoint of the century, was well aware of the links between the Scottish and American traditions of perceived cultural and linguistic marginality, leading him to remark that 'In respect of those circumstances which affect style, the position of Americans is much like that of Scotsmen;

and the results have not been very dissimilar.'[46] The recent volume *Launch-site for English Studies* details more fully links between literary teaching in St Andrews and colonialism.[47] As the chapters of this present book indicate, the university teaching of literary texts written in English has been bound up with issues of colonialism (both internal and external) from its origins in eighteenth-century Scotland, and in its subsequent exporting abroad, and it continues to be so, albeit from a much more sceptical perspective in the work of such different critics as Edward Said and Edna Longley, Terry Eagleton and Homi Bhabha. To make such a point aligns some of the emphases of this book with Alan Richardson's presentation of English teaching in schools as a form of colonialism in his study *Literature, Education, and Romanticism* (1994), but it would be naive to emphasize only the negative side of the process.[48] As I have argued in *Devolving English Literature*, the literary climate of the eighteenth-century Scottish universities helped shape such masterpieces as Boswell's *Life of Johnson* and the works of Scott with their explorations of Britishness.[49] To contend that the university development of English as a subject was simply oppressive and to be rejected is to ignore the easy access to reading and (crucially) writing in an emerging world language which study of the new subject encouraged. Yet from at least the time of Robert Fergusson and Robert Watson, of James Macpherson and Hugh Blair, the subject became a site of complex negotiations, and not infrequently conflicts between native and Anglocentric pressures; these continue to the present day and are evident in contemporary writing from inside and outside academia. The early chapters of this book deal with a university subject in which what we would now call creative writing, composition and rhetoric were closely fused with criticism. This fusion is striking and relevant to modern debates about the relation between these areas and modern university literary teaching. Going beyond the work of Adam Potkay, Martin Moonie in particular reminds us how important were issues of gender and sexuality to the emergence of literary studies in a climate where such teachers as William Barron stressed the need for 'manliness and dignity'.[50] As later chapters of this book look at the export of the new university subject, readers may appreciate more fully just how the university teaching of English spread across the globe, and how it conditioned the emergence of the modern English departments in England. From its beginnings, as today, the subject was somewhat fluid in its precise definition, so that an eighteenth-century university principal might worry that William Barron's was a subject for which 'every well

educated young man is considered as qualified.'[51] This book provides
detail and arguments which are relevant not only to the history of a
key modern discipline, but also to contemporary debates about that
discipline's changing nature. In the late twentieth century when developments in both theory and technology have brought the processes of
reading, speaking and writing into a conjunction where each may appear
a form of the other, the emergence of the study of 'Rhetoric and Belles
Lettres' in eighteenth-century Scottish universities and its subsequent
export and development may help inform not only the past but also
the present and future shape of what we do when we do 'English'.

NOTES

1 Chris Baldick, *The Social Mission of English Criticism, 1842–1932* (Oxford:
  Clarendon Press, 1983); Terry Eagleton, *Literary Theory, An Introduction*
  (Oxford: Blackwell, 1983), pp. 17–53; Gerald Graff, *Professing Literature: An
  Institutional History* (Chicago and London: University of Chicago Press,
  1987).

2 Robert Crawford, *Devolving English Literature* (Oxford: Clarendon Press, 1992),
  pp. 16–44; Franklin E. Court, *Institutionalizing English Literature: The Culture
  and Politics of Literary Study, 1750–1900* (Stanford: Stanford University Press,
  1992); Winifred Bryan Horner, *Nineteenth-Century Scottish Rhetoric: The American
  Connection* (Carbondale: Southern Illinois University Press, 1993); Thomas
  P. Miller, *The Formation of College English: Rhetoric and Belles Lettres in the
  British Cultural Provinces* (University of Pittsburgh Press, 1997).

3 St Andrews University Minutes, vol. III, pp. 41–7, St Andrews University
  Muniments UY 452 3. For a published account which prints Stuart's
  correspondence quoted here, see J. Maitland Anderson, 'The "Princely
  Chandos" and the University of St Andrews', *The Scottish Review* 25 (1895),
  41–70.

4 Charles Rollin, *De la manière d'enseigner et d'étudier les Belles-Lettres*, 4 vols.
  (Paris: J. Estienne, 1726–8), vol. I, title page.

5 Adam Potkay, *The Fate of Eloquence in the Age of Hume* (Ithaca and London:
  Cornell University Press, 1994).

6 Richard Terry, 'The Eighteenth-Century Invention of English Literature:
  A Truism Revisited', *British Journal for Eighteenth-Century Studies* 19 (1996),
  47–62.

7 George MacKenzie, *The Lives and Characters of the Most Eminent Writers of
  the Scots Nation*, 3 vols. (Edinburgh: James Watson, 1708–22), vol. I, pp.
  481–7.

8 Information from Charles Stuart's Doctor's Diploma, St Andrews University Muniments UY 232 2; R. W. Innes Smith, *English-Speaking Students
  of Medicine at the University of Leyden* (Edinburgh: Oliver and Boyd, 1932),

p. 226 (I am grateful to Mr Robert Smart for this reference); Anderson, 'The "Princely Chandos" and the University of St Andrews', pp. 43–4; C. H. Collins Baker and Muriel I. Baker, *The Life and Circumstances of James Brydges, First Duke of Chandos, Patron of the Liberal Arts* (Oxford: Clarendon Press, 1949), pp. 100–3; Anon., *The Record of the Royal Society of London*, fourth edition (London: The Royal Society, 1940), p. 395.

9 Anderson, 'The "Princely Chandos" and the University of St Andrews', p. 45.

10 Charles Stuart to Robert Ramsay, 28 November 1720, St Andrews University Muniments UY 232 2.

11 Charles Stuart to Francis Pringle, 23 January 1721, St Andrews University Muniments UY 232 2.

12 MacKenzie, *Writers of the Scots Nation*, vol. i, p. xli.

13 Francis Pringle to Mr Bayne, 1736, fair copy in St Andrews University Muniments MS. LF 1111.P8C99, p. 88.

14 *Ibid.*; Douglas Duncan, *Thomas Ruddiman: A Study in Scottish Scholarship of the Early Eighteenth Century* (Edinburgh: Oliver and Boyd, 1965), pp. 54, 57, 97–121.

15 St Andrews University Minutes, vol. iii, p. 46.

16 These and subsequent analyses of borrowings are derived from my examination of the St Andrews University Library Receipt Books now held among the St Andrews University Muniments and detailing the borrowings of students and professors between 1737 and 1759 (LY 205 1–3), then the borrowing of professors between 1773 and 1781 and 1792 (LY 206 2–3), and cross-checked where appropriate with the Shelf Catalogue 1734–63 (LY 105/6) and the Author Catalogue 1763 (LY 105/7).

17 James Maitland Anderson, *The Matriculation Roll of the University of St Andrews 1747–1897* (Edinburgh: Blackwood, 1905), pp. 2–3. On the relevant history of the University of St Andrews see Anderson's introduction to *The Matriculation Roll*, and Ronald Cant, *The University of St Andrews, A Short History*, 3rd edn (St Andrews University Library, 1992).

18 Crawford, *Devolving English Literature*, pp. 16–44. See also Charles Jones, *A Language Suppressed: The Pronunciation of the Scots Language in the 18th Century* (Edinburgh: John Donald, 1995).

19 James Boswell, *The Life of Samuel Johnson* (1791; repr. 2 vols., London: Dent, 1973), vol. i, p. 264 (6 July 1763).

20 Miller, *The Formation of College English*, chapter 3.

21 *Ibid.*, chapter 5.

22 For the fullest accounts of Watson's life and lectures see Paul G. Bator, 'Robert Watson (1730–1781)' in Michael G. Moran, ed., *Eighteenth-Century British and American Rhetorics and Rhetoricians: Critical Studies and Sources* (Westport, CT, and London: Greenwood Press, 1994), pp. 245–59; and Paul G. Bator, 'The Unpublished Rhetoric Lectures of Robert Watson, Professor of Logic, Rhetoric, and Metaphysics at the University of St. Andrews, 1756–1778', *Rhetorica* 12 (1994), 67–113.

23 'Scotland' (anonymous article), *Scots Magazine* 21 (December 1759), 661.
24 In the St Andrews University Library Receipt Book 1748–53 it is these men who most often authorize Watson's borrowings.
25 Robert Watson, 'A Treatise on Rhetorick' [1758], St Andrews University Muniments MS PN 173.W1, pp. 1–2.
26 *Ibid.*, p. 3.
27 *Ibid.*, p. 13.
28 Robert Fergusson, *The Poems*, ed. Matthew P. MacDiarmid, 2 vols. (Edinburgh and London: Blackwood for the Scottish Text Society, 1954 and 1956), vol. II, pp. 182–5. See also Robert Crawford, 'Robert Fergusson's Robert Burns' in Robert Crawford, ed., *Robert Burns and Cultural Authority* (Edinburgh: Edinburgh University Press, 1997), pp. 1–22.
29 Robert Watson, 'Introduction to Logic & Rhetoric', St Andrews University Muniments MS BC6.W2, p. 183.
30 Details of Barron's career and curriculum are drawn from the corrected proof copy of a printed obituary of c. 1805 now in St Andrews University Muniments (MS 36260).
31 William Barron, *Lectures on Belles Lettres and Logic*, 2 vols. (London: Longman, Hurst, Rees, and Orme; and Edinburgh: Bell and Bradfute, 1806), vol. I, pp. 541–2.
32 *Ibid.*, p. 541.
33 William Barron, *An Essay on the Mechanical Principles of the Plough* (Edinburgh: Balfour, 1774), Advertisement.
34 William Barron, *History of the Colonization of the Free States of Antiquity, Applied to the Present Contest between Great Britain and her American Colonies, with Reflections concerning the Future Settlement of these Colonies* (London: Cadell, 1778), pp. 134 and 142–3.
35 William Barron, *History of the Political Connection between England and Ireland from the Reign of Henry II to the Present Time* (London: Cadell, 1780), p. 200.
36 Barron, *Lectures on Belles Lettres*, vol. I, pp. 12–13.
37 *Ibid.*, vol. I, pp. 34–36.
38 *Ibid.*, vol. I, p. 120.
39 *Ibid.*, vol. I, p. 131.
40 In addition to evidence from Library Borrowings Registers, the signatures of several early nineteenth-century St Andrews students on the volumes of Barron's *Lectures* in St Andrews University Library indicate continuing use of his work there.
41 Library Receipt Book, Professors, 1801–1816, St Andrews University Muniments, LY 206 5, pp. 107–9.
42 Gauri Viswanathan, *Masks of Conquest: Literary Study and British Rule in India* (London: Faber and Faber, 1989), pp. 3 and 49; Library Receipt Book, Students, 1816–25, St Andrews University Muniments LY 207 14, pp. 464–5 and 200–1.
43 *Ibid.*, p. 464; Viswanathan, *Masks of Conquest*, p. 54.
44 Alexander Duff, *New Era of the English Language and English Literature in India* (Edinburgh: John Johnstone, 1837), p. 30.

45 See Robert Crawford, 'Internationalizing the Subject' in Robert Crawford, ed., *Launch-site for English Studies: Three Centuries of Literary Teaching at the University of St Andrews* (St Andrews: Verse, 1997).

46 William Spalding, *The History of English Literature* (Edinburgh: Oliver & Boyd, 1853), p. 409.

47 See note 45 above.

48 Alan Richardson, *Literature, Education, and Romanticism: Reading as Social Practice, 1780–1832* (Cambridge University Press, 1994).

49 Crawford, *Devolving English Literature*, pp. 45–110.

50 Potkay, *The Fate of Eloquence*; Barron, *Lectures*, vol. 1, p. 603.

51 Principal George Hill of St Andrews University to the Right Hon. Henry Dundas, 1 March 1799, St Andrews University Muniments MS 4782.

CHAPTER I

From Rhetoric to Criticism

Neil Rhodes

Any attempt to trace the origins of an academic discipline has to be informed by an awareness of how subjects transform themselves over long periods of time. In the case of 'English', while it is clear that the subject did not begin, suddenly, with the creation of chairs in late-nineteenth-century Oxbridge, its earlier emergence in the mid-eighteenth-century Scottish universities must also be placed in the historical perspective of evolving disciplines. Our perception of this is at present extremely unclear, since eighteenth- and nineteenth-century scholars tend to regard the rhetorically based learning of Renaissance academies as remote from their own concerns, while studies of the development of Rhetoric by Renaissance specialists are liable to peter out early in the seventeenth century. My title is intended both to supply that gap and to echo Grafton and Jardine's 1986 study, *From Humanism to the Humanities*, which demonstrates how an educational programme in the humanities, designed to train a social elite, emerged from the moral and intellectual ideals of humanism in the fifteenth and sixteenth centuries. This was to be transformed by the French belleletrism of the late seventeenth century which had a direct influence on the Scottish rhetoricians, and which led in turn to an anxiety about the very term 'rhetoric', now regarded as archaic and mechanical. Such anxiety about nomenclature is not trivial or superficial. It arises from an awareness that a subject has been transformed to a point where it needs to be redefined. The condition of English Studies in the late twentieth century bears obvious witness to this, and from that perspective we may also notice the irony that, while the term 'rhetoric' has become an increasing part of our academic discourse, the term 'belleletrism' is used exclusively now in a pejorative sense to denote an anti-intellectual form of literary appreciation. A further irony which arises from an examination of the way in which the subject has evolved is the recognition that, *pace* complaints from traditionalists that

English was suddenly infected by new ideas from Paris in the late 1960s, it was effectively *created* by new ideas from Paris. This essay, then, argues that academic English emerges from the transition from Rhetoric to Criticism, and that it does so, paradoxically, in the context of the French connection with Scotland.

The study of literature had always been associated with rhetoric as part of a training in eloquence, but until the eighteenth century a co-requisite was the mastery of a foreign language. For the Roman schoolboy the language was Greek, and for the Renaissance schoolboy, firstly at any rate, Latin. What is more, the acquisition of that linguistic proficiency became, in the Renaissance, a form of puberty rite in which young boys were inducted into an all-male, Latin-speaking world, with corporal punishment as part of the initiation process.[1] The issue of gender, then, is inseparable from the story of the evolution of Rhetoric as an academic subject, and its eventual replacement by Criticism. The issue is also relevant when we consider the objectives involved in mastering the art of rhetoric. The Renaissance had inherited from Cicero and Quintilian an ideal of eloquence as civic discourse, with the orator as the perfect embodiment of the *vir civilis*, and the public functions of eloquence ensured that it was by definition a virile accomplishment. In the public sphere, female eloquence would almost invariably have been translated into its negative counterparts, shrewishness or loquacity, since to speak out (*e-loquor*) in that context would not have been appropriate. And to the issue of gender we must also add that of social rank, since the almost superhuman attributes expected of the true orator, as well as the political power which they conferred, implied a certain degree of nobility in the eloquent speaker. The implication is present in Quintilian's requirement that the orator be a good man, capable of moving his audience to virtue. The ideals of eloquence, and also the status of rhetoric, the vehicle through which these ideals could be achieved, reached their highest point of prestige in the sixteenth century.[2] In an academic context they were reinforced by educational theorists, among them Erasmus, who were exploiting the new technology of printing to produce textbooks designed to help the student in his acquisition of the art of rhetoric. At the same time, however, that print was being used as a facilitator for Rhetoric, it was also both transforming it and diminishing it. Print transferred attention from oral to written discourse, dealing a body blow to the art of memory, the fourth part of classical rhetoric, in the process. With the production of multiple copies (a travesty of the Renaissance concept of *copia* in eloquence), print helped to erode the elitist and specifically masculine character of Rhetoric, and the same effect was achieved by the increase in the number of books written in or translated into the vernacular. So when we follow the development of Rhetoric into Criticism, and hence the emergence of English as a subject , we are bound to address a number of intimately related topics: the replacement of the learned language by the vernacular, issues of gender and class, and the shift in emphasis from speaking to writing and, eventually, reading.

We can now relocate to Paris where, in the mid sixteenth century, the ability of Rhetoric to realize a 'dream of eloquence which would cover the whole range of the human mind'[3] was polemically challenged by the philosopher and pedagogue, Pierre de la Ramée, better known as Ramus. (Translating yourself into Latin gave you added authority, and in this instance had the effect of conspicuous masculinization.) Having graduated MA in 1536 with a thesis notoriously attacking Aristotle, Ramus was appointed, in 1551, Regius Professor of Philosophy and Eloquence at the Collège de France in Paris, a title which was very much his own invention and which had no successors. In spite of his Latinized name he was quite in favour of the vernacular, and his most influential work, the *Dialectique*, was first published in French in 1555 and *then* adapted into Latin.[4] The most far-reaching aspect of this book was the radical surgery which Ramus performed on classical Rhetoric, removing its first two parts (*inventio* and *dispositio*) and reassigning them to dialectic, while leaving Rhetoric with only *elocutio* (style or expression) and *pronuntiatio* (delivery); *memoria* was to become redundant. This is the way in which Ramus's contribution to the evolution of Rhetoric is usually described, but it would be misleading to think of his aims as anti-humanist or anti-rhetorical. He was chiefly concerned to establish more specifically what Rhetoric was supposed to cover in its contribution to those Renaissance ideals of eloquence inherited from Cicero and Quintilian. The principle here, as throughout his work, was one of simplification and practicality, and it was also as an aid to understanding that the *Dialectique* and his Paris lectures were illustrated by examples from poetry. In the case of the *Dialectique* this meant modern poetry in the vernacular by Ronsard, Du Bellay, Marot and others, and at the end of that work he spells out precisely what Rhetoric was concerned with: 'all the tropes and figures of style, all the graces of delivery, which is the whole of rhetoric, distinct and separate from dialectic'.[5] Like most other educational reforms Ramus's were attacked at the time as trivializing and shallow, but they were

nonetheless to have profound importance for the subsequent development of Rhetoric.[6] As Brian Vickers has observed: the 'reforms of
Ramus and Talon may indeed have separated rhetoric from dialectic,
but in their systematic development of *elocutio*, and their espousal of the
vernaculars, the Ramists had a beneficial influence in applying rhetoric
to literature'.[7] The first evidence of this in the English-speaking world
comes from Scotland.

Ramus was one of the best-selling authors of the Renaissance, as
the thousand or so editions of his works listed in Ong's *Ramus and Talon
Inventory* bear witness, and he achieved the widest influence on the educational curricula of the late sixteenth and seventeenth centuries.
There are more translations of the *Dialectica* (i.e. the Latin version of
the *Dialectique*) into English than into any other language, and the first
of these is by the Scot, Roland MacIlmaine, a scholar from St Andrews
University, who published *The Logike of the Moste Excellent Philosopher P.
Ramus, Martyr* and a Latin edition of the same work in 1574. Although
the introduction of Ramism to the English-speaking world is usually
credited to Gabriel Harvey, who produced no translation of Ramus,
Ramism in fact established itself at St Andrews before Cambridge.[8]
James Stewart, Earl of Mar and Moray, and Regent of Scotland from
1567, was a St Andrews graduate who had studied under Ramus at
Presle, while Andrew Melville, Principal of St Mary's College, St
Andrews, and MacIlmaine himself had both attended Ramus's classes
in Paris. One effect on MacIlmaine was to encourage him to produce
a vigorous defence of the vernacular in his introduction to the *Logike*:

Heare I will speake nothing of the envious, that thinkethe it not decent to
wryte any liberall arte in the vulgar tongue, but woulde have all thinges kept
close eyther in the Hebrewe, Greke, or Latyne tongues . . . Did Cicero, who
was a Latinist borne write his Philosophie and Rethoricke in the Greke tongue,
or was he content with his mother tongue? . . . Shall we then thinke the
Scottyshe or Englishe tongue, is not fitt to write any arte into? no in dede . . .
But thou wilt saye, our tongue is barbarous, and theirs is eloquent? I aunswere
thee as Anacharsis did to the Athenienses, who called his Scithian tongue
barbarous, yea sayethe he, Anarcharsis is barbarous amongest the Athenienses,
and so are the Athenienses amongest the Scythyans, by the which aunswere
he signifieth that every mans tongue is eloquent ynoughe for hym self, and
that others in respecte of it had as barbarous . . .[9]

The treatise is then illustrated with passages of poetry, English
translations from Virgil, Ovid and Catullus (though not from modern
French poetry), and MacIlmaine's reference to the Scottish tongue is

supported by his admission of Scotticisms which would have shocked his eighteenth-century successors. MacIlmaine's *Ramus*, then, affirms both the status of the vernacular and the pedagogical value of poetry, while Ramus's work as a whole has been described by Grafton and Jardine as transformational in the history of Western education: 'we turn to Ramus in pursuit of the crucial moment of transition when (we maintain) "humanism" became the "humanities" . . . he heralds the age of standardized classroom teaching and the best-selling textbook'.[10] And we might add to this the proposition that Ramus is also responsible for the transition from Rhetoric to Criticism.

That proposition needs to be referred not only to the concentration on *elocutio* in Ramist rhetoric, but also to another aspect of his work which is of direct relevance to the question of evolving academic disciplines. This is Ramus's aim of eliminating repetition through the overlapping of subject categories, which is what led to his separation of *inventio* and *dispositio* in the first place, and his insistence that subjects be taught with regard to their intrinsic elements. MacIlmaine renders this as follows: 'The third documente which thou shalt note herein observed, is, that thou intreate of thy rules which be generall generallye, and those which be speciall speciallie, and at one tyme, without any vaine repetitions . . .'.[11] It is one of the many paradoxes involved in the Scottish invention of English Literature that the subject should have been created by a process of narrowing down and hiving off, but that, in the late twentieth century, in the entire academic curriculum it is the subject with the least sense of sharp boundaries or intrinsic elements. In the late seventeenth century, however, it was emerging from another Parisian innovation, which took the name Belles Lettres, and which occupies the interim between Rhetoric and Criticism. The term seems to have been invented by the Jesuit author René Rapin, who refers to 'belles lettres' in the expanded titles of two books, *Les Comparaisons des grands hommes de l'antiquité* . . . and *Les Réflexions sur l'eloquence* . . . , both published in 1684.[12] But if Rapin was responsible for the term Belles Lettres, the moment of transition for Rhetoric was effectively announced by Bernard Lamy in his treatise *L'Art de parler*, which was published anonymously in Paris in 1675. It was translated into English the following year and reissued in 1696 and 1708. The French version also went into a third edition (1688) in which the author's name was revealed and the title changed to *La Rhétorique, ou l'art de parler*, and for the fifth edition of 1712 the work itself was 'revised and augmented'. Lamy's work is described by Barbara Warnick, author of the first monograph to deal with the influence of French belleletrism on eighteenth-century Scottish Rhetoric, as a 'transitional rhetoric', and she attributes what she calls 'the eclipse of invention' to Lamy. Rather oddly, there is only one mention of Ramus at the end of Warnick's book.[13] Lamy was indeed influential, but the transitional aspect of his work might best be illustrated somewhat differently. In the course of revision his conception of Rhetoric changed, and in the fifth edition it appears as follows: 'The art of speaking is very useful and has a very extensive application. It comprises everything that in French is called Belles Lettres; in Latin and Greek philology, the Greek word means love of words. To know Belles Lettres is to know how to speak, to write, *or to judge those who write*' (my emphasis).[14] That sequence of speaking, writing and critical reading defines the moment at which Rhetoric becomes Criticism.

While Lamy's work had some success in what we may now call 'Britain' – the third London edition appeared in the year following the Union of the Scottish and English parliaments – it was Charles Rollin who was principally responsible for the naturalization of the term 'belles lettres' in English with the translation of his four-volume work *De la manière d'enseigner et d'étudier les belles lettres* in 1734. Rollin was also to have a powerful influence in the academy. Like Ramus he was Professor of Eloquence in the Collège de France in Paris, but with the job description 'Eloquence and Belles Lettres' rather than Ramus's 'Philosophy and Eloquence', a distinction which offers a paradigm of the subject development we have been tracing. And he underlines the transition from Rhetoric to what he calls 'the reading and exploration of authors', and earlier, 'the perusal of good authors', without which, he says, rhetoric is 'lifeless and barren'.[15] This is all specifically designed for an academic audience. The last part of Rollin's work consists of 'an account of the government of the classes and college: how to manage the conduct of youth', while the title declares that the work is 'Illustrated with Passages from the most famous Poets and Orators, Ancient and Modern, with Critical Remarks on them, designed more Particularly for Students in the Universities'. And the whole project may be summed up by the statement: 'I shall principally endeavour to form the taste of young persons . . . The taste, as it now falls under our consideration, that is, with reference to the reading of authors and composition.'[16] Here, the crucial concept of 'taste' sets the agenda for the early academic study of English literature. Through a combination of literary criticism and what we would now call creative writing, the student acquires certain standards of 'politeness' (another crucial concept) which will fit him for easy intercourse in society. That this agenda appealed to the Scottish universities is demonstrated in the case of St Andrews by the frequency with which Rollin's work was borrowed from the University Library.

Although St Andrews had made plans for a Chair of Eloquence as early as 1720, it seems likely that Edinburgh was the first university to introduce the new French belleletrism into the academic curriculum. This was the doing of John Stevenson, appointed Professor of Logic and Metaphysics in 1730, whose own copies of Lamy (the fifth edition) and Rollin now repose in Edinburgh University Library.[17] Stevenson's lectures do not survive, but some of his students' essays do, and they include such topics as 'Taste' and 'Rules of Conversation'.[18] Meanwhile, outside the university there were developments which would lead directly to the formation of the Regius Chair of Rhetoric and Belles Lettres, effectively the first Chair of English. In 1748 Adam Smith, who had returned to Scotland after ten years in a comatose Oxford, was appointed to give a series of public lectures in Edinburgh on Rhetoric and Belles Lettres, lectures which Smith modelled on Rollin. The prime mover behind this appointment was Henry Home, Lord Kames, lawyer and man of letters, and a leading member of the Edinburgh Philosophical Society. Smith's lectures were highly success-ful, and when he left for Glasgow in 1751 Kames found a successor in Robert Watson. In 1756 Watson in turn left to take up the Chair of Logic, Rhetoric and Metaphysics at St Andrews, and Kames again kept the Edinburgh lectures running with the appointment of Hugh Blair. The continued popularity of the lectures prompted the Town Council to recommend that a Chair of Rhetoric be established in the university, with Blair as the incumbent, and this was finally settled in 1762 through the offices of the Earl of Bute, a close adviser to George III. Blair himself was responsible for the title of the chair, suggesting that 'to give it a more modern air, the title of Belles Lettres might be added'.[19] The one person to be put out by these developments was Stevenson, whose position was summed up in an article in *The Scots Magazine* of 1802:

His critical lectures, it must be owned, contributed a large share towards the production of the more polished and refined, but not more useful, aca-demical discourses of the late Dr Blair: and it was not without reason, that the institution of a separate chair for a Professor of Rhetoric and Belles Lettres was complained of, by the respectable veteran, as an encroachment upon his province.[20]

Since Stevenson had taught not only Blair, but also John Witherspoon, who lectured on Rhetoric at the College of New Jersey, later Princeton, where he became President in 1768, his feelings are understandable.

The roles of Smith and Blair in the formation of English Studies are well known, and they are discussed elsewhere in this volume, so it is worth saying a little more about Robert Watson, not least because it is Watson who first explicitly replaces Rhetoric with 'Criticism' in the university curriculum. Watson's lectures at St Andrews survive in two manuscript notebooks in the University Library, dated 1758 and 1762, and there is a further manuscript in Edinburgh University Library catalogued under 1764.[21] Watson starts his first lecture with the Ramist pronouncement (compare MacIlmaine above) that

The first thing to be done in every Science, is to fix the notion of the Science itself . . . many Rules of this Art [i.e. rhetoric] are of a General nature, and therefore ought to be delivered as general . . . it is proposed in the first place to mention those rules which are common to all the different kinds of discourse, and then mention those which are peculiar to each particular kind.

Watson then states his intention of abandoning theory for practice:

By the Rules of Rhetorick are meant Nothing else, but Observations concerning the Particulars which render Discourse excellent & usefull. It is not proposed to deliver them in the Form of Rules, but in the form of general Criticisms illustrated by Examples from Authors. To what follows then you may give the Name of Rhetorick, or Criticism as you please; if they deserve the one they will deserve the other also.[22]

If we can trace the moment at which Rhetoric in effect becomes Criticism back to Lamy, this is probably the moment at which the two forms are first claimed to be interchangeable, and certainly so in the context of a university lecture.

By replacing theory with practice, and substituting Criticism for Rhetoric, what Watson is actually offering is practical criticism. It is practical because it is concerned with particular verbal effects, it is combined with exercises in composition, and its stated objective is to improve the taste of the students. Those students would have heard Watson's discussion of literary style with reference to vocabulary; to tropes and figures such as metaphor, allegory, personification and periphrasis; and to literary forms such as tragedy, epic and comedy. They would also have heard illustrations from English authors including Shakespeare, Milton, Swift and Pope. The objective of social improvement at which this programme of education was aimed is repeated by

Watson's successor at St Andrews, William Barron, who published
his own *Lectures on Belles Letters and Logic* in 1781: 'Rhetoric and criticism
are a branch of the pleasures of the imagination . . . these pleasures are
felt and relished by men in all ages of society, but particularly in
periods of refinement. – They prevent the abuse of riches. – They
occupy the mind with innocence, if not with dignity, and oppose or
retard the degeneracy of nations.'[23] Barron's title is also significant
since it dispenses with the term 'rhetoric', presumably on the grounds
that it has been superseded. The term was certainly falling into dis-
favour, and earlier, at Glasgow, Adam Smith had dismissed most rhetorics as 'generally a very silly set of Books and not at all instructive'.[24]
But Barron does not instead choose the term 'criticism'. The person
who does is the patron of Watson, Smith and Blair, Lord Kames.
Kames's *Elements of Criticism* appeared in 1762, going through eleven
editions to 1839, and it may fairly be said to have established the
nomenclature up to the present day.

As Watson's teaching was getting under way, the St Andrews University Library bought Thomas Sheridan's *British Education* (1756), a
book which supplies a crucial dimension to the emergent subject of
English. Sheridan was an Irishman who had also delivered a *Course of
Lectures on Elocution* at Edinburgh in 1761, published the following year
by subscription, the subscribers including Kames and Kames's son,
George Home, a pupil of Watson's at St Andrews. Sheridan's *British
Education* is important for English in several ways. Firstly, he argues
that English offers a better education than Classics: 'The learned languages are no longer the sole repositories of knowledge; on the contrary, the English is become an universal magazine not only of antient
but of all modern wisdom . . . how is it possible to account for the
absurd notions of so many parents, that Greek and Latin are still the
high roads to fortune, because they were so two centuries ago . . .'[25]
He then argues that Britain has greater means than Greece or Rome
of making its language universal, through modern commerce and the
democratization of literature by print, but that in order to achieve this
it has to be corrected and standardized. He also argues that 'As the
chief glory of a people arises from their authors, the propagation of
their language is necessary to the displaying of that glory in it's full
lustre',[26] and it follows from this that the best authors must be studied
in depth: '[on Milton] Let us therefore apply ourselves seriously, and
with diligence, to a study capable of affording us such delight. Let us
no longer think, that to learn to read is sufficient, but to read well . . .'[27]

Finally, if all this is done, 'Nothing but the most shameful neglect in the people can prevent the English from handing down to posterity a third classical language, of far more importance than the other two.'[28] Sheridan's *British Education* complemented Watson's Rhetoric lectures and provided an intellectual agenda for them, and while Sheridan's programme for English is idealistic, in Scotland it was also useful. University English was firstly concerned with the inculcation of correct taste and standards of expression for social ends. English literature was the medium through which the newly Britished Scots might become socially assimilated with England and enjoy the commercial benefits of the expanding British Empire. In that respect, it had a practical appeal for the middle classes, who would surely have endorsed the following description of a good educator: 'He proposed as a test of an education that it should prove "useful" – that it should repay those who undertook it with skills applicable outside the universities. He thereby won the approval of a mercantile class determined to get value for money from their "investment" in their sons' education.'[29] 'He' in this account, however, is not Robert Watson, or any other Scot, in fact, but Peter Ramus as described by Grafton and Jardine.

The role of St Andrews in the development of the new subject of English offers a paradigm of the social and cultural conditions which led to its emergence in Scotland more widely in the years, roughly speaking, 1756–63. What is specific to St Andrews is the contribution of MacIlmaine to the dissemination of Ramist pedagogy, and the later redescription of Rhetoric as Criticism by Robert Watson. But we can also extrapolate from the university's response to the social conditions created by the new British state some more general observations about the subject as a whole, especially with regard to the issues of nomenclature and gender raised at the start of this chapter. English, when it came to establish itself in the English universities, especially Oxford, was popularly and dismissively typecast as a 'women's subject'. This was because it was thought to lack the masculine discipline and factual precision required to study the classics, and the labelling echoes a similarly gendered perception of the transition from Rhetoric to Belles Lettres to Criticism in the eighteenth century. Women were not, of course, admitted to universities in eighteenth-century Scotland, and the educational objective of acquiring good taste by reading polite literature can be referred in the first instance to the social and ethnic requirements of gentrification. But there is also an underlying principle of feminization at work here. With the arrival of Belles Lettres

– the form itself suggests a feminization of the subject – persuasive eloquence in the arena of public life is replaced by the more feminine activities of reading and conversation, which are associated in turn with the rise of the novel. This development has been discussed in depth in an excellent recent study by Adam Potkay, who describes a 'querelle between conversation and eloquence in the eighteenth century which led to calls, by David Hume in particular, for a revival of the "Sublime and pathetic" eloquence of the great classical orators' to counteract the 'calm, elegant, and subtle' tenor of modern feminized eloquence.[30] We might add to this the point that the gradual trans-formation of Rhetoric itself can also be construed in gendered terms. The removal of its first two parts to the masculine province of logic left it principally with the feminine ornaments of its third part, *elocutio*, while its final part, *pronuntiatio*, which in its classical form included *actio*, also experienced a metamorphosis. Stentorian tones and vigorous gestures were hardly well adapted to the drawing-room, and *pronuntiatio* became the more refined art of elocution in the modern sense outlined by Sheridan ('the just and graceful management of the voice, counten-ance, and gesture in speaking').[31] The art of speaking well dwindled to the art of being well-spoken. These are the cultural conditions in which English emerges as an academic subject, and as the French have traditionally been blamed for the importation to Britain of things effeminate, so they may now be blamed for the Scottish invention of English Literature.

This last remark is not merely facetious. French literature was rou-tinely caricatured in feminine terms by contrast with the manly 'British Muse' (Sheridan's term), and Watson's students at St Andrews would have read in Sheridan that they should 'leave to the shallow French their rouge and white paint, but let the British red and white appear in its genuine lustre, as laid on by nature's own pencil'.[32] And Shake-speare was routinely invoked to illustrate the point. In his *Essay upon English Tragedy* (1757), William Guthrie of Brechin writes excitedly: 'Where is the Briton so much of a Frenchman as to prefer the highest stretch of modern improvement to the meanest spark of Shakespeare's genius. Yet to our eternal amazement it is true, that for above half a century the poets and patrons of poetry in England, abandoned the sterling merit of Shakespeare for the tinsel ornaments of the French academy.'[33] And he also makes the rather Wildean observation that 'It is not Shakespeare who speaks the language of nature, but nature rather speaks the language of Shakespeare.'[34] Guthrie's enthusiasm was timely. The Scottish advocacy of Shakespeare, and the accompanying appeals to manliness and 'nature', was a bid for a share in the national genius of the new British state,[35] and we are confronted by the double paradox that university English was invented by Scots as a result of French rhetorical influence, but that Scottish literary criticism disparaged French authors by comparison with their English counterparts in order to establish their British credentials. While the Scots assimilated French belleletrism for their own educational purposes, this was not an indebtedness they particularly wished to acknowledge. This is everywhere apparent in Kames's *Elements of Criticism*. Kames may have chosen the term 'criticism' not only because he wished to avoid the outmoded 'rhetoric', but also because he wished to avoid the French 'belles lettres'. He begins by attacking Bossuet for his adherence to rules, and asserts that 'human nature [is] the true source of criticism'.[36] While Corneille has 'accustomed the French ear to a style, formal, pompous, declamatory', the English prefer 'the more natural language of Shakespeare'[37] and 'Shakespeare's soliloquies may justly be established as a model'.[38] It was this last remark especially, in which Racine's *Phèdre* is unfavourably compared with *Hamlet*, that provoked Voltaire's sarcastic review of the *Elements* in the *Gazette Littéraire* (April 1764). Ridiculing the English obsession with nature, he proclaims: 'It is an admirable result of the progress of the human spirit that today rules for taste for all the arts, from the epic poem to gardening, come to us from Scotland. The human spirit is extending itself daily, and we should not give up hope of getting poetics and rhetorics from the Isles of Orkney.'[39] It is somewhat ironic, in view of the Scots' concern with correct taste and standardized English, that Voltaire's dismissive conclusion to the review ('Chacun à son goût') should have entered the English language in its French form.

The dual sympathy and antagonism between the French and British muses in the formation of English as a subject has finally to be placed in the context of international politics. Robert Crawford has referred to the promotion of English in Scotland as part of a process of internal colonization which would enable the Scots to take part in the British imperial enterprise. It is surely not a coincidence that the period which saw the emergence of academic English, the period 1756–63, is that of the Seven Years War, the first major Anglo-Scottish imperial war against the French. Nor is it insignificant that success in the two main theatres of that war, North America and India, was to be an important stepping stone for the establishment of English as an international language, as Sheridan had advocated in *British Education*. In 1759, as the young George Home studied that book and digested Professor Watson's Rhetoric lectures, he would also have heard news of Wolfe's victory at Quebec, which secured Canada for the British Empire and, more particularly, for Scotland. Three or four years later, referring to his review of the elder Home's *Elements of Criticism*, Voltaire wrote to the Count and Countess of Argental: 'As long as the British have been content to take our vessels and seize Canada and Pondicherry, I have been content to maintain a noble silence. But now that they push barbarity to the point of finding Racine and Corneille ridiculous, I have to take up arms.' Voltaire's error was not to realize that the colonial losses he was willing to tolerate would in fact lead to the international domination of French by the language and literature of Britain.[40]

NOTES

1 See Walter J. Ong, 'Latin Language Study as a Renaissance Puberty Rite' in *Rhetoric, Romance and Technology* (Ithaca, NY: Cornell University Press, 1971), pp. 113–41.

2 On Renaissance ideals of eloquence see Neil Rhodes, *The Power of Eloquence and English Renaissance Literature* (Hemel Hempstead: Harvester Wheatsheaf, 1992); Wayne A. Rebhorn, *The Emperor of Men's Minds: Literature and the Renaissance Discourse of Rhetoric* (Ithaca and London: Cornell University Press, 1995); Quentin Skinner, 'Classical Eloquence in Renaissance England' in *Reason and Rhetoric in the Philosophy of Hobbes* (Cambridge University Press, 1996), pp. 17–211.

3 R. R. Bolgar, *The Classical Heritage and its Beneficiaries* (Cambridge University Press, 1958), p. 273.

4 See Walter J. Ong, *Ramus, Method and the Decay of Dialogue* (Cambridge, MA: Harvard University Press, 1958), pp. 25–7; *Ramus and Talon Inventory* (Cambridge, MA: Harvard University Press, 1958), pp. 178–80.

5 Pierre de la Ramée, *Dialectique*, ed. Michel Dassonville (Geneva: Libraire Droz, 1964), p. 152. (Translations from French are my own.)

6 See Anthony Grafton and Lisa Jardine, *From Humanism to the Humanities: education and the liberal arts in fifteenth- and sixteenth-century Europe* (London: Duckworth, 1986), p. 167.

7 Brian Vickers, *In Defence of Rhetoric* (Oxford: Clarendon Press, 1988), p. 206.

8 See Karl Josef Höltgen, 'Roland MacIlmaine and Early Ramist Influence in Britain' forthcoming in *Explorations in Renaissance Culture*; W. S. Howell, *Logic and Rhetoric in England, 1500–1700* (New York: Russell and Russell, 1961), pp. 179–89.

9 Peter Ramus, *The Logike*, trans. Roland MacIlmaine; ed. Catherine M. Dunn (Northridge, CA: San Fernando Valley State College, 1969), p. 9.

10 Grafton and Jardine, *From Humanism to the Humanities*, p. 162.

11 Ramus, *The Logike*, p. 5.

12 See W. S. Howell, *Eighteenth-Century British Logic and Rhetoric* (Princeton University Press, 1971), pp. 520–1.

13 See Barbara Warnick, *The Sixth Canon: Belletristic Rhetorical Theory and its French Antecedents* (Columbia, SC: University of South Carolina Press, 1993).

14 'L'Art de parler est tres-utile, & d'un usage fort étendu. Il renferme tout ce qu'on appelle en François Belles Lettres: en Latin et en Grec Philologie, ce mot Grec signifie, l'amour des mots. Savoir les Belles Lettres, c'est savoir parler, écrire, ou juger de ceux qui écrivent . . .' Bernard Lamy, *La Rhétorique, ou l'Art de parler*, 5th edn (Amsterdam, 1712), p. 4.

15 Charles Rollin, *Method of Teaching and Studying the Belles-Lettres*, 4 vols. (London, 1734), vol. III, p. 48; vol. III, p. 2.

16 Rollin, *Method*, vol. I, pp. 47–9.

17 See Peter France, *A Thing Called Rhetoric: Eloquence, Literature and Taste in Edinburgh 1583–1995* (Edinburgh: Edinburgh University Library, 1995), p. 15, catalogue of an exhibition prepared for the International Society for the History of Rhetoric conference, 1995.

18 See Thomas P. Miller, *The Formation of College English: Rhetoric and Belles Lettres in the British Cultural Provinces* (University of Pittsburgh Press, 1997).

19 See Paul G. Bator, 'The Formation of the Regius Chair of Rhetoric and Belles Lettres at the University of Edinburgh', *Quarterly Journal of Speech* 75.1 (1989), 40–64.

20 'Account of the Late Duke Gordon, M.A.', *The Scots Magazine* 64 (1802), 22.

21 See Paul G. Bator, 'The Unpublished Rhetoric Lectures of Robert Watson, Professor of Logic, Rhetoric, and Metaphysics at the University of St. Andrews, 1756–1778', *Rhetorica* 12 (1994), 67–113.

22 Robert Watson, 'A Treatise on Rhetorick' [1758], St Andrews University Muniments MS PN173.W1, pp. 1–2. I have adopted the singular form 'Criticism' from the 1762 MS, which appears to be a correction of the plural recorded in 1758.

23 William Barron, *Synopsis of the Lectures on Belles Lettres and Logic Read in the University of St Andrews* (Edinburgh, 1781), pp. 4–5.

24 Adam Smith, *Lectures on Rhetoric and Belles Lettres*, ed. J. C. Bryce (Oxford: Clarendon Press, 1983), p. 26.

25 Thomas Sheridan, *British Education: Or, The Source of the Disorders of Great Britain* (London, 1756), pp. 218, 221.

26 *Ibid.*, p. 268.

27 *Ibid.*, p. 263.

28 *Ibid.*, p. 367.

29 Grafton and Jardine, *From Humanism to the Humanities*, p. 168.

30 Adam Potkay, *The Fate of Eloquence in the Age of Hume* (Ithaca and London: Cornell University Press, 1994), pp. 24–5.

31 Thomas Sheridan, *A Course of Lectures on Elocution* (London, 1762), p. 19.

32 Sheridan, *British Education*, p. 365.

33 William Guthrie, *Essay upon English Tragedy* (London, 1757), p. 10. Guthrie also produced the first English translation of Quintilian (1756) which Watson refers to in his 'Treatise on Rhetorick' [1758], I, 114.

34 Guthrie, *Essay upon English Tragedy*, p. 11.

35 Watson refers to Shakespeare and Milton as 'British'; vol. II, p. 7.

36 Henry Home, Lord Kames, *Elements of Criticism* (Edinburgh, 1762), vol. I, pp. 15–16.

37 *Ibid.*, vol. II, p. 159.

38 *Ibid.*, p. 218.

39 'C'est un effet admirable des progrès de l'esprit humain qu'aujourd'hui il nous vienne d'Écosse des règles de goût dans tous les arts, depuis le poëme épique jusqu'au jardinage. L'esprit humain s'étend tous les jours, et nous ne devons pas désespérer de recevoir bientôt des poétiques et des rhétoriques des îles Orcades.' Voltaire, *Oeuvres complètes* (Paris, 1879), xxv, 161–2. See also France, ed. *A Thing Called Rhetoric*, p. 12.

40 'Tant que les Anglais se sont contentés de prendre nos vaisseaux et de s'emparer du Canada et de Pondicheri, j'ai gardé un noble silence. Mais à présent qu'ils poussent la barbarie jusqu'à trouver Racine et Corneille ridicules, je dois prendre les armes.' *Voltaire's Correspondence*, ed. Theodore Besterman (Geneva: Institut et Musée Voltaire, 1953–65), vol. LIV, p. 42.

CHAPTER 2

Adam Smith, Samuel Johnson and the institutions of English

Ian Duncan

Initially delivered (1748–51) before an audience of professional gentlemen in Edinburgh, and subsequently (1751–63) as the 'private' course in the curriculum of Logic and Moral Philosophy at the University of Glasgow, Adam Smith's *Lectures on Rhetoric and Belles Lettres* constitute the first significant university programme devoted to the analysis of English literary discourse. Although scholars have begun to acknowledge Smith's foundational place in the early history of English, they by no means agree on the role he plays there.[1] It seems that the meaning of the *Lectures* as a historical event depends on the cultural field in which they are viewed. Franklin E. Court and Thomas P. Miller insist on separating 'the development of English studies' from an 'English literary history' which, in Miller's account especially, becomes the false destiny from which the discipline must be rescued. Both critics (following Gerald Graff) narrate the fall from a socially and politically responsive pedagogy into 'belleletrism', a romantic cult of appreciation, and the Arnoldian tradition that has dominated English Studies since the late nineteenth century. Their argument draws on an earlier, specialist tradition of commentary on Smith's lectures, by Vincent M. Bevilacqua and W. S. Howell, which recounts the ascendancy of a 'new rhetoric' in eighteenth-century Britain.[2] The new rhetoric turns away from traditional goals of inculcating civic virtue through persuasive eloquence and imitation of the Ancients, towards an emphasis on the stylistic formation of polite discourse and the cultivation of sensibility in modern civil society – 'literary' values, in short. Most of the credit (or blame) for codifying a belleletristic conception of English Studies falls on Hugh Blair, who attended the first series of Smith's lectures and would occupy the first university chair of 'Rhetoric and Belles Lettres' at Edinburgh in the 1760s. Blair examined the manuscript of Smith's lectures while preparing his own set, which he had published in 1783; Blair's lectures were disseminated on both sides of the Atlantic well into the nineteenth

century, and their influence was widely recognized. But Smith's lectures were not published until 1963, following their rediscovery in the
problematic form of a student's notes, and the nature of their influence
remains controversial.[3] Most commentators affirm a continuity between
Smith and later developments, except for Court, who draws a contrast
between Smith's 'pragmatic and political concerns' and Blair's new
regime of taste and sensibility; while Miller finds Smith already instituting the reduction of 'rhetoric' to 'literature' that Blair merely perfected.
Court's emphasis on Smith's capable modernity comes closer however
to the rhetorical historian Howell's insistence on the innovative force
of Smith's work as rhetoric, while Miller amplifies Bevilacqua's 'anti-
rhetorical' view of a Smith programmatically devoted to the aesthetic
transformation of the human sciences.[4]

The present essay, while drawing on the learning and insights of
these disciplinary histories, will not attempt a new account of Smith's
contribution to the tradition of eighteenth-century Rhetoric as it entered
the modern academy (nor adjudicate, thus, between the different views
of Smith's relation to Blair – a topic that more properly belongs to the
reassessment of Blair). It is important to note, however, that the British
academic tradition of Belles Lettres did not exist yet; there is a risk (from
which Miller's powerful study is not entirely free) of ideologically stream-
lining if not foreclosing texts by reading them through a discourse that
was formalized after their time, even though they might have occupied
an originary relation to it. Instead, I propose to reattach Smith's lectures
to literary history outside the academy – to the wider contemporary
horizon of discourses and genres, then undergoing revolutionary
transformation – in order to address their significance in the late-
eighteenth-century formation of a cultural subject called 'English literature'. In my view, Smith's originality lies in his account of the rhetorical
function of literary discourse in a modern culture, rather than in an
aesthetic conversion of rhetoric. A larger politics of literacy, overlapping
with but by no means limited to the aesthetic, informs the *Lectures
on Rhetoric and Belles Lettres*, which represent one of the first analytical
descriptions of literacy as a modern, secular technology of subject-
formation. The modernizing turn of the *Lectures* becomes particularly
clear if we set them beside another 'institution of English literature',
one that has been long granted canonical if not foundational status in
literary histories. This, the version of literature that would dominate the
twentieth-century academy as 'the English critical tradition', occupies
a very different site of production in mid-eighteenth-century Britain.

As its scholars have noted, the invention of English as an academic discipline coincided historically with a complex, socially dispersed formation of discursive institutions that together would constitute the larger institution of 'English literature'; this movement in turn belongs to a wholesale restructuring of the public sphere throughout the eighteenth century, and the emergence of the domain that contemporary theorists – notably Smith himself – would call 'civil' or 'commercial society'. These new institution-making activities included the antiquarian collection and poetic imitation of ancestral and popular vernacular forms (romance and ballad revivals), the assembly of canons of 'British poets', and the production of literary histories and biographies and scholarly editions. Such projects were largely bookseller-driven, often explicitly nationalist in their agenda, and facilitated by economic and legal developments such as the end of perpetual copyright in 1774; they took place not in the academy but Grub Street, the industrializing marketplace of printed texts.

In an influential account of these developments, Alvin Kernan has credited Samuel Johnson with giving authoritative definition to the institutional features of a modern literary culture in the commercial mode of production.[5] Johnson's career dramatizes the modern formation of the professional man of letters; at its crux, the *Dictionary of the English Language* (1755) marks the turn from an obsolescent patronage system to the marketplace, the new site of literary production as a heroic individual labour. Johnson's own writings, from the 'Letter to Chesterfield' to the 'Preface to the Dictionary', track and justify this movement. At the same time, in the *Dictionary* itself and later projects such as the edition of Shakespeare (1765) and the 'Lives of the English Poets' (1781), Johnson definitively erects the institutional superstructure of 'English Literature', a national vernacular language regulated by a native canon of classical authors. Kernan describes the genesis of a 'print-based romantic literary system centering on the individual creative self' which constitutes 'literature' out of the author's struggle with the material conditions of his production. Johnson's excellence and celebrity provide for a heroic rendering of this formation (pathos and all), as opposed to the ironical version that the counter-example of a Savage or Chatterton or Macpherson might supply.[6]

In the 'Preface to the Dictionary' Johnson distinguishes the conditions of his enterprise not only from 'the patronage of the great' but also from 'the shelter of academic bowers' – meaning, primarily, the French and Italian institutions set up to codify the national language, rather than Oxford and Cambridge.[7] Johnson's remark directs us to the institutional site of literary production, even as it sets aside the efficacy of institutions to represent (let alone fashion) a national culture, at least in Great Britain. Instead, the exemplary labour of the individual author will precipitate the forms of national culture in a commercial society. But nation-building was very much the business of the Scottish universities, devoted to the pedagogic reconstruction of national identity in a modern, post-national epoch. And crucially, the Scottish academy provided Adam Smith with a viewpoint from which commercial society could be theorized as a topic, not just endured as a predicament. Smith was able to conceptualize the market because he occupied an institutional position at least nominally outside it, allowing an intellectual engagement with market forces that could take place under the assumption that it was not directly determined by them. At the same time, the economic, political and cultural links between the Scottish universities and their towns, closer than in their English counterparts, facilitated the affirmative philosophical engagement with modernity, as we can see from the evolution of Smith's lectures: a private venture delivered to a city audience before being instituted in a receptive academy. This municipally responsive college setting accommodated a professional career which Smith came to understand as a unified intellectual project rather than as a series of commercial engagements. Late in life (1785) Smith expressed his ambition of composing a grand synthesis of the human sciences, which would include 'A Philosophical History of all the different branches of Literature, of Philosophy, Poetry, and Eloquence'.[8] Smith did not live to publish it in book form, but he had begun to realize something like this project, engaging a 'universal' array of disciplines and discourses, across the civic and pedagogical domain of the university curriculum – in contrast to Johnson's iteration of the printed commodity-text as the sole medium of literary expression. The *Lectures on Rhetoric and Belles Lettres* constitute an important, continuous stage in this career. They were Smith's first professional exercise, before he became a university professor, while the record of them that has survived dates from 1762–3, after the publication of *The Theory of Moral Sentiments* and contemporaneous with the *Lectures on Jurisprudence* out of which would grow *The Wealth of Nations*. Participating in this larger curricular and philosophical domain, the *Lectures on Rhetoric and Belles Lettres* are thoroughly informed by terms, themes and associations developed elsewhere in Smith's work: the ethical psychology of *The Theory of Moral Sentiments*, the historical and materialist sociology of *The Wealth of Nations*.

Through the academy, then, and as part of the project of a comprehensive theory of modernity, Smith's *Lectures on Rhetoric* theorize a constitutive function for literary discourse in commercial society, in contrast to the Romantic anti-modernism that formulates Johnson's situation as a literary producer in the marketplace. The nation-building purpose of the lectures, as has been well noted, was to provide post-Union Scottish students with a command of metropolitan discourse that would enable them to enter the imperial professions and pass as 'British' (rather than Scottish) subjects. The making of metropolitan identity is the project of ambitious provincials rather than those who already inhabit the metropolis. As has also been well noted, the term 'improvement' denotes both Smith's pedagogic imperative and the animating principle of his theoretical history – it names both the progress of civilization and the strategy of access to it.[9] With the applied sciences in mind, we can call Smith's Rhetoric a *cultural technology*, a repertoire of the tropes of individual and national self-fashioning, directed towards the achievement of a modern, metropolitan identity: an identity not natural but artificial, although based on a scientific grasp of the principles of human nature, and not inherited but forged.

The site of this formation is literacy in English. Smith's lectures equate English with literary discourse as such – like Latin, the imperial language of administration, business and education. As Crawford notes, such an equation entailed the pedagogic dismissal of a native vernacular culture; Smith's expulsion of the Scots poetic tradition to a barbaric darkness, in Lecture 23, makes him one of the founders of a literary schizophrenia deplored by modern nationalist critics.[10] Yet we should also note the expansive thrust of an argument that insists on the cultural and performative status of national identity, as a condition not fixed by birth but made, learnt and practised – in short, as a competence. Smith's *Lectures*, and the generic reorientation of Rhetoric from eloquence to politeness, take part in a larger intellectual shift in late-eighteenth-century Scotland, the distinctive regional version of the institution of 'literature' already mentioned. This involves the programmatic realignment of the national culture upon a conception of literacy, set against (yet in crucial ways dependent upon) a 'primitive' orality.[11] A sense of this larger national movement will help us to grasp the positive as well as the exclusionary strategy of Smith's lectures, requiring measures more grandly conceived than drills in English elocution or a weeding out of Scotticisms. They promoted a structural and systematic subject-fashioning oriented to the emergent domains of modernity; their distinctive innovation lies in their advocacy of the constitution of a new kind of modern subject through the techniques of literacy – specifically, they constitute the modern subject as a *reader*. Even in the secondhand, fractured text of the *Lectures* that has come down to us, we can read an impressive early analysis of the rhetorical and psychological dynamics that twentieth-century theorists, notably Marshall McLuhan and Benedict Anderson, have ascribed to the construction of modern national subjectivity in print culture.[12]

Far from cordoning off 'literature' as a closed semiotic system or fetishizing it as a finished object, in the manner of a high aesthetics, Smith's *Lectures on Rhetoric* insist on the social, historical and functional dynamism of literary discourse. They constitute 'belles lettres' as a rhetoric, a resource for improvement – less national monument than imperial technology, less a museum of wonderful relics than a store of commodities to trade in. Smith himself welcomed Johnson's *Dictionary* very much in these terms, as a warehouse of good English, while criticizing it for being insufficiently systematic.[13] The *Lectures* include modern English prose writers in their range of citations, in contrast to Johnson's announced policy in the *Dictionary* (which he by no means strictly followed) of favouring the Elizabethan and Jacobean authors as native classics and proprietors of a pure language. Smith's magazine of examples – functional, provisional, open-ended – is to be distinguished, therefore, from a 'canon' in the sense we have come to take for granted, and indeed the *Lectures* show little concern with hierarchies of taste and canon-formation.

The example of Johnson clarifies Smith's account of literature as a technology of representation by which readers constitute themselves as modern subjects in a commercial society. Conversely, the example of Smith illuminates Johnson's role at the origins of an English critical tradition bearing an ideology – a barely secularized theology – of Romantic anti-modernity, the establishment of which in the modern curriculum has been described by recent criticism.[14] The absence of the eighteenth-century Scottish academy from the received history of English has rested on a corresponding neglect of the rhetorical conception of literary discourse as a technique, part of a larger cultural technology. As Raymond Williams showed forty years ago, the Arnoldian figure of culture (derived in turn from Newman's *The Idea of a University*) came to mark a class-based division of intellectual labour in modern industrial capitalism, sustained until very recently in the postwar British distinction between universities and polytechnic colleges.[15] Culture defines the anti-materialist, anti-utilitarian polemic of the English critical tradition, which drafted Johnson into the regiment of Romantic and Victorian critics at odds with industrial modernity and 'political economy'. Thus, Smith, Hume, and other 'Scotch philosophers' do not merely belong to the tradition of materialism, utilitarianism and political economy, against which 'culture' is the reaction-formation: they are its founding fathers.

One of the signal omissions of the English critical tradition has been its failure, at least until the twentieth century, to have had anything very interesting to say to the history of the novel, as though official neglect or depreciation on the part of the critics (from Johnson through Arnold to T. S. Eliot) had drawn a line around that compromised genre of modern bourgeois culture. Actual novel criticism remains a comparatively humble sideline, at least until Henry James. It would seem, in short, that the main current of critical discourse only involved the form once it had sunk from its cultural pre-eminence (or else risen from Victorian commercialism to a respectable Modernist aestheticism). But to turn to Smith and Hume is to read theoretical mappings of modernity of an unmatched lucidity and sophistication; here, rather than in the official critical tradition, are to be found the philosophical conditions of novelistic practice, and of related modern forms such as history and biography. Like the novel, the ascendant model of the techniques he recommends, Smith's own discourse is dynamically homologous with modernity, reflecting upon its key topics of commerce and sympathy, and playing an important part in the establishment of a distinctively modern 'professional-managerial' culture. After a description of some of the key elements of Smith's analysis of literary discourse, this essay will go on to examine the ways in which the *Lectures on Rhetoric and Belles Lettres* opened theoretical space around the prose genres that would dominate modern literature.

First, however, Johnson. The 'Preface to the Dictionary' announces the author's arrival at a new space of literary production, outside patronage and the academy, defined by the marketplace and booksellers' genres. This new space is a desert, 'a gloom of solitude', and the arrival in it a sentence to hard labour – in theological terms, a fall. In the English language, 'copious without order, and energetic without rules' (p. 307), Johnson glimpses a postlapsarian shadow of the archangel's view of Eden: 'Wild above rule or art, enormous bliss' (*Paradise Lost*, VI. 297). The language has been 'suffered to spread, under the direction of chance, into wild exuberance; resigned to the tyranny of time and fashion; and exposed to the corruptions of ignorance, and caprices of innovation' (p. 307). Our legacy is the georgic imperative of cultivation: 'perplexity [is] to be disentangled and confusion to be regulated'. Out of this wilderness will arise, by the lexicographer's pains, the national and monumental order of the *Dictionary*.

But Johnson knows that a fixed, total order of representation cannot be made in an unstable world. English is an organic entity, 'the boundless chaos of a living speech', generated across time and space by human usage, subject to increase and decadence. The lexicographer may no more 'imagine that his dictionary can embalm his language and secure it from corruption and decay' than he may hope to 'change sublunary nature, and clear the world at once from folly, vanity, and affectation' (p. 324). In a Smithian review of the rise of commercial society, Johnson attends to the relation between modernization and linguistic change:

> Commerce, however necessary, however lucrative, as it depraves the manners, corrupts the language; they that have frequent intercourse with strangers, to whom they endeavour to accommodate themselves, must in time learn a mingled dialect, like the jargon which serves the traffickers on the Mediterranean and Indian coasts. This will not always be confined to the exchange, the warehouse, or the port, but will be communicated by degrees to other ranks of the people, and be at last incorporated with the current speech. (p. 325)

In Smith's account such a history will produce the conditions for material improvement, refinement of manners, and linguistic propriety; but in Johnson's it unfolds a categorical depravity and corruption.

Brought to recognize the imperfection of his materials and the unattainability of his goal, Johnson resorts to a provisional rather than absolute settlement. Appropriately he cites Hooker, whose *Laws of Ecclesiastical Polity* exemplify an English 'constitutional' discourse of conservative moderation and compromise – seeking to contain innovation, rather than refusing to countenance it, by the appeal to tradition. This constitutional discourse expresses itself as a characteristic *temper* rather than as a set of strategies:

> If the changes that we fear be thus irresistible, what remains but to acquiesce with silence, as in the other insurmountable distresses of humanity? It remains that we retard what we cannot repel, that we palliate what we cannot cure. Life may be lengthened by care, though death cannot ultimately be defeated: tongues, like governments, have a natural tendency to degeneration; we have long preserved our constitution, let us make some struggles for our language. (pp. 326–7)

Virtue lies in the stoic's stance of resistance to an inevitable fate. The solitary judgement, vulnerable to fits of passion and imagination, cleaves to the forms of purity even as it recognizes their transience in a fallen world. As is the way with these tragic scenarios, the very pathos of Johnson's alienated, strenuous solitude turns out to be redemptive; pathos is, so to speak, the surplus value that accrues back to the author as the aura of his inalienable identity in the face of death. The 'work' is the image of the man, incorporated in the book although – since the poet is 'doomed at last to wake a lexicographer' (p. 322) – confined to its margins. Johnson concludes the 'Preface' on an austere note of ascetic refusal, as one who has outlived his present: 'I have protracted my work until most of those whom I wished to please have sunk into the grave, and success and miscarriage are empty sounds; I therefore dismiss it with frigid tranquillity, having little to fear or hope from censure or from praise' (p. 328). Epitaph-wise the author consigns himself to posterity and the poets of a classical past.

For Johnson labour has value in that it expresses an embattled and pathetic individuality. But for Smith – it is his famous axiom – labour acquires value through the act of exchange. Exchange is the foundational trope of Smith's philosophic system, the key term in his revolutionary theory of modernity. If, according to *The Wealth of Nations*, 'the propensity to truck, barter, and exchange one thing for another' defines human nature, then modernity, in the form of commercial society, represents a realization rather than a corruption of our being. *The Theory of Moral Sentiments* makes sympathetic exchange the foundation of moral sentiment; what we now call 'intersubjectivity' generates the ethical and social imagination. Smith's model of intersubjectivity, as David Marshall has argued, is grounded on nothing but its own motion of exchange – not, for instance, on a moral or psychological overflow in either of the subjects.[16] In this spirit, the *Lectures on Rhetoric and Belles Lettres* offer a conjectural account of 'the first formation of languages' (the only part of the lectures that Smith published in essay form). Smith represents the primal scene of language formation as a *dialogue*:

Two savages, who had never been taught to speak, but had been bred up remote from the societies of men, would endeavour to make their mutual wants intelligible to one another, by uttering certain sounds, whenever they meant to denote certain objects.[17]

Far from being a pure source sullied by commerce, language occupies a homologous relation with it, since each is the contingent medium of the other, the response to an original privation.

Crucial to Smith's dialogical and intersubjective conception, the faculty of sympathy governs 'perspicuity of style', the topic of the early lectures. Even though it represents a 'naturall order of expression' (p. 6), perspicuity denotes no natural condition but an artificial construction, a convention, the style of metropolitan elites (pp. 4–5). This is because of the status of that 'natural order' as a representation, apprehended through the social framing of sympathy and custom rather than through any proximate access to the world. Language is transparent not to 'things' but to 'sentiment':

When the sentiment of the speaker is expressed in a neat, clear, plain and clever manner, and the passion or affection he is poss<ess>ed of and intends, *by sympathy*, to communicate to his hearer, is plainly and cleverly hit off, then and then only the expression has all the force and beauty that language can give it. (p. 25)

The task of Rhetoric, accordingly, is to activate this intersubjective circuit – to be 'interesting'. Its topics should 'interest us greatly by the Sympatheticall affections they raise in us' (p. 90); an author should regulate his narration 'in proportion to the impression it makes' (p. 93). The classical schemes and tropes are only noteworthy as instruments of this affective evocation, and Smith dismisses the traditional taxonomies of them.

Smith places far more emphasis on a new description of the techniques of sympathetic identification, which are above all *narrative* techniques. After the opening account of style, and before the closing discussion (Lectures 22–30) of the traditional branches of eloquence, Smith devotes the central portion of the course (Lectures 12–21) to the modern administrative medium of written prose. Smith recommends a particularistic rhetoric (famously deplored by Johnson) of mixed character and circumstantial detail. Especially momentous, though, is his prescription of 'subjective' and 'indirect' discourses. Smith distinguishes between 'direct' and 'indirect' modes of representation in order to privilege the 'indirect method' over an objective, enumerative accounting (Lecture 13). More than a stylistics (what will later be called 'free indirect discourse'), the indirect method is the major device of Smith's technology of subject-formation, formally embedding, and so activating, the dialogical principle he has found at the root of language. The indirect method turns upon the mediation of the representation through the response of a represented subject: 'describing the effects [a] quality produces on those who behold it' (p. 67). The author places a figure within the scene as the reader's mirror or proxy, serving to situate and integrate the rhetorical effect: the swains and hermits inserted into landscapes by Titian or Salvatore Rosa, Virgil or Milton, convey a more precise and profound emotion than would the depiction of the landscape alone. Turning to narrative ('the more complex and important actions of men', p. 85), Smith elaborates 'the Generall rule that when we mean to affect a reader deeply we must have recourse to the indirect method of description, relating the effects the transaction produced both on the actors and Spectators' (pp. 86–7). A figure made familiar by *The Theory of Moral Sentiments* – the 'impartial spectator' that regulates the ethical imagination in civil society – takes literary form as the medium that bonds the reader with the narrative event.

Smith begins to theorize a literary construction of subject positions that has preoccupied much recent cultural criticism. To compare Smith's insight with one of the most exhaustively codified modern accounts, the 'indirect method' anticipates the techniques of 'interpellation' and 'suture' designated by Althusserian criticism, by which an individual subject is enfolded into a collective ideological formation. Smith's originality lies in the recognition of a subject-formation that takes place through the techniques of literacy, and is dialogical in its operation: the activation of 'sentiment' occurs in a sympathetic transaction *between* the representation and the reader or audience, as opposed to its being found 'in' either the text or the reader's psychology. With this understanding, characteristic of the general model of intersubjectivity mentioned earlier, Smith goes beyond the period's fashionable formulation of the Longinian sublime, which at times he may echo ('The ancients carry us as it were into the very circumstances of the actors, we feel for them as it were for ourselves', p. 96).

Early in the lectures, Smith extends the consideration of style from linguistic practice to the more ambitious socializing project of the construction of a persona (Lectures 8–11). Literary representation is a key resource for a work of self-fashioning conceived in aesthetic rather than ethical terms, of strength and propriety. This labour occupies the reflexive sympathetic and linguistic circuit between self and audience, between composition and reception. Once again we encounter a principle familiar from *The Theory of Moral Sentiments* (I. i. 3–4): the agreeable man inhabits the field of sympathy by a rigorous tuning of his temper to what he conceives to be the pitch of those about him. The passage is worth quoting at length:

For what is that makes a man agreable company, is it not, when his sentiments appear to be naturally expressed, when the passion or affection is
properly conveyed and when their thoughts are so agreable and naturall that
we find ourselves inclined to give our assent to them. A wise man too in
conversation and behaviour will not affect a character that is unnaturall to
him . . . He will only regulate his naturall temper, restrain within just bounds
and lop all exhuberances and bring it to that pitch which will be agreable to
those about him. But he will not affect such conduct as is unnaturall to his
temper tho perhaps in the abstract they may be more to be wished.

In like manner what is agreable in Stile; it is when all the thoughts are
justly and properly expressed in such a manner as shews the passion they
affected the author with, and so that all seems naturall and easy. He never
seems to act out of character but speaks in a manner not only suitable to the
Subject but to the character he naturally inclines to. (p. 55)

The 'naturall' occupies a double site: both an 'original' temper or character and a social appearance or representation. Smith's attention to the
dialectical and performative circuit of the production of identity resists
both the essentialist notion that there is a prior self that expresses itself
through transparent cultural forms, and the nominalist view that there
is no self except what is constituted by representation. What is 'naturall' is
produced, instead, through a strenuous disciplinary conjunction of 'affection', 'appearance' and 'assent'. The sympathetic imagination constitutes
a shared site of mediation and negotiation in which the self forges itself
through a series of responsive adjustments and repositionings.

The practice of style requires an intellectual as well as an emotional
discipline, as Smith shows through a remarkable critique of Shaftesbury
(Lecture 11), whom he anatomizes in contrast to the successful personae
wrought by Addison and Swift. In an argument that in many of its
moves anticipates Arnold, Smith claims that Shaftesbury's failure to
achieve a commanding persona reflects a double failure of critical
engagement: Shaftesbury neither came to terms with the Puritanism of
his upbringing, nor participated in the advanced intellectual movement
of the day, natural philosophy. A constitutional weakness, the combined
consequences of neurasthenia and cultural deracination, governed his
recourse to the fine arts and to a compensatorily ornate and pompous
style. In presenting Shaftesbury's case as so richly overdetermined, the
issue of a mixed cultural, psychological and physiological symptomato-
logy, Smith amplifies the dialogical principle to encompass the self's
critical understanding of the historical field of its own production. Our
own projects of self-fashioning, we understand, are to be informed by
a comparable reckoning with the forces that shape us.

The concern for the integrity of the subject, as a rigorously yet precariously achieved dynamic construct, yields Smith's almost obsessive concern with effects of unity and continuity:

We should never leave any chasm or Gap in the thread of the narration even tho there are no remarkable events to fill up that space. The very notion of a gap makes us uneasy for what should have happened in that time. (p. 100)

Tis not then from the interruption of the deception that the bad effect of such transgressions of the unity of time proceed; It is rather from the uneasiness we feel in being kept in the dark with regard to what happened in so long a time. . . . We make a jump from one time to another without knowing what connected them. (p. 122)

The student-notes format is no doubt responsible for making Smith's anxiety seem like fussiness; but the suggestion of a representational *horror vacui* remains. The 'uneasiness' does not derive from 'the interruption of the deception' – for we always know we are dealing with a representation – but from a breach in knowledge, as though a loss of consciousness itself has occurred. As Smith's editor points out, the argument here relies upon the principle, crucial to Smith's philosophy and its basis in Humean epistemology, of the imaginary interconnectedness of the field of sensation.[18] In the *Treatise of Human Nature* Hume maintains that a continuum of customary associations constitutes not only our knowledge of the world, but our coherence as subjects in it: 'our notions of personal identity, proceed entirely from the smooth and uninterrupted progress of the thought along a train of connected ideas'.[19]

Smith thus cleaves to the neoclassical unities of time, space and action because they secure an internal, subjective unity for the reader. This has important consequences for the domain of representation. In a brief history of historians, Smith commends Tacitus for recognizing 'that the incidents of private life tho' not so important would affect us more deeply and interest us more than those of a publick nature' (p. 113). This is because the representation of private life concentrates the affections, producing the desired effect of psychological unity: 'In Private calamities our passions are fixt on one, as it were concentrated and so become greatly Stronger than when separated and distracted by the affecting circumstances that befell the severall persons involved in a common calamity' (p. 113).

Private life is conspicuously the mimetic domain of the novel, rather than of history, in this, the age of Richardson and Fielding. In one of the historical accounts of modernization outlined in the *Lectures on Rhetoric*,

Smith describes a cultural shift in the sources of 'interest' away from the superstitious wonders that fascinated pre-modern societies:

As the marvellous could no longer please authors had recourse to that which they imagind would please and interest most; that is, to represent such actions and passions as, being affecting in themselves, or displaying the delicate feelings of the Human heart, were likely to be most interesting. (p. 111)

The shift explains a common theme of eighteenth-century criticism, the succession of 'the novel' upon 'romance': 'Novells which unfold | the tender emotions or more violent passions in the characters they bring before us succeeded the Wild and extravagant Romances which were the first performances of our ancestors in Europe' (p. 111).[20] The change occurs as the progress of civilization, with its consequences of 'Luxury, and Refinement of manners', gives people leisure to 'turn their attention to the motions of the human mind' (p. 112). Smith's conjectural and analogical reasoning makes it clear that the representation of sentiment and private life – the peculiar stuff of the novel – is a structurally modern phenomenon, the product of advanced civilizations, as characteristic of contemporary France as of imperial Rome. The argument is congruent with the brief history of literary forms sketched later (Lecture 23), which charts a progress across three cultural stages. Poetry is the invention of primitive societies, an oral art emerging from song and dance and so close to cultural origins. But '[it] is always late before prose and its beauties come to be cultivated' (p. 136). The product of a commercial society and the division of labour, 'Prose is naturally the Language of Business; as Poetry is of pleasure and amusement. Prose is the Stile in which all the common affairs of life all Business and Agreements are made' (p. 137). The 'cultivation' of prose – its investment with the complex aesthetic effects associated with poetry – accompanies the still later stage of (once more) opulence, leisure and refinement of manners.

Smith does not formally admit the novel into his pedagogy; that curricular innovation would take place elsewhere in eighteenth-century Scotland, as Paul Bator's essay will indicate later in this book. If anything Smith deprecates the genre for its lapses from narrative rigour. Novelists are practically obliged to violate the unities and resort to the meretricious devices of suspense, since 'newness is the only merit in a Novel and curiosity the only motive which induces us to read them' (p. 97). Nevertheless Smith provides generous theoretical accommodation for the 'rise of the novel', identified by a series of influential twentieth-century critics (Bakhtin, Lukács, Benjamin, Ian Watt) as the typical genre of modern culture, and more recently implicated in the invention of a feminine, domestic sphere of subject-fashioning.[21] My argument has been suggesting that *The Lectures on Rhetoric and Belles Lettres* specify many of the formal techniques of novelistic discourse (also taken up by associated, 'novelized' genres such as history and biography), the most consequential of which furnish the technology of subject-formation perfected by modern realist fiction. Scott's Waverley novels play a decisive part in that development, and many of their most characteristic innovations can be traced back to Smith. To take a notable example, Scott's mixed, indirect narrative mode deploys a 'blank' hero, the passive spectator rather than heroic agent of historical events, to focus the subjectivity of his reader.[22]

Scott's intellectual formation took place in the late-Enlightenment milieu of Smith and his successors; he studied at Edinburgh University under Dugald Stewart and Hugh Blair, although it appears he did not attend Blair's Rhetoric and Belles Lettres course.[23] Scott provides a good example of how intellectual influence may be disseminated indirectly in a culture. As Gillian Beer has remarked apropos of Darwin, 'ideas are even more influential when they become assumptions embedded in the culture than while they are the subject of controversy. . . . Ideas pass more rapidly into the state of assumptions when they are *unread*'.[24] One student who did however attend Smith's *Lectures on Rhetoric* (at Glasgow, 1759–60) was James Boswell, and we have his own testimony that they informed his biographical technique. Boswell realizes Smith's prescriptions – more brilliantly, no doubt, than Smith could have imagined – in his attention to particularistic detail, in his use of the indirect method including a literal representation of dialogue and the placing of a spectatorial proxy ('Boswell'), and in his didactic attention to character as a product of the subject's interaction with his material and cultural conditions.[25] Johnson's eminence as the supreme instance of English literary character rests, in other words, on canons of perspicuity devised by Adam Smith.

NOTES

1 See, especially, Robert Crawford, *Devolving English Literature* (Oxford: Clarendon Press, 1992); Franklin E. Court, *Institutionalizing English Literature: The Culture and Politics of Literary Study, 1750–1900* (Stanford University Press, 1992); Thomas P. Miller, *The Formation of College English: Rhetoric and Belles Lettres in the British Cultural Provinces* (University of Pittsburgh Press, 1997).

2 Vincent M. Bevilacqua, 'Adam Smith's Lectures on Rhetoric and Belles Lettres', *Studies in Scottish Literature* 3: 1 (1965), 41–60. W. S. Howell, 'Adam Smith's Lectures on Rhetoric: An Historical Assessment' in Andrew S. Skinner and Thomas Wilson, eds., *Essays on Adam Smith* (Oxford: Clarendon Press, 1975), pp. 11–43.

3 Bevilacqua argues that although unpublished, the lectures were widely circulated and 'had the effect of a book', influencing among others Blair, Kames and Reid ('Adam Smith's Lectures', pp. 45, 59), a view with which J. C. Bryce, the editor of the *Lectures* for the Glasgow edition, concurs. Howell speculates that 'Rhetorical theory in the nineteenth century might have taken a better turn than it did, had Adam Smith's lectures been available to stand beside the works of Campbell and Blair' ('Adam Smith's Lectures on Rhetoric', p. 43). Court asserts that although Blair acknowledged a debt to the lectures, 'Smith's influence had no long-term measurable consequence' (*Institutionalizing English Literature*, p. 32). Miller absorbs the lectures into the general programme of Smith's thought and the general tendency of Scottish Enlightenment moral philosophy; Smith is 'the most important example of how the trend toward belletrism in rhetoric was paralleled by the movement of moral philosophy toward the social sciences'.

4 Court, *Institutionalizing English Literature*, pp. 19, 29–35. Howell, 'Adam Smith's Lectures on Rhetoric', pp. 42–3. For a different account of the shift from eloquence to aestheticism, see Adam Potkay's recent argument that the new politeness entails a studied nostalgia for primitive virtue and the sublime: *The Fate of Eloquence in the Age of Hume* (Ithaca and London: Cornell University Press, 1994).

5 Alvin Kernan, *Printing Technology, Letters, and Samuel Johnson* (Princeton University Press, 1987; reprinted in 1989 as *Samuel Johnson and the Impact of Print*).

6 See Susan Stewart, *Crimes of Writing: Problems in the Containment of Representation* (New York: Oxford University Press, 1991) and Richard Holmes, *Dr Johnson and Mr Savage* (London: Hodder & Stoughton, 1993), to take two different contemporary styles of literary history.

7 *The Oxford Authors: Samuel Johnson*, ed. Donald Green (Oxford University Press, 1984), p. 328. Future references to the 'Preface to the Dictionary' in this edition will be given in the text.

8 In a letter to Rochefoucauld, 1 Nov. 1785; cited in the editors' introduction, *Essays on Adam Smith*, p. 2.

9 For both points see, especially, Kurt Heinzelman's valuable essays, 'Rhetoric, Economics and the Scene of Instruction' in *L'imaginaire économique*, ed. Philippe Desan, *Stanford French Review* 15 (1991), 349–71; and 'The Last Georgic: Adam Smith and the Scene of Writing' in *Texts in Contexts: Adam Smith's Wealth of Nations*, ed. Stephen Copley and Kathryn Sutherland (Manchester University Press, 1995), pp. 171–94.

10 Crawford, *Devolving English Literature*, pp. 31–3. For the nationalist tradition of criticism see my essay, 'North Britain, Inc.', *Victorian Literature and Culture* 23 (1995), 335–46.

11 See Penny Fielding, *Writing and Orality: Nationality, Culture and Nineteenth-Century Scottish Fiction* (Oxford: Clarendon Press, 1996), pp. 8–12; and 'Writing at the North: Rhetoric and Dialect in Eighteenth Century Scotland' (unpublished essay).

12 Marshall McLuhan, *The Gutenberg Galaxy: The Making of Man in a Typographic Age* (University of Toronto Press, 1962), pp. 244–50; Benedict Anderson, *Imagined Communities: Reflections on the Origin and Spread of Nationalism* (London: Verso, 1985), pp. 28–49. Both Court and Miller discuss the programme of subject-formation in the *Lectures on Rhetoric and Belles Lettres*, which they read through the lens of Smith's ethical psychology and economic theory. In my view, there is a crucial distinction between the *reader* and *spectator* as figures for the Smithian subject; the former allows for a degree of critical activity unacknowledged in the latter.

13 Smith's review, originally published in the *Edinburgh Review*, no. 1 (1755), is reprinted in vol. III of the Glasgow Edition of Smith's works: *Essays on Philosophical Subjects*, ed. W. P. D. Wightman and J. C. Bryce (Oxford: Clarendon Press, 1980), pp. 232–41.

14 See Gerald Graff, *Professing Literature: An Institutional History* (University of Chicago Press, 1987) for North American developments, and Chris Baldick, *The Social Mission of English Criticism, 1848–1932* (Oxford: Clarendon Press, 1983) for Britain.

15 Raymond Williams, *Culture and Society, 1780–1950* (New York: Columbia University Press, 1958).

16 See David Marshall, *The Figure of Theatre: Shaftesbury, Defoe, Adam Smith and George Eliot* (New York: Columbia University Press, 1986).

17 'Considerations concerning the first formation of Languages, and the different genius of original and compounded Languages' (1761), in Adam Smith, *Lectures on Rhetoric and Belles Lettres*, ed. J. C. Bryce (Oxford: Clarendon Press, 1983), p. 203. Future references to this edition will be given in the text.

18 *Lectures on Rhetoric and Belles Lettres*, 'Introduction', p. 13; Bryce refers to 'The History of Astronomy', *Essays on Philosophical Subjects*; see esp. pp. 37–47.

19 David Hume, *A Treatise of Human Nature* (Harmondsworth: Penguin, 1969), p. 308. For the argument, see esp. Book 1, Part IV, Sections ii and vi.

20 See the many examples collected in Ioan Williams, ed., *Novel and Romance 1700–1800: A Documentary Record* (London: Routledge and Kegan Paul, 1970).

21 See Mikhail Bakhtin, *The Dialogic Imagination: Four Essays* (Austin: University of Texas Press, 1981); Georg Lukács, *Theory of the Novel* (Cambridge, MA: MIT Press, 1971); Walter Benjamin, 'The Storyteller' in *Illuminations* (New York: Schocken Books, 1968); Ian Watt, *The Rise of the Novel* (Berkeley: University of California Press, 1957); Nancy Armstrong, *Desire and Domestic Fiction: A Political History of the Novel* (New York: Oxford University Press, 1987).

22 See Alexander Welsh, *The Hero of the Waverley Novels* (Princeton University Press, 1992), which surveys the history of commentary on the figure.

23 See Arthur Melville Clark, *Sir Walter Scott: The Formative Years* (Edinburgh: Blackwood's, 1969), p. 119, n. 1.

24 Gillian Beer, *Darwin's Plots: Evolutionary Narrative in Darwin, George Eliot and Nineteenth-Century Fiction* (London: Routledge & Kegan Paul, 1983), pp. 4, 6.

25 See Gordon Turnbull, 'Boswell in Glasgow: Adam Smith, Moral Sentiments and the Sympathy of Biography' in Andrew Hook and Richard B. Sher, eds., *The Glasgow Enlightenment* (East Linton: Tuckwell, 1995), pp. 163–75.

CHAPTER 3

The 'eloquence of the Bar': Hugh Blair's Lectures, professionalism and Scottish legal education

Rajit S. Dosanjh

'I am powerful. And I am only the least of the doorkeepers. From hall to hall there is one doorkeeper after another, each more powerful than the last. The third doorkeeper is already so terrible that even I cannot bear to look at him.' These are difficulties the man from the country has not expected; the Law, he thinks, should surely be accessible at all times and to everyone...

– Franz Kafka, 'Before the Law'[1]

In his most famous essay, 'Tradition and the Individual Talent', T. S. Eliot argues that new works of art change the way we perceive history. They force us to find new connections between past and present, to weave new narratives of interpretation. '[T]he past', he says, is 'altered by the present as much as the present is directed by the past.'[2] Although Eliot is referring explicitly to the dynamics of the literary canon, his words are equally relevant to the history of English Literature *as an academic discipline*. In recent years, new scholarship has effectively transformed our understanding of this history by moving its point of origin from nineteenth-century England to eighteenth-century *Scotland*. As a result, both Adam Smith and Hugh Blair have emerged as key figures in the development of English Literature within the academy. Robert Crawford, for example, describes Smith as 'a progenitor of English Studies' and claims that his lectures on rhetoric (given first in Edinburgh and later at Glasgow University) stand 'at the root of what constitutes the university canon of English Literature'.[3] After Smith, he says, the subject spread throughout Scottish academia but 'was most celebrated at Edinburgh University' where Hugh Blair gave a course of lectures that 'both acknowledge a debt to Smith's work and take it further'.[4] Franklin Court offers a similar account: 'In the history of English studies, Smith was pivotal and innovative'; he was followed by Blair, who made 'the next notable eighteenth-century attempt to teach English literature'.[5]

Even as they affirm Blair's place in history, these descriptions imply that his work lacks the foundational importance of Smith's, its connection to present-day methods and concerns. According to Court, Smith pioneered a form of sociological criticism while Blair championed an outmoded critical approach, one preoccupied with 'interior, egocentric matters of taste'. Whereas Smith 'assimilated literature to a much broader cultural context', Blair 'presided over interpretations and the values derived from them largely for their own sake'.[6] Court thus establishes a tidy dichotomy between Smith's *critical theory*, which situated itself in the gritty realities of commerce and ethics, and Blair's *literary criticism*, which distanced itself from such worldly concerns. What follows, however, is an attempt to show that Blair's critical practice was not as isolated from its 'cultural context' as Court's interpretation suggests.

Like Smith, Blair addressed the role of literary study within other academic and professional economies. Crawford has argued that Blair's teachings were aimed at reinforcing the attitudes towards language and literature associated with the project of linguistic 'improvement' pursued by Scottish elites during the eighteenth century. In this instance, 'improvement' meant removing the linguistic differences between Scotland and England said to be preventing full economic and political integration after the Union. Crawford writes that Blair's *Lectures on Rhetoric and Belles Lettres* represents 'a skilled effort at cultural translation, turning Scottish material of an unacceptable kind into a form acceptable to a new British audience'.[7] This may be so, yet, as I will argue, Blair's own project was as much about the maintenance of institutional and professional power, and the *fixing* of difference, as it was about 'improvement' and the *elimination* of difference. His *Lectures* – particularly his discussion of 'eloquence' – sanctioned the efforts of Enlightenment Scotland's most powerful professional association, the Faculty of Advocates, to confine legal education to the university, thereby insulating the practice of law from the 'lower' ranks of Scottish society.[8] In other words, Blair authorized the Faculty's use of the university as an instrument of social exclusion. Seen in this light, his discourse appears just as 'modern' as Smith's, just as relevant to current critical practice. It provides valuable evidence that the university subject of English Literature has always been 'interdisciplinary' to some extent; that it has always found some of its own purpose in its relationship to other fields and professions.

Academic institutions and professional associations deal in the same commodity, namely, certification of knowledge. They therefore negotiate between the same competing interests. On one hand, they must ensure that 'competency' appears available to all. Only then can they preserve the authority of their endorsement (which depends upon it being seen as a proof of knowledge rather than as a sign of privilege). On the other hand, these institutions must ensure that 'incompetence' survives by limiting access to credentials. Only then can they guarantee continued demand for their services and continued meaning for the distinctions they manufacture. It is this common tension between eliminating and preserving certified difference that connects Blair's *Lectures* to changes in the Faculty of Advocates' entrance requirements during the eighteenth century – changes that are emblematic of academia's links with the development of a culture of professionalism.

Nicholas Phillipson has described how, in the late seventeenth century, members of the ruling class of Scotland came to see the study of law as 'the principle science of the polite world'.[9] They pursued formal legal training in increasing numbers: law, they believed, could establish and enforce the codes of social conduct necessary for Scotland to join the community of 'polite' nations. With its status elevated by the elite, the Scottish legal profession began to define its role not only in terms of civil administration but social and cultural leadership as well. It was during this period that the Faculty of Advocates fashioned an identity for itself as the representative of the 'polite world' in Scottish society, an identity it would claim for the next two centuries.

Perhaps the greatest proponent of the Scottish advocate as cosmopolitan and civic leader was Sir George Mackenzie of Rosehaugh, Dean of the Faculty from 1682 until 1689. Throughout his tenure, Mackenzie encouraged formal legal training for all advocates. He pushed for the creation of legal professorships at Scottish universities and played a leading role in the founding of the Advocates' Library in Edinburgh (which eventually gave rise to the National Library of Scotland). In his speech inaugurating the Library in 1689, Mackenzie brings together competing notions of law – as the expression of a common culture and as the private domain of qualified professionals. He makes the Library a symbol of the connection between law and a wider culture of enlightenment. After assuring his audience that the shelves have been kept 'chastely devoid of works dealing with irrelevant subjects', he goes on to describe the collection as 'all the fruits of Greek and Roman wisdom together with everything that the riper experience of later ages had added to their discoveries, and all that the great galaxy of the learned has made common property for the common good'.[10] The relevant knowledge for legal practice seems to be nothing less than the 'common' intellectual heritage of Europe. 'Three branches of learning are the handmaidens of Jurisprudence,' he declares, 'namely, History, Criticism, and Rhetoric; for which reason our catalogue abounds in Greek and Roman historians. From them the sources and development of laws as also the abilities of their makers, can be discerned.'[11] Mackenzie argues that the work of lawyers is informed by disciplines and creative endeavours far beyond the narrow sphere of technical rules and forms of process. The Library is envisioned as the foundation of a community linked by shared knowledge rather than shared origins: 'Formerly, educated men of an inquiring turn of mind, even if they were wealthy, lacked abundance of every kind of writing which has now been assembled here with consummate care and system. All now enjoy it in common, as men did in the golden age; all gain unlimited instruction at no expense, and riches without inquietude.'[12] The Library promotes education for *all* male citizens, regardless of economic status. It emancipates knowledge from its previous captivity, uniting literate men in their free and equal access to learning. It is a cultural reserve: through its open doors legal knowledge becomes public knowledge, 'common property'.

This idealistic rhetoric, however, can not escape its context. It is, after all, the *Advocates'* Library that Mackenzie is inaugurating and he makes sure to balance his imagery of universal access with descriptions of the Library as the sole property of the legal profession, there to foster its exclusive mastery over the law. There are certain advantages, he says, in developing a corps of legal specialists and the Library will make these apparent. They were obvious to

our great Justinian, when he commended to legal students the study of law on the grounds that their prescribed course, when completed, would enable them successfully to conduct their country's affairs in the departments to be entrusted to them. It was thus that the Roman state flourished, not so much by the valor of its armies, as by the justice of its laws.

Classism and classicism converge as visions of universal access give way to a defence of bureaucratic division. The Library will help train legal *professionals* able to manage the affairs of a nation. It will link modern Scotland to Justinian's Rome, a society that improved through the competence of its administrators. As we have seen, Mackenzie was Dean of the Faculty at a time when it was becoming more and more socially exclusive, when those who Phillipson describes as 'the natural leaders of the political nation' formed a significant part of its membership.[13]

So even as Mackenzie offers the ideal of the Library, and legal knowledge itself, as 'common property', the profession that puts this knowledge to work, *that gives it power,* has already distanced itself from the 'common' social and economic life of the community it serves. When justifying the Library to the public, Mackenzie denies this separation; when speaking to his colleagues, he affirms its necessity.

As Phillipson points out, immediately following the Union of 1707 members of the Faculty stepped back from their self-constructed image as cultural leaders, focusing instead on their more limited role as legal specialists.[14] Yet by the middle of the eighteenth century, Robert Dundas, Dean of the Faculty, could say with confidence that 'there was no science or part of polite and useful Learning for the knowledge of which some in the Faculty were not distinguished'.[15] The Faculty was once again asserting its cultural authority and its connection to European intellectual life. To ensure that its members were qualified to play a prominent role in the 'polite world', the Faculty revived the broad definition of legal competence set down by Mackenzie. Speaking in 1748, Dundas advises the Faculty to guarantee that its future members:

maintain and preserve that character and reputation that they had long held, and still possessed not only for knowledge of the Civil or Roman and municipal Laws and Constitution of their country, but of the other valuable branches of learning that are requisite to accomplish & adorn the Character of Gentlemen, and were indeed necessary to render them completely qualified for the exercise of their Profession.[16]

The boundaries of legal knowledge once again extend beyond technical proficiency, local expertise. Like Mackenzie, Dundas links the practice of law with breadth of learning: proper legal education encompasses all parts of 'polite' culture and produces advocates with the 'Character of Gentleman'. He judiciously avoids any mention of class or economic preconditions: all that is required to attain the right character is the right education, nothing else.

Dundas goes on to emphasize the need for comprehensive qualifications, saying that prospective entrants 'should take pains to acquire the other Sciences and accomplishments becoming the Character of Gentlemen, particularly not to neglect Academical learning, before they should apply themselves to study the municipal laws of their Country'.[17] The practice of law requires not only 'municipal' training, but an education that transcends political borders, that concerns the *community* of nations. Yet the phrase 'Academical learning' suggests that there are limits to this shared intellectual territory. Knowledge once described as 'common property' is now located behind the walls of the modern Academy, the university.

What remained only an implication in 1748 became more explicit over the course of the next two decades as the Faculty took steps to make university attendance a clear requirement for membership.[18] Those conducting the Faculty's entrance examinations were advised to ask specific questions concerning 'Universal History', the 'Law of Nature and Nations', and 'Roman Antiquities' – courses offered at the University of Edinburgh. On 30 November 1756, for example, this resolution was passed:

The Faculty of Advocates considering that for some years past the Colleges upon Universal History and Roman Antiquities have not been regularly attended; and also considering that it concerns the honour of the Faculty that their Members should be versant in every part of literature . . . they do therefore recommend to the private Examinators upon the Civil Law to examine the Candidates upon the History and Antiquities of the Roman Law; and they hereby order a Copy of this their resolution to be sent to all the professors in the University of Edinburgh in order that the same may be intimated to the Students at their different Colleges.[19]

The University of Edinburgh appears as an extension of the Faculty itself, as a secure repository for the intellectual wealth required of its members. The approved site of legal education is being shifted away from individual tutorials, towards the university; away from private transactions, towards the regulated sale of knowledge.[20]

Two decades later, the Faculty made further attempts to compel university attendance, prompted by the controversy over its acceptance of John Wright as an advocate in 1781.[21] Wright started out as a shoemaker in the small town of Greenock, near Glasgow, but went on to become a preacher and a private teacher of law and mathematics. Although he met all existing requirements for entry, his admission faced stiff opposition. As Henry Cockburn writes, the Faculty was 'then a highly aristocratic body, and used to curl up its birse at every plebeian who tried to enter'.[22] James Boswell gives this account of the controversy: 'There was a debate in the Faculty of Advocates whether we should oppose Mr. John Wright's petition to come among us, he being of low origin and gaining his livelihood as a teacher . . . I was keen for him, being of the opinion that our Society has no *dignity*, and must receive every man of good character and knowledge.'[23]

Although the Faculty did eventually accept Wright, in 1785 it established a committee to review its membership requirements, hoping to avoid such embarrassing situations in the future. In its report, the committee explains that the practice of law 'implies a publick Trust, of a high and important Nature'. The Faculty should therefore limit its membership to only those individuals who possess 'that enlightened understanding, and those liberal Sentiments which are acquired, by an early Course of well directed Study, and an early Admission into useful and respectable Society'.[24] The committee warns the Faculty to maintain its long tradition of requiring 'a Knowledge of the learned Languages and Philosophy, in a word that liberal education which is necessary to form the Scholar and the Gentleman'. Each applicant should be made to provide 'proper Evidence to the Dean of Faculty of his having attended the Classes of an University Seven Years; three Years whereof at the law Classes'.[25] In addition, each applicant should furnish 'satisfying Evidence that he is not above Twenty Seven Years of Age'.[26] As John Cairns has observed, this combination of educational requirements and age restrictions was intended to prevent members of the 'less wealthy classes' from becoming qualified advocates.[27] The Faculty has completed its move away from the promise of free knowledge to a more prohibitive definition of legal training, all the while maintaining the rhetoric of openness by exploiting concepts of 'character', 'scholarship' and, most importantly, 'liberal education'. In reality, the business of exclusion has been simply handed over to the university. And when governed by such a restrictive institution, knowledge that supposedly allows access to a universal community becomes an obstacle to economic and social equality.

While the Faculty of Advocates encouraged professional training at Edinburgh University, changes in the curriculum itself were adding to the vocational character of the institution where Hugh Blair would eventually give his course on Rhetoric and Belles Lettres. During the same period that saw the establishment of chairs of Civil and Scots law, the number of students completing their degrees declined remarkably. For much of the eighteenth century, only one or two students received a Master of Arts each year.[28] This development, brought on by the elimination of the Regenting system in 1708, was not confined to the Arts: the only Law degrees awarded during the eighteenth century were honorary ones.[29] Presumably, students were attending only those classes they thought necessary for professional practice or attainment of 'polite learning'. And, as we have seen, professional advocacy required both legal and 'liberal' education. It is not surprising, then, that Blair's course, and literary study in general, should have been so popular with students at the university.

In 1783, after more than two decades of teaching, Blair published his *Lectures on Rhetoric and Belles Lettres*, a collection of readings intended to give to 'the world' what had previously been available only to his students, namely, knowledge of how to appreciate and make use of great literature. In the introduction, Blair foregrounds the ideas of European refinement and Scottish professionalism that shaped education at Edinburgh during the eighteenth century. Referring to 'language, style, and composition', he declares: 'in all the polished nations of Europe, this study has been treated as highly important, and has possessed a considerable place in every plan of liberal education'.[30] Here, Blair is vindicating the university's decision to create a Chair of Rhetoric and Belles Lettres: like the Advocates Library, it will help to secure Scotland's connection to the wider, 'polite', world.[31] He is also reassuring the reader that literary study is important and socially advantageous. Just as Mackenzie and Dundas had done, Blair imagines a transnational community united by similar intellectual values and educational practices. And once again, access to this community depends upon the acquisition of a specific body of knowledge. The study of Rhetoric and Belles Lettres encourages independence from one's immediate verbal surroundings: 'They who have never studied eloquence in its principles, nor have been trained to attend to the genuine and manly beauties of good writing, are always ready to be caught by the mere glare of language.'[32] Blair claims to be providing the 'rules and instructions' necessary to avoid being led astray by 'what chances to be fashionable and popular, how corrupted soever, and erroneous, that may be'.[33] His is offering, in other words, a way to move past parochial standards towards universal principles of truth and beauty, principles that transcend the vagaries of time and place.

This wider sphere of reference, however, is available only to the properly qualified. According to Blair, an authentic understanding of rhetoric and literature requires knowledge of the other disciplines that make up the 'liberal' curriculum. This point is emphasized when Blair describes the position his subject 'is entitled to possess in academical education':

the study of Rhetoric and Belles Lettres supposes and requires a proper acquaintance with the rest of the liberal arts. It embraces them all within its circle, and recommends them to the highest regard. The first care of all such as wish either to write with reputation, or to speak in public so as to command attention, must be, to extend their knowledge; to lay in a rich store of ideas relating to those subjects of which the occasions of life may call them to discourse or to write. Hence, among the ancients, it was a fundamental principle, and frequently inculcated . . . that the orator ought to be an accomplished scholar, and conversant in every part of learning.[34]

The issue of education immediately turns Blair's attention away from matters of cultural integration towards more local concerns over personal 'reputation' and professional distinction. He iterates the need for 'solid' education: 'Knowledge and science must furnish the materials that form the body and substance of any valuable composition. Rhetoric serves to add the polish; and we know that none but firm and solid bodies can be polished well.'[35] Without eloquence, however, knowledge is mute: 'without being master of those attainments, no man can do justice to his own conceptions; but how rich soever he may be in knowledge and in good sense, will be able to avail himself less of those treasures, than such as possess not half his store'.[36] Eloquence, the product of rhetorical and literary study, makes difference visible. It frees 'academical' knowledge from silence, giving it the power to differentiate the truly 'qualified' from the 'incompetent'. Indeed, the purpose of liberal knowledge seems to have changed from the expansion of community to the spread of difference.

Once the academic foundation has been laid, eloquence becomes a valuable asset in professional life. Blair explains that '[t]o speak or write perspicuously and agreeably, with purity, with grace and strength, are attainments of the utmost consequence to all who propose, either by speech or writing, to address the public'.[37] He names 'the Bar' as one of the 'three great scenes of eloquence', the others being 'popular assemblies' and 'the pulpit'.[38] Blair, in effect, adds rhetoric and literature to the catalogue of learning required of the advocate. In his discussion of 'the eloquence of the Bar' we find the same dichotomy between unity and division that marks his introduction: restrictions on access to the knowledge necessary to practice legal eloquence undermine the transcendence it supposedly offers. Blair advises prospective advocates to improve their rhetorical skills, describing the courtroom as the perfect arena for personal advancement:

It is no small encouragement to eloquence at the bar, that of all the liberal professions, none gives fairer play to genius and abilities than that of the advocate. He is less exposed than some others, to suffer by the arts of rivalry, by popular prejudices, or secret intrigues . . . Interest and friends may set forward a young pleader with peculiar advantages beyond others, at the beginning; but they can do no more than open the field to him . . . Spectators remark, judges decide, parties watch; and to him will the multitude of clients never fail to resort, who gives the most approved specimens of his knowledge, eloquence, and industry.[39]

Using examples from works of literature, Blair makes eloquence available for appropriation, thereby leaving only 'knowledge' and 'industry' to determine the extent of professional success. There seem to be no unexplained conditions or arbitrary rules to prevent the rise of the advocate. In this way, Blair's image of the courtroom is interestingly similar to numerous descriptions of the Union offered by members of the Scottish ruling class during the eighteenth century. Writers such as Lord Kames, John Sinclair and Alexander Wedderburn portrayed the Union as a vast community without rigid social distinctions, as a free market offering the prospect of unlimited political and commercial success for *all* ambitious Scots so long as they played by its social and linguistic rules.[40]

Achievement in the Union and courtroom is linked to rhetorical skill; but this skill, it turns out, is not so easy to acquire. The very instrument that would clear the way to a wider world of opportunity and allow the free play of identities becomes, for most, an obstacle to upward mobility, reifying difference. Professional eloquence requires other forms of knowledge, knowledge which Blair's *Lectures* cannot provide by itself. What is needed is that combination of liberal and technical education available only from the university. An advocate, says Blair, must possess a 'profound knowledge of his own profession. Nothing is of such consequence to him, or deserves more his deep and serious study.'[41] As we have seen, by the time Blair began teaching, the Faculty of Advocates had already established that 'deep and serious study' of law could only take place at a university, through officially endorsed courses. Beyond vocational training, however, Blair asserts that whosoever wants to 'plead at the bar must make himself thoroughly master . . . of all the learning and experience that can be useful in his profession, for supporting a cause, or convincing a judge.'[42] But what, exactly, is this necessary 'learning and experience'? Blair explains that all public speakers – including lawyers – 'ought to have, what we call, a liberal education; and to be formed by a regular study of philosophy, and the polite arts'.[43] Upon first glance, this appears to be merely another endorsement of 'polite' learning – the type of civilized ambiguity that the Faculty of Advocates could offer in those halcyon days before John Wright. Yet it is the idea of regulation that gives Blair's words specific meaning. Only academic institutions can provide 'regular' education. Only they can enforce standards, control curricula and, most importantly, limit access to certification.

It was this desire for order and control that led members of the Faculty to name the university as the only authorized source of legal knowledge. Just as they had done, Blair uses the idea of 'liberal education' to make academic institutions central to professional training. To join a world without fixed boundaries, to practise the 'eloquence of the Bar', prospective advocates must first gain entry to these exclusive sites of education. Like Mackenzie and Dundas, Blair conceals the restrictiveness of the educational institution by employing the rhetoric of common knowledge, common access. Where once the Advocates' Library and its holdings had promised to make education available to all at 'no expense', now Blair's *Lectures* promises to teach all the principles of legal eloquence. But behind this apparently open door to knowledge and opportunity stand other barriers to stop those, like John Wright, who would dare to enter the community of the learned without the proper social and economic credentials. By reading Blair's *Lectures* alongside the Faculty's evolving discourse of qualification we have seen that even from its early establishment, the university subject of English Literature has been linked to other fields of professionalism, such as law, which appropriate academic institutions as instruments of often strict social regulation – thereby ensuring that 'improvement' does not open too many doors.

NOTES

I am indebted to John W. Cairns for his work on the history of legal education in Scotland – an invaluable resource. I am also grateful to Angus Stewart, QC, and Catherine Smith for their courtesy in granting me permission to examine and cite the records of the Faculty of Advocates. Finally, I would like to thank the Marshall Aid Commemoration Commission for their generous support of my studies.

1 Franz Kafka, *The Complete Stories*, ed. N. N. Glatzer, trans. W. and E. Muir (New York: Schocken Books, 1971), p. 3.

2 T. S. Eliot, *Selected Essays* (London: Faber and Faber, 1972), p. 15.

3 Robert Crawford, *Devolving English Literature* (Oxford University Press, 1992), pp. 28, 29.

4 *Ibid.*, p. 33.

5 Franklin E. Court, *Institutionalizing English Literature: The Culture and Politics of Literary Study, 1750–1900* (Stanford University Press, 1992), p. 28.

6 *Ibid.*, p. 30.

7 Crawford, *Devolving English Literature*, p. 36.

8 For a concise explanation of the Faculty of Advocates' role in the Scottish legal system and eighteenth-century society, see John Stuart Shaw, *The Management of Scottish Society, 1707–1764* (Edinburgh: John Donald Publishers, 1983), pp. 18–40.

9 N. T. Phillipson, 'Lawyers, Landowners, and the Civic Leadership of Post-Union Scotland', *Lawyers in their Social Setting*, ed. D. N. MacCormick (Edinburgh: W. Green & Son, 1976), pp. 171–94 at 181.

10 *Ibid.*, p. 62.

11 *Ibid.*, p. 73.

12 Sir George Mackenzie, *Oratio Inauguralis In Aperienda Jurisconsultorum Bibliotheca*, ed. J. W. Cairns and A. M. Cain, trans. J. H. Louden (Edinburgh: Butterworths, 1989), p. 62. For more on Mackenzie and the founding of the Advocates' Library, see John W. Cairns, 'Sir George Mackenzie, the Faculty of Advocates, and the Advocates' Library', *ibid.*, pp. 18–35.

13 Phillipson, 'Lawyers', p. 174. See also G. Donaldson, 'The Legal Profession in Scottish Society in the Sixteenth and Seventeenth Centuries', *Lawyers in their Social Setting*, pp. 152–70.

14 Phillipson, 'Lawyers', p. 184.

15 *The Minute Book of the Faculty of Advocates, 1661–1712* and *1712–1750*, ed. J. M. Pinkerton (2 vols., Stair Society, 29 and 32, Edinburgh, 1976 and 1980), vol. II, p. 225 (3 Nov. 1748).

16 *Ibid.*

17 *Ibid.*

18 See John W. Cairns, 'The Formation of the Scottish Legal Mind in the Eighteenth Century: Themes of Humanism and Enlightenment in the Admission of Advocates', *The Legal Mind: Essays for Tony Honoré*, ed. N. MacCormick and P. Birks (Oxford University Press, 1986), pp. 253–79, at 265.

19 'Minutes of the Faculty of Advocates 1751–1783', *FR* 2, National Library of Scotland, p. 84.

20 For a description of Scottish legal education in the late seventeenth and early eighteenth centuries, see Ian Simpson Ross, *Lord Kames and the Scotland of his Day* (Oxford University Press, 1972), pp. 11–26.

21 See Cairns, 'Scottish Legal Mind', p. 267.

22 Henry Cockburn, *Journal of Henry Cockburn*, 2 vols. (Edinburgh: Edmonston and Douglas, 1874), vol. II, p. 153.

23 James Boswell, *Boswell, Laird of Auchinleck*, The Yale Editions of the Private Papers of James Boswell, ed. J. W. Reed and F. A. Pottle (New York, Toronto and London: McGraw-Hill, 1977), pp. 413–14.

24 'Miscellaneous Papers of the Faculty of Advocates', Box 23 (iii) – 27, *FR 339*ʳ, National Library of Scotland. The folder entitled 'Papers, 1776–99', contains two drafts of the 'Report of the Committee appointed to prepare Regulations, respecting the Course of Studies, necessary to be followed, and the other Qualifications, which ought to be required, in those who wish to become Members of the Faculty'.

25 *Ibid.*
26 *Ibid.*
27 Cairns, 'Scottish Legal Mind', p. 268.
28 *Ibid.*, p. 265.
29 *Ibid.*, p. 290.
30 Hugh Blair, *Lectures on Rhetoric and Belles Lettres*, a new edition, 3 vols. (Edinburgh, 1811), vol. I, p. 3.
31 Blair occupied the Chair of Rhetoric and Belles Lettres from its founding in 1760 until his retirement in 1784. See Paul Bator, 'The Formation of the Regius Chair of Rhetoric and Belles Lettres at the University of Edinburgh', *Quarterly Journal of Speech* 75 (1989), 40–64.
32 Blair, *Lectures*, vol. I, p. 9.
33 *Ibid.*, pp. 7, 9.
34 *Ibid.*, p. 4.
35 *Ibid.*, p. 5.
36 *Ibid.*, p. 6.
37 *Ibid.*, p. 6.
38 *Ibid.*, vol. II, p. 213.
39 *Ibid.*, pp. 253–4.
40 See Crawford, *Devolving English Literature*, pp. 22–7.
41 *Ibid.*, p. 250.
42 *Ibid.*, p. 432.
43 *Ibid.*

CHAPTER 4

Hugh Blair's Ossian, Romanticism and the teaching of Literature

Fiona Stafford

When I. A. Richards laid down his *Principles of Literary Criticism* in the 1920s, he began by bulldozing away the critical tradition of Western Europe on the grounds that Aristotle, Longinus, Horace, Boileau, Dryden, Addison, Wordsworth, Coleridge, Carlyle and Arnold had produced nothing more than 'a few conjectures, a supply of admonitions, many acute isolated observations, some brilliant guesses, much oratory and applied poetry, inexhaustible confusion, a sufficiency of dogma, no small stock of prejudices, whimsies and crotchets, a profusion of mysticism, a little genuine speculation, sundry stray inspirations, pregnant hints and random *apercus*'.[1] No one, in short, had tackled what Richards regarded as the central aesthetic question: 'What is the value of the arts?'

In his list of great critics, Richards failed to mention the man who was, in effect, the first Professor of English Literature in a British university: Hugh Blair, who was appointed to the newly created Chair of Rhetoric and Belles Lettres in Edinburgh in 1760, and whose *Lectures* were to be printed and reprinted for the next century.[2] The reason may be merely that by the 1920s, Blair's work had become less familiar – or less highly esteemed – than that of those in Richards' roll-call (although as late as 1911 an abridged version served as the textbook for an American writing course).[3] But it was certainly a convenient omission, for anyone turning to the *Lectures on Rhetoric and Belles Lettres* in 1783 would have found Blair addressing the very question that Richards was to claim for himself – 'What is the value of the arts?'

Rather than dismiss earlier aesthetic views in order to emphasize the importance of his own enquiry, however, Blair freely acknowledged his debts to earlier critics and, adopting a tone of quiet authority, delivered his views as if they were self-evident truths:

Speech is the great instrument by which man becomes beneficial to man: and it is to the intercourse and transmission of thought, by means of speech, that we are chiefly indebted for the improvement of thought itself. Small are the advances which a single unassisted individual can make towards perfecting any of his powers. What we call human reason is not the effort or ability of one, so much as it is the result of the reason of many, arising from lights mutually communicated, in consequence of discourse or writing.

It is obvious, then, that writing and discourse are objects intitled to the highest attention.[4]

The direct and unequivocal manner in which Blair attempted to justify the study of literature is curiously compelling and probably accounts for much of his enormous and enduring popularity. While a late-twentieth-century teacher of English Literature might nurse a secret suspicion that defences of literary criticism generally stem from doubts about its real significance in the modern world, Blair set out his subject with all the zealous optimism of a pioneer.

The very circumstances which led first to his invitation to lecture on Rhetoric to Edinburgh students and, latterly, to his election to the new chair, must have contributed to the confident tone of Blair's intro-duction. For until the middle decades of the eighteenth century, the study of literature in English had had no formal place on the univer-sity curriculum. It was only with the success of Adam Smith's 1748–49 course of Lectures on Rhetoric that the real need for the development of literary criticism as an academic discipline became apparent.[5] The extraordinary advances being made by Blair's fellow intellectuals, in philosophy, history, chemistry and the physical sciences, demanded effective communication and so, far from seeming trivial in compar-ison, the 'arts of discourse and writing' began to be seen as crucial to the collective endeavour.

The improvement of oral and written discourse was necessary not only for the exchange of ideas and dissemination of knowledge, but also to enable Scottish intellectuals to achieve their full potential and reach an international audience. As John Home observed in 1756, when at-tempting to secure a Chair of Rhetoric for his friend Adam Ferguson, 'Eloquence in the Art of speaking is more necessary for a Scotchman than any body else as he lies under some disadvantages which Art must remove.'[6] Although such a remark may be interpreted as a sign of the general embarrassment about the Scottish tongue that many modern critics have emphasized in their accounts of eighteenth-century Scotland, it is also indicative of a new ideal of wide communication, which probably owed as much to John Locke as to the Union.[7] The desire for a Chair of Rhetoric may be seen not so much as a product of social underconfidence, as of a belief in the importance of the intellectual advances being made in Edinburgh, and of the need to communicate the new ideas to the widest possible audience. In the *Edinburgh Review*, for example, which was founded in 1755 to promote belles lettres in Scotland, the preface isolates the 'difficulty of a proper expression' and inadequate printing as the 'two considerable obstacles' which had 'long obstructed the progress of science', the implication being that the study of language and literature was essential to the continuing development of any field of knowledge.[8] The physical distance between Edinburgh and other major intellectual centres meant that writing, whether through correspondence or publication, was the only adequate medium for ideas.

Apparently unafflicted by the kinds of opposition that were to beset those who strove to establish academic courses in English in the late nineteenth and early twentieth centuries, then, Blair's lectures drew energy from the intellectual environment in Edinburgh, and offered themselves as a vital contribution to the improvement of society.[9] And this is the foundation of Blair's pre-emptive answer to I. A. Richards – that without the arts of 'discourse and writing', all intellectual development would cease, and with it the progress of society itself.

Although the Introduction to the *Lectures* stresses the fundamental importance of the subject, it is characteristic of Blair to include further justification on the grounds of entertainment, and moral improvement of a particularly enjoyable kind:

Such studies have also this peculiar advantage, that they exercise our reason without fatiguing it. They lead to enquiries acute, but not painful; profound, but not dry nor abstruse.[10]

Throughout, the tone is inviting rather than demanding, the method of instruction one of infectious enthusiasm rather than intimidation. Indeed, Blair's own rhetorical strategy was to present himself as a student, learning the principles of composition from the study of those texts that he considered to represent the best models of English, and passing on his discoveries to others. Literary criticism is thus made an active, dialogic experience, motivated by the desire to facilitate intellectual exchange, and developing through a continuous programme of reading and writing. In this dynamic process, the ideal reader is drawn in and impelled towards independent activity through the perpetual encouragement to read, think and communicate (even if the less active might be tempted to follow Blair's own analyses uncritically).

Blair's emphasis on the communication of knowledge, though part of Locke's massive legacy to the eighteenth century, is also indebted specifically to Adam Smith's Lectures on Rhetoric, which he had originally attended as a student of Divinity in Edinburgh, and read in manuscript when composing his own series.[11] It is also typical of the intellectual environment in which he worked, where human beings were perceived as essentially sociable – both from a theoretical point of view, in the philosophy of Frances Hutcheson, Adam Smith and David Hume and, more practically, as the leading intellectuals met frequently at clubs and dinners to discuss their work and ideas.[12] Blair, furthermore, was a Minister of the Church of Scotland, and thus saw human society as part of a divinely orchestrated and active universe, in which each individual had a responsibility to make his contribution:

Look around you, and you will behold the universe full of active powers. Action is, to speak so, the genius of nature. By motion and exertion, the system of being is preserved in vigour. By its different parts always acting in subordination one to another, the perfection of the whole is carried on. The heavenly bodies perpetually revolve. Day and night incessantly repeat their appointed course. Continual operations are going on in the earth, and in the waters. Nothing stands still. All is alive, and stirring, throughout the universe. – In the midst of this animated and busy scene, is man alone to remain idle in his place? Belongs it to him, to be the sole inactive and slothful being in the creation, when he has so much allotted him to do; when in so many various ways he might improve his own nature; might advance the glory of the God who made him; and contribute his part to the general good?[13]

It is clear from this sermon 'On Idleness' that notions of action, improvement and participation were fundamental to the moral vision promoted by Blair, in which no one existed independently of his fellow men:

We are all connected with one another by various relations; which create a chain of mutual dependence, reaching from the highest to the lowest station in society. The order and happiness of the world cannot be maintained, without perpetual circulation of active duties and offices, which all are called upon to perform in their turn.[14]

As a consequence, speech ('the great instrument by which man becomes beneficial to man') is central to human action, its improvement a moral imperative. Since Blair's solution to the problem of perfecting communication was the analysis of carefully chosen texts, literary criticism became a contribution not only to the progress of society, but also to the fulfilment of God's purposes for mankind.

Blair's conception of criticism as part of a much larger intellectual enterprise meant that rather than parcelling off 'Literature' from other academic disciplines, he recommended the study of earlier writings to all rational beings. Reading the 'best models' was not so much a way of equipping the would-be writer with a storehouse of usable phrases and stylistic devices as a means of teaching any reader to think. Good writing, according to Blair, is both a signal and a consequence of clear thought and sound logic:

True rhetoric and sound logic are very nearly allied. The study of arranging and expressing our thoughts with propriety, teaches to think, as well as to speak, accurately. By putting our sentiments into words, we always conceive them more distinctly. Every one who has the slightest acquaintance with composition knows, that when he expresses himself ill on any subject, when his arrangement becomes loose, and his sentences turn feeble, the defects of his style can, almost on every occasion, be traced back to the indistinct conception of the subject; so close is the connection between thoughts, and the words in which they are clothed.[15]

This echoes the opening defence of language studies, which had argued that 'the improvement of thought itself' was the result of the 'intercourse and transmission of thought, by means of speech'. Such ideas had received wide currency after the publication of Locke's *Essay Concerning Human Understanding* in 1690, with its emphasis on clear communication and the problems inherent in language, but Blair was also indebted to a number of more recent works on language, which he cited in his sixth lecture, on 'The Rise and Progress of Language'.[16] Although Blair avoided the more radical implications of the idea that thought might be dependent on language,[17] it is central to his justification of the study of English, for if thought itself was to be improved by discourse, the study of language was fundamental to all intellectual activity.

In the substantial series of lectures on language, grammar and sentence structure which follow from the premise that language and thought are interdependent, Blair's method of exposition throughout is to give examples of the various grammatical points – to demonstrate language *in action* – a practice that leads in turn to lectures devoted to the critical analysis of particular texts. Blair's literary criticism is thus deeply conscious of its usefulness to the individual reader as well as society. This sense of fulfilling a special social role informs not only the comments on particular texts but also those in the later lectures on entire genres, where 'Historical writing' or 'Descriptive poetry' are evaluated according to their respective benefits to mankind.

Although Blair's lectures appear to develop coherently from the notion that the 'whole power' of discourse 'is derived from the significancy of words',[18] his own prose betrays a certain anxiety about language itself. The very choice of metaphor in the introductory passage on rhetoric and thought ('so close is the connection between thoughts and the words in which they are clothed') suggests that words – as a form of clothing – have the potential to conceal rather than reveal the body of thought beneath. This idea of language as the 'dress' of thought was an eighteenth-century commonplace; but although Dryden had used it positively, if playfully, when recommending the avoidance of obscenity in drama ('expressions therefore are a modest cloathing of our thoughts, as Breeches and Petticoats are of our bodies'), the philosopher, Berkeley, was fully alert to the misleading tendencies of language and urged his reader to 'use his utmost endeavours, to obtain a clear view of the ideas he would consider, separating from them all that dress and encumbrance of words which so much contribute to blind the judgement and divide the attention'.[19]

Blair's own anxiety about the possibility of words becoming corrupted emerges plainly in his sermon 'On Sensibility':

a word, which in modern times we hear in the mouth of every one; a quality, which every one affects to possess; in itself, a most amiable and worthy disposition of mind; but often mistaken and abused; employed as a cover, sometimes, to capricious humour; sometimes to selfish passions.[20]

Here, the relationship 'between thoughts and the words in which they are clothed' has been 'abused', the words becoming a mere 'cover' for things that the speaker wishes to hide. 'True sensibility', according to Blair, is a spontaneous impulse from the heart, distinguishing its possessors from those who act merely from a sense of duty or self-interest. To combat the deceptions inherent in words, Blair turns inward to discover the 'instinctive feeling' that is to determine the value of the utterance. It is only when words match the feelings of the speaker that they are to be trusted by others and indeed, one of Blair's reasons for promoting literary criticism was the notion that it helped with the difficult task of 'distinguishing accurately between the specious and the solid'.[21]

Blair's emphasis on the disposition of the speaker is closely related to his account of the 'Rise and Progress of Language' which, though acknowledging a 'Divine original', describes a gradual development from the 'cries of passion' by which primitive man communicated his basic desires and fears, to a simple kind of nomenclature involving

socially agreed names for things, to the infinitely more complicated
modern systems of symbols, which had largely lost any relationship to
the physical world.[22] Although the improvement of language may
depend on thought, it is clear that Blair sought its origins in feeling
rather than reason, and much of his work displays a tendency similar
to that evident in the sermon 'On Sensibility', to recover the emotional
basis of language as a means of determining truth. His critical judge-
ments, for example, reveal an admiration for those works that appear
to convey emotion most directly, such as Macpherson's *Ossian* ('the
Poetry of the Heart'), or familiar letters ('There, if any where, we look
for the man, not for the Author').[23]

Although the empirical account of the progress of language is part
of the case for literary criticism, it also leads to a number of difficulties,
particularly when Blair attempts to deal with metaphor. For while
'figures' were part of the early development of language, necessary to
enable primitive man to begin communicating more complicated ideas
even with a limited vocabulary, they were less easy to justify as instruments of communication in a modern language. If the images used
by Ossian or the Hebrew poets were the 'natural' forms of expression
for those early societies where 'want of proper names' combined with
lively imaginations to produce a language 'bold, picturesque, and meta-
phorical', those employed by more recent poets, such as Cowley, were
more likely to 'puzzle the reader, and instead of illustrating the thought,
render it perplexed and intricate'.[24] The progress of language, in Blair's
account, though essential to intellectual development, was hardly con-
ducive to the composition of poetry:

Language is become, in modern times, more correct, indeed, and accurate;
but, however, less striking and animated: In its antient state, more favourable
to poetry and oratory; in its present, to reason and philosophy.[25]

Although Blair recognized the power of metaphor and, viewing it as
the language of 'the passions', celebrated it as the form of speech
through which the feelings could be conveyed most directly, an underlying unease can be discerned from the opening comment that figures
'always imply some departure from simplicity of expression'.[26] Once
again, the clothing metaphor is in evidence, as Blair distinguishes
between plainer and more picturesque kinds of language:

Simple Expression just makes our idea known to others; but Figurative Language, over and above, bestows a particular dress upon that idea; a dress
which both makes it to be remarked, and adorns it.[27]

Since this sentence follows from a discussion of the derivation of the word 'Figures', in which Blair suggests that 'as the figure or shape of one body distinguishes it from another, so these forms of Speech have, each of them, a cast or turn peculiar to itself', the inherent ambiguities of metaphor are well demonstrated. Figures are at once the 'body' and the 'dress', and while this could be interpreted as a sophisticated argument for the impossibility of dividing language from thought, it is also possible to regard it as an indication of a fundamental uncertainty over the nature of language, characteristic of the intellectual context in which Blair was working.

In the context of Blair's own work, however, the issue of whether metaphors were conveying ideas or merely providing a 'dress which both makes it to be remarked, and adorns it' was perhaps more closely connected with his larger concern with the purpose of Rhetoric and Belles Lettres. For despite its self-confident tone, Blair's introductory lecture nevertheless displays an awareness of a widespread suspicion of 'the arts of writing and discourse', and their association in the minds of many of his contemporaries with ostentation and deceit:

I am far from denying, that rhetoric and criticism have sometimes been so managed as to tend to the corruption, rather than to the improvement, of good taste and true eloquence. But sure it is equally possible to apply the principles of reason and good sense to this art, as to any other that is cultivated among men. If the following Lectures have any merit, it will consist in an endeavour to substitute the application of these principles in the place of artificial and scholastic rhetoric; in an endeavour to explode false ornament, to direct attention more towards substance than show, to recommend good sense as the foundation of all good composition, and simplicity as essential to all true ornament.[28]

As Blair set out his own 'principles', he explicitly addressed some of the difficulties attendant on his subject: the dangers of linguistic pleasure becoming an end in itself; of language as merely a means of display for the writer; and, most worryingly, the tendency of discourse to deceive or manipulate the audience. These had been central issues for late-seventeenth-century writers as diverse as Robert South, who had warned of the '*bewitchery*, or fascination in words', and John Milton, who created an additional temptation for the hero of *Paradise Regained* in order to have him dismiss 'all the oratory of Greece and Rome' in favour of the 'majestic unaffected style' of the Hebrew prophets.[29]

Ironically, the rejection of Rhetoric had a distinguished classical tradition. In the *Gorgias*, Plato had articulated many of the perennial

objections to the art of oratory, making Socrates dwell on its spurious-
ness ('no more than a knack acquired by routine').[30] Although the attack
had found an equally influential opponent in Aristotle whose work on
oratory, together with that of Quintilian, had provided Blair with much
of the material used to justify the study of Rhetoric, the suspicion of an
art devoted to the persuasion of others was hard to dispel entirely.[31]
The formality of medieval Rhetoric, with its complicated rules and labels,
had also contributed to the association between rhetoric and artifice,
so that by the early eighteenth century a new approach began to emerge
and established itself in opposition to the 'artificial and scholastic' discipline of the past.[32] As W. S. Howell has suggested, the work of Adam
Smith and George Campbell, especially, contributed to the expansion of
Rhetoric to include a greater range of literary discourse, generally plainer
in style and less marked by ceremonial and syllogistic structures.[33]

The old objections to scholastic Rhetoric can nevertheless be discerned in the background of many of Blair's comments on discourse,
as he makes his case for the usefulness of his subject, its foundation in
practical application rather than rule-following and the persistent
emphasis on 'simplicity' rather than ornament:

Good sense, clear ideas, perspicuity of language and proper arrangement of
words and thoughts . . . are the foundations of all solid merit, both in speaking
and writing.[34]

The recognition that language, when improperly used, could provide
a mask for misleading the reader also informs Blair's advocacy of oral
forms of discourse which, far from being associated with insincere
speech-making are celebrated as the most direct indicators of meaning.

In his lecture on 'The Rise and Progress of Language', Blair emphasized the continuing value of speech even in modern society where
written discourse had long been the medium of authority, and was
rapidly becoming the main channel for intellectual traffic:

The voice of the living Speaker, makes an impression on the mind, much
stronger than can be made by the perusal of any Writing. The tones of voice,
the looks and gesture, which accompany discourse, and which no Writing can
convey, render discourse, when it is well managed, infinitely more clear, and
more expressive, than the most accurate Writing. For tones, looks, and gestures, are natural interpreters of the sentiments of the mind. They remove
ambiguities; they enforce impressions; they operate on us by means of sympathy, which is one of the most powerful instruments of persuasion. Our
sympathy is always awakened more by hearing the Speaker, than by reading
his works in our closet.[35]

In Blair's account of language, speech retains a closer affinity than writing to the discourse of early man, whose utterances were stimulated by desire, accompanied by gesture and intended to communicate directly. Where writing – and especially print – obliterates body language, and thus makes words less amenable to the intuitive test of truth, speech is accompanied by the 'tones, looks and gestures' that 'remove ambiguities' and give access to the inner feelings of the speaker.[36]

This enthusiasm for the spoken informs much of Blair's criticism, from his series on 'Eloquence' to the lectures on poetry. Indeed, when writing on the 'Nature of Poetry', Blair commented that it was 'hardly possible to determine the exact limit where Eloquence ends, and Poetry begins'.[37] Both shared the same foundation in the 'passions', and thus represented modes of discourse through which one man could convey his emotions most effectively to another, and in doing so, awaken sympathetic feelings. The desire to find a common root for different kinds of discourse led Blair once again to speculate on the origins of society, where the division of disciplines had yet to take place and where communication was unencumbered by the complicated considerations facing modern writers:

> Poetry . . . in its ancient original condition, was perhaps more vigorous than it is in its modern state. It included then, the whole burst of the human mind; the whole exertion of its imaginative faculties. It spoke then the language of passion, and no other; for to passion it owed its birth. Prompted and inspired by objects which to him seemed great, by events which interested his country or his friends, the early Bard arose and sung.[38]

Unlike modern authors who studied poetry as an art 'for reputation and for gain', the poet of early society sung 'the native effusions of his heart'. Just as Blair regarded the power of eloquence to lie in its 'conviction', so he judged poetry by its capacity to convey genuine feeling.

Given Blair's theoretical assumptions, it is not difficult to see why he should have been so enthusiastic about the discovery of *Ossian*, since Macpherson's translations appeared to substantiate many of his own linguistic and aesthetic ideas. Indeed, his critical views reached the reading public long before the publication of his *Lectures* through the influential *Critical Dissertation on the Poems of Ossian*, which contained a condensed version of much of the material being delivered in the Edinburgh lecture room. In *Ossian*, Blair found all the 'vehemence and fire, which are the soul of poetry', thus confirming his views on the association between great poetry and early society.[39] His ideas of language, too, were borne out by the Ossianic metaphors which seemed to be drawn entirely from the Highland landscape, but used with ingenuity to convey more complicated things:

The language has all that figurative cast, which, as I before shewed, partly a glowing and undisciplined imagination, partly the sterility of language and the want of proper terms, have always introduced into the early speech of nations.[40]

Above all, the figure of Ossian himself is admired, the power of his concise style deriving from the strong emotions of the poet ('Ossian appears every where to be prompted by his feelings; and to speak from the abundance of his heart'[41]). Although Ossian embodies all the strength of the early poet, as a 'professed bard, educated with care . . . to all the poetical art then known' he also fulfils the more progressive ideals that inform both the *Lectures* and the *Sermons*.[42] Blair's image of the Celtic bard, whose natural abilities have been improved by listening to the best poetry of the past, and who can, as a consequence, convey his own words most effectively to the rest of the tribe, has much in common with his view of the modern man of letters, who perfects his own discourse through the study of earlier writings. Ossian combined the strong feelings of early man with the beneficial discipline of the oral bardic tradition, through which only the most powerful compositions could survive, and thus represented a model not only for critical analysis, but also for personal emulation.

There is, however, a certain irony in Blair's celebration of Ossian, and the oral tradition of the bards, since his only acquaintance with the poetry came through written English translations. This difficulty was neatly skirted through the ingenious suggestion that if Ossian could still 'command', 'transport' and 'melt the heart', even when 'stripped of his native dress', then his work must be that of the true genius, and comparable with the greatest poetry in the world.[43] The loss of orality, however, was more difficult to overcome, as was the problem of the poetry's transmission, since Ossian represented the last of his race and therefore had no successor to receive his words. Although this was to cause problems for the defence of *Ossian*'s authenticity, the very sense of the poetry's vulnerability seems to have been part of its appeal for Blair.[44] His efforts to ensure the retrieval of the vanishing traditions of the Scottish Highlands were entirely compatible with his views of the progress of language and society, in which the early stages, for all their inherent powers, must eventually be superseded. Despite the advances of civilization, however, the qualities of early society were still enormously valuable and needed to be studied to ensure continuing development. The image of the aged Ossian, poised at the end of an heroic age, could thus convey both its inherent value, and its inevitable disappearance. And it was perhaps the consciousness of loss, of the elusiveness of the oral ideal, that attracted Blair so strongly to Macpherson's *Ossian*, with its eighteenth- (rather than exclusively third-) century preoccupations.

For although Blair frequently praised speech over writing in his *Lectures*, he was also fully aware of its limitations. In the same lecture that praised the 'tones, the looks and gestures' of oral discourse, Blair admitted that speech was not only 'confined within the narrow circle of those who hear our words', but also 'fugitive and passing; you must catch the words the moment they are uttered, or you lose them for ever'.[45] These were undoubtedly among the considerations that led him at last to publish his own *Lectures* and *Sermons*, even though he had been presenting oral versions, with all the attendant advantages, for many years. Just as the voices of Highland tradition seemed to require the solidity of writing in order to survive, so Blair's words needed to be published if they were to extend beyond his immediate circle. With his retirement from professional life, the lectures would either be forgotten, or survive in the disjointed, unreliable forms copied down by students who had attended his courses. Although the publication was partly motivated by financial considerations, the preface to the *Lectures* attributes the decision to the prevalence of unauthorized copies:

The publication of them, at present, was not altogether a matter of choice. Imperfect Copies of them, in Manuscript, from notes taken by Students who heard them read, were first privately handed about; and afterwards frequently exposed to public sale. When the Author saw them circulate so currently, as even to be quoted in print, and found himself often threatened with surreptitious publications of them, he judged it to be high time that they should proceed from his own hand, rather than come into public view under some very defective and erroneous form.[46]

Ironically, the prized medium of oral communication seemed to have resulted in a somewhat inexact reception of Blair's ideas, and so he was forced to resort to letters, in order to establish the real meaning of his discourse. The opening emphasis on the lectures having been delivered in Edinburgh for twenty-four years prior to publication, however, gives readers the sense of an ending, even before they have reached the Introduction. It is as if an evolving text has suddenly been turned to stone and, in the course of becoming resistant to error, has also become resistant to growth.

Once in the public domain, Blair's *Lectures* and *Sermons*, though now
in forms approved by the author, could become the property of any
one who wished to buy them. And, although the sales indicate that
their publication benefitted a vast number of readers, it is also clear
that they were not always used in ways that Blair might have wished.
In *Mansfield Park*, for example, Mary Crawford observes light-heartedly
that any preacher should have the sense to prefer Blair's sermons to
his own, thus demonstrating that far from encouraging fresh composition, Blair's work could be used as a substitute.[47] Once published, Blair's
words of wisdom were also available for extraction and inclusion in
popular anthologies such as Vicesimus Knox's *Elegant Extracts* or Alfred
Howard's *Beauties of Literature* series, while abridgements of the *Lectures*
found their way into nineteenth-century school textbooks.[48] Thus the
written word, once detached from its author, could be used either to
cover up an absence of ability, or to distort the original meaning by
the removal of the surrounding text.

The wider dissemination of Blair's *Lectures* also involved an inevitable separation from the environment in which they had developed.
This was particularly significant in relation to the emphasis on orality
and the active, dialogic nature of discourse. Publication meant that the
Lectures lost not only the accompanying visual image of the Moderate
Presbyterian divine, but also his distinctively Scottish intonation and the
room full of sympathetic listeners, responding with the special insight
of a local audience. Given the well-known concern about 'Scotticisms'
current among the Edinburgh intellectuals of the mid eighteenth century, the escape from an oral transmission in non-standard English
may have seemed an additional argument for publication.[49] However,
it is noticeable that when Blair lectured on 'Pronunciation, or Delivery',
his own emphasis was still on the persuasiveness of a 'natural' rather
than 'artificial manner': 'Whatever is native, even though accompanied
with several defects, yet is likely to please; because it shows us a man;
because it has the appearance of coming from the heart.'[50] This advice,
however, must have sounded rather differently in the ears of his students from its silent effect on unknown readers. For although the title page
makes clear Blair's position as 'Minister of the High Church and Professor of Rhetoric and Belles Lettres in the University of Edinburgh',
there is little explicit internal reference to Scotland or to Blair's other
professional activities, while the only Scottish text to be lionized is
Macpherson's *English* translation from the Gaelic. As soon as Blair's
words went on sale in London bookshops, the particular conditions in

which they had originally been formed were erased; they then began to acquire the impersonal authority of the textbook, and could be placed on the shelf next to Johnson's *Dictionary*.

It was thus the movement from orality to print that turned Blair's *Lectures* into the Anglicizing, institutionalizing project for which he has been criticized in the twentieth century by those who interpret his admiration for certain writers as contributory to the formation of a literary canon, in which a particular kind of English is the criterion of excellence. Franklin Court, for example, sees Blair's preference for Addison and Longinus as indicative of an ideology 'situated firmly within the idea of cultural and racial supremacy', while Robert Crawford has linked the *Lectures* to the development of 'English studies in England' seeing them as an effort of 'cultural conversion, of Anglicizing upwardly mobile Scots to make them acceptable Britons.'[51] Blair's own repeated preference for the spoken and the natural has a certain irony in this context.

Although the detachment of Blair's texts from their native environment may have rendered the *Lectures* an instrument of cultural imperialism, it is also possible to regard their publication as a liberating development for many readers. For despite the advantages of oral communication, it is also a medium that limits meaning, not only through the inevitable restrictions of the lecture space and the human voice, but also, perhaps, through the dominant presence of the speaker. Blair's theory of literature, after all, is based on an ideal of clear communication, and a related assumption that the definitive meaning of the discourse is that determined by its author. This is why the worry over words is so persistent, and why Blair repeated the need to 'remove ambiguities' by looking at the speaker. The preference for oral delivery may be interpreted as a desire to maintain control of the thoughts being communicated, and therefore of the minds receiving them.

The publication of Blair's *Lectures* in the 1780s, however, meant that his words could be interpreted independently by individual readers, who were free to concentrate on those passages that particularly appealed. In the decade of the French Revolution, Blair's work would find an extraordinarily diverse audience, and while numerous people turned to his *Sermons* for reassurance at a time of national crisis, radical readers such as William Blake were more attracted by his critical emphasis on the freedom of early society and the importance attached to the role of the bard as a public figure and defender of ancient liberties.[52]

For William Wordsworth, caught between his disillusionment with the course of the French Revolution and continuing commitment to the improvement of society, Blair offered a host of congenial ideas that were to find echoes in one of the most famous contributions to British Romanticism, the 1800 Preface to *Lyrical Ballads*.

Coleridge borrowed the second volume of the *Lectures* in February 1798 and, as Duncan Wu has observed, 'there is something on nearly every page of Blair's *Lectures* that would have interested Wordsworth and Coleridge, and which ties in with various statements they made subsequently'.[53] Indeed, many scholars have noted the influence of Blair's *Lectures* on *Lyrical Ballads*, the very title of which suggests ideas of strong feeling, oral transmission and communal discourse. Wordsworth's definition of the poet as 'a man speaking to men' is strongly reminiscent of Blair's ideal, and for Michael Baron, the question of 'how poetic language can be like spoken language' represents the 'central topic' of the Preface to *Lyrical Ballads*.[54] The equally characteristic emphasis on both 'the spontaneous overflow of powerful feelings' and more restrained qualities such as 'good sense' and 'rational sympathy' has much in common with Blair's admiration for Ossian, in which a primitive degree of enthusiasm seemed balanced by the cultivation of finer feelings.[55] Blair's views on literary language, too, find echoes in Wordsworth's simultaneous rejection of any 'falsehood of description', and retention of figures of speech 'prompted by passion'; but it is the passage justifying the choice of 'low and rustic life' that perhaps contains the most striking parallels:

The language, too, of these men is adopted . . . because such men hourly communicate with the best objects from which the best part of language is originally derived; and because, from their rank in society and the sameness and narrow circle of their intercourse, being less under the influence of social vanity they convey their feelings and notions in simple and unelaborated expressions.[56]

Although the account of his poetic strategy has obvious resemblance to Blair's ideas on the development of language and the association of poetry with the early stage when words corresponded more closely to things, Wordsworth's paragraph continues with a crucial sentence that suggests a rejection of the more negative tendencies of Blair's linguistic theory:

Accordingly, such a language, arising out of repeated experience and regular feelings, is a more permanent, and a far more philosophical language, than that which is frequently substituted for it by poets.

Where Blair's view of the origins of language had led him to the pessimistic conclusion that while poetry flourished in early society, the accuracy of a sophisticated language was better suited to prose, Wordsworth borrowed only the aspects of Blair's work that suited his own purposes. To argue that simple language could also be philosophical effectively overturned Blair's stadialist view of the progress of literature, and restored poetry to the status of the highest moral and intellectual pursuits. Wordsworth's discovery, too, in the British countryside, of the same vital qualities that Blair had consigned to the remote past, redeemed poetry from antiquity and reclaimed the language of passion for contemporary society. Despite its debts to Blair's *Lectures* and, indeed, to a host of eighteenth-century works, *Lyrical Ballads* transformed many of the more problematic aspects of mid-century aesthetics into a manifesto for the modern poet, and was thus, perhaps, more likely to inspire creative writing than critical prose.

Discussions of Blair's influence on Wordsworth have generally focussed on *Lyrical Ballads*, but it is also possible to trace analogies in the later work. The *Essays upon Epitaphs*, for example, with their central emphasis on 'sincerity' as the key to literary style, are strongly reminiscent of Blair's preoccupation with the 'Man, not the Author' and his notion of an ideal correspondence between a man and his words. It is in these essays, too, that Wordsworth betrays a similar anxiety about the unreliable nature of language, and the moral implications of its capacity to deceive:

Words are too awful an instrument for good and evil to be trifled with: they hold above all other external powers a dominion over thoughts. If words be not . . . an incarnation of the thought, but only a clothing for it, then surely will they prove an ill gift; such a one as those poisoned vestments, read of in the stories of superstitious times, which had power to consume and to alienate from his right mind the victim who put them on.[57]

Although Wordsworth was as concerned as Blair about the connection between language and thought, he can again be seen to evoke the eighteenth-century metaphor of dress only to reject it. For Wordsworth, true feeling is conveyed through 'those expressions which are not what the garb is to the body but what the body is to the soul', thus redeeming words from being external, sheddable covers for thoughts, and turning them into living powers.[58] Writing, for Blair, whether in his linear narrative of society or his personal history, seemed to entail the end of a living, spoken discourse with its accompanying body language of gestures and physical expressions. For Wordsworth, in the *Essays upon Epitaphs*, at least, inscription could be a form of 'incarnation', through which words perpetuated the body in the grave.

Without the publication of his *Lectures*, then, Blair's ideas would have been limited to his original audiences. And, while there have been readers to whom this might have been welcome, there were plenty of eighteenth-century writers who drew on his work, uninhibited by any personal knowledge of the man or his views. If contemporary scholars feel compelled to historicize or politicize Blair's texts, readers of two centuries ago were content to borrow and reconstitute his ideas, which were themselves drawn from a vast range of earlier writings. Writing, for all Blair's anxieties, was still closer to the oral tradition in that authors were more relaxed about citing sources, perhaps regarding existing texts as channels of truth rather than as property, or applying their ideals of sociability and community to literary discourse. Although the burgeoning book trade, together with the new aesthetic emphasis on originality, was beginning to affect literary practice, it was still possible for those now designated 'Romantic' to take what they wanted from published material and make it their own. Evaluation of Blair's achievement is thus very difficult, because so many of the ideas that characterize his work were part of the general intellectual climate, making the attribution of particular thoughts, and thus of influence, somewhat speculative. Like many a popular lecture series, Blair's digested current literary and philosophical trends and reproduced them in a form accessible to a wide audience. To judge him by late-twentieth-century standards of political correctness may thus be inappropriate, since he can neither be credited with, nor held responsible for, the ideas he promoted. But the restoration of Blair's texts to their contexts is itself complicated by the long period of maturation: if his *Lectures* belong in one sense to the Scotland of the 1750s, their eventual appearance in London and Edinburgh in 1783 makes Blair an early British Romantic prose writer. The oral Blair of the 1750s and 1760s may be impossible to reconstruct perfectly, but neither can the published Blair of the 1780s be an entirely adequate respresentation. But whether Blair's *Lectures* are 'Fragments' like the broken pieces of Macpherson's *Ossian*, or true epitaphs, representing an 'incarnation' of the vanished speaker, is hard to determine. Blair's answer to the problem would undoubtedly have been to recommend the study of literary criticism.

NOTES

1 I. A. Richards, *Principles of Literary Criticism*, 3rd edn (London: Kegan Paul, 1929), p. 6.
2 Blair became the Regius Professor two years later through the influence of the Earl of Bute. See Richard B. Sher, *Church and University in the Scottish Enlightenment: The Moderate Literati of Edinburgh* (Edinburgh University Press, 1985), pp. 109–16. For further biographical information see Robert M. Schmitz, *Hugh Blair* (New York: King's Crown Press, 1948); John Hill, *An Account of the Life and Writings of Hugh Blair, D. D.* (London, 1807).
3 Hugh Blair, *Lectures on Rhetoric*, ed. G. Kleiser (New York: Funk and Wagnalls Co., 1911). In 1914, W. P. Mustard quoted from Blair's *Lectures* in the introduction to his edition of *The Piscatory Eclogues of Jacopo Sannazaro* (Baltimore: Johns Hopkins University Press), but added 'Blair was much more familiar with the opinions of Johnson and Fontenelle than with the Latin original', p. 25. For further unfavourable comments from the early twentieth century, see Schmitz, *Hugh Blair*, p. v.
4 Hugh Blair, *Lectures on Rhetoric and Belles Lettres*, 2 vols. (London and Edinburgh, 1783).
5 Adam Smith, *Lectures on Rhetoric and Belles Lettres*, ed. J. C. Bryce (Oxford: Clarendon Press, 1983). See also Wilbur S. Howell, *Eighteenth-Century British Logic and Rhetoric* (Princeton University Press, 1971), pp. 536–76; Franklin E. Court, *Institutionalizing English Literature: The Culture and Politics of Literary Study, 1750–1900* (Stanford University Press, 1992), pp. 13; 17–30.
6 Home to Milton, August 1756, NLS 16696: p. 74, cited by Sher, *Church and University*, p. 108.
7 See, for example, David Craig, *Scottish Literature and the Scottish People, 1630–1830* (London: Chatto and Windus, 1961), pp. 40ff; Robert Crawford, *Devolving English Literature* (Oxford: Clarendon Press, 1992), pp. 22–44.
8 *Edinburgh Review* 1 (1755), preface, iii. The shortlived magazine contained work by Hugh Blair and his colleagues.
9 On the foundation of English Literature courses, see, for example, C. Baldick, *The Social Mission in English Criticism, 1848–1932* (Oxford: Clarendon Press, 1983); T. Eagleton, *Literary Theory: An Introduction* (Oxford: Basil Blackwell, 1983), pp. 17–53; G. Graff and M. Warner (eds.), *The Origins of Literary Studies in America* (New York and London: Routledge, 1989).
10 Blair, *Lectures*, vol. I, p. 10.
11 Schmitz, *Hugh Blair*, p. 62; Howell, *Eighteenth-Century British Logic*, pp. 543–4.
12 See J. Dwyer and R. B. Sher (eds.), *Sociability and Society in Eighteenth-Century Scotland* (Edinburgh: The Mercat Press, 1993); D. D. McElroy, *Scotland's Age of Improvement: A Survey of Eighteenth-Century Literary Clubs and Societies* (Washington State University Press, 1969).
13 Hugh Blair, *Sermons*, 5 vols. (Edinburgh and London: 1777–1801), vol. III, pp. 176–7.
14 *Ibid.*, p. 179.

15 Blair, *Lectures*, vol. I, pp. 3–4.

16 *Ibid.*, vol. I, pp. 97–8. Among the authorities cited are Smith, Harris, Condillac, Rousseau, de Brosses, Beauzée, Batteux, Warburton and Girard.

17 For the further implications of this idea, which Blair might have borrowed from Condillac's *Essai sur l'origine des connaissances humaines* (1746), see Hans Aarsleff, *The Study of Language in England, 1780–1860* (Princeton University Press, 1967); *From Locke to Saussure* (London: Athlone Press, 1992). For discussion of its persistent interest to philosophers of language, see M. Dummett, *The Seas of Language* (Oxford: Clarendon Press, 1993), pp. 166–87.

18 Blair, *Lectures*, vol. I, p. 96.

19 Dryden, preface to *All for Love* (1678), *The California Edition of the Works of John Dryden*, ed. H. T. Swedenberg et al., 20 vols., vol. XIII, ed. M. E. Novak (Berkeley and Los Angeles: California University Press, 1984), p. 11. George Berkeley, introduction to *Principles of Human Knowledge* (1710), *Philosophical Works*, ed. M. R. Ayers (London: Dent, 1975), p. 86.

20 Blair, *Sermons*, vol. III, p. 23.

21 Blair, *Lectures*, vol. I, p. 9.

22 *Ibid.* vol. I, pp. 97–125. In his influential discussion of pre-Romantic views of language, which includes Blair, M. H. Abrams emphasized the influence of Lucretius through Vico and Blackwell, rather than those Enlightenment theorists acknowledged by Blair himself, *The Mirror and the Lamp* (London, Oxford and New York: Oxford University Press, 1953), pp. 79–83.

23 Blair, *A Critical Dissertation on the Poems of Ossian* (1763), in James Macpherson, *The Poems of Ossian*, ed. Howard Gaskill (Edinburgh University Press, 1996), p. 356; *Lectures*, vol. II, 298.

24 Blair, *Lectures*, vol. I, pp. 283, 303.

25 *Ibid.*, vol. I, pp. 124–5.

26 *Ibid.*, p. 273.

27 *Ibid.*, pp. 274–5.

28 *Ibid.*, p. 3.

29 Robert South, *Twelve Sermons preached on Several Occasions*, London, 1692, cited by Robert DeMaria, *Johnson's Dictionary and the Language of Learning* (Oxford: Clarendon Press, 1986), pp. 156–7; John Milton, *Paradise Regained*, pp. 359–60.

30 Plato, *Gorgias*, 463, translated by W. Hamilton (Harmondsworth: Penguin, 1971), p. 44.

31 For a full discussion of the long-running debate over rhetoric, see Brian Vickers, *In Defence of Rhetoric* (Oxford: Clarendon Press, 1988).

32 James Murphy, *Rhetoric in the Middle Ages: A History of Rhetorical Theory from Saint Augustine to the Renaissance* (Berkeley and Los Angeles: University of California Press, 1981).

33 Howell, *Eighteenth-Century British Logic*, pp. 441–694.

34 Blair, *Lectures*, vol. I, p. 368.

35 *Ibid.*, p. 136. See also M. T. Clanchy, *From Memory to Written Record, England 1066–1307*, 2nd edn (Oxford: Basil Blackwell, 1993); Walter J. Ong, *Orality and Literacy* (London and New York: Methuen, 1982); Penny Fielding,

Writing and Orality: Nationality, Culture, and Nineteenth-Century Scottish Fiction (Oxford: Clarendon Press, 1996).

36 Blair's views resemble those of contemporary philosophers of the progress of society, but see also South, *Twelve Sermons*, p. 593, for warnings of the possibilities of deceit by '*Actions*, and *Gestures*'. The importance of body language to oratory was also a key part of Thomas Sheridan's course on elocution, given in Edinburgh in 1756 – see Tony Crowley, *Language in History* (London and New York: Routledge, 1996), pp. 81–7 for a recent discussion.

37 Blair, *Lectures*, vol. II, p. 313.

38 *Ibid.*, vol. II, p. 322.

39 Blair, *Critical Dissertation*, p. 345. On Blair's role in the discovery of Ossian, see Schmitz, *Hugh Blair*, pp. 42–60; Sher, *Church and University*, pp. 242–61; S. Rizza, 'A Bulky and Foolish Treatise? Hugh Blair's *Critical Dissertation* Reconsidered', *Ossian Revisited*, ed. Howard Gaskill (Edinburgh University Press, 1991), pp. 129–46; F. Stafford, *The Sublime Savage: James Macpherson and The Poems of Ossian* (Edinburgh University Press, 1988), pp. 96–102.

40 Blair, *Critical Dissertation*, p. 354.

41 *Ibid.*, p. 381.

42 *Ibid.*, p. 352.

43 *Ibid.*, p. 399.

44 David Hume was particularly troubled by the transmission of poetry from the third century, and prompted Blair's early attempt to collect evidence of the authenticity of Ossian, which was published in the 1765 edition of *The Works of Ossian*. See David Raynor, 'Ossian and Hume', *Ossian Revisited*, pp. 147–63.

45 Blair, *Lectures*, vol. I, p. 136.

46 *Ibid.*, preface. The passage includes a footnote reference to an article on Addison in the *Biographia Britannica*. Notes taken by students attending Blair's lectures survive in manuscripts held at the Universities of Edinburgh (EUL MS Dc. 10.6; Dc. 3.43); Aberdeen (AUL MS 131); Glasgow (GUL MS Murray 1); Louisiana State; and the National Library of Scotland (NLS MS 5834–5; 850), and the Bodleian Library, Oxford (Bod. MS Eng. Misc 716/1–2). I am indebted to Martin Moonie for this information.

47 Jane Austen, *Mansfield Park*, ed. R. W. Chapman, 3rd edn (London: Oxford University Press, 1934), p. 92.

48 Ironically, the second edition of *Elegant Extracts: or useful and entertaining Passages in Prose selected for the Improvement of Scholars at Classical and other Schools in the Art of Speaking, in Reading, Thinking, Composing, and in the Conduct of Life* (London, 1785), began by recommending the purchase of Blair's *Lectures* and *Sermons*, while including as an introductory essay to the collection Blair's lecture on 'Pronunciation, or Delivery'. See also *Essays on Rhetoric Abridged Chiefly from Dr Blair's Lectures on that Science* (London, 1784); *Sentimental Beauties and Moral Delineations from the Writings of the Celebrated Dr Blair* (London, 1782); Alexander Jamieson's *A Grammar of Rhetoric, and Polite Literature* (London, 1818), also includes extensive quotation from Blair.

49 See note 7, above, and for a recent discussion, James Basker, 'Scotticisms and the Problem of Cultural Identity in Eighteenth-Century Britain', Dwyer and Sher, *Sociability and Society*, pp. 81–95.

50 Blair, *Lectures*, vol. II, p. 224.

51 Court, *Institutionalizing English Literature*, p. 33; Crawford, *Devolving English Literature*, p. 42.

52 Jon Mee has examined the influence of Blair and Ossian on Blake in *Dangerous Enthusiasm: William Blake and the Culture of Radicalism in the 1790s* (Oxford: Clarendon Press, 1992), pp. 77–120.

53 *Wordsworth's Reading, 1770–1799* (Cambridge University Press, 1993), pp. 181–2. See also G. L. Little, 'A Note on Wordsworth and Blair', *Notes and Queries*, ns 7 (1960), 254–5; *The Prose Works of William Wordsworth*, ed. W. J. B. Owen and J. W. Smyser, 3 vols. (Oxford: Clarendon Press, 1974), vol. I, pp. 167–88; E. C. Knowlton, 'Wordsworth and Blair', *Philological Quarterly* 6 (1927), 277–81.

54 Michael Baron, *Language and Relationship in Wordsworth's Writing* (London and New York: Longman, 1995), p. 13. References to Wordsworth's preface are from *Lyrical Ballads*, ed. Michael Mason (London and New York: Longman, 1992).

55 *Lyrical Ballads*, pp. 82, 66, 79.

56 *Ibid.*, pp. 66, 60–1.

57 'Essay III', *Essays upon Epitaphs* (composed 1809–10), in William Wordsworth, *Selected Prose*, ed. John O. Hayden (Harmondsworth: Penguin, 1988), p. 361.

58 *Ibid.*, pp. 360. See also Baron, *Language and Relationship*; Frances Ferguson, *Wordsworth: Language as Counter-Spirit* (New Haven and London: Yale University Press, 1977); J. Douglas Kneale, *Monumental Writing: Aspects of Rhetoric in Wordsworth's Poetry* (Lincoln and London: University of Nebraska Press, 1988).

CHAPTER 5

The entrance of the novel into the
Scottish universities

Paul G. Bator

In an earlier chapter Ian Duncan has revealed how Adam Smith's work in particular helped develop a theoretical framework in which the novel could gain increasing prominence inside and outside academia. This chapter counterpoints Duncan's, supplying detailed evidence to show how eagerly the teachers and students of Rhetoric and Belles Lettres in the eighteenth-century Scottish universities responded to the novel. While the professors of Rhetoric and Belles Lettres expressed standard reservations about aspects of the novel's propriety, it is far from the case that those involved in the development of the fledgling academic subject of English scorned the emerging genre of extended prose fiction. Close examination of lecture notes, library circulation records and student literary society activity shows how quickly the novel was taken into the mainstream system of university education in Scotland.[1] That this marginalized species of prose fiction was accorded direct attention should not surprise us, for the production and consumption of novels, or popular romances, was at its pinnacle at precisely the same time that the neo-Renaissance discipline of Rhetoric – under the francophile shift toward a belletristic expansion of Rhetoric's domain – reconfigured and re-established its long-standing position as a primary university subject. While recognizing the role and importance of Adam Smith's ideas for a theory of fiction, this chapter suggests that it was in the more marginal universities of St Andrews and Aberdeen, at least as much as in Smith's Glasgow or Blair's Edinburgh, that early academic interest in the novel was most clearly manifested.

The impetus for acknowledgement and initial critical treatment of the novel came from without and within the university. Public clamour in Scotland for the popular English works of the day such as *Pamela*, *Evelina*, *Robinson Crusoe*, *Tom Jones* and *Joseph Andrews*, the establishment of circulating libraries in Edinburgh, Glasgow and Aberdeen, weekly reviews of the novels in *The Monthly Review* and *The Critical Review*, private manor library acquisition of the latest romances and novels, literary society discussions, and the increasing authorship, sales, distribution and consumption of novels throughout Britain at the mid point of the century – together opened doors for the entrance of this new breed of prose fiction into academic quarters. The libraries of the four major universities in Scotland all began acquiring and lending novels from the outset, thus simultaneously whetting student and professorial appetite for reading and discussion of this new course of fiction. Private library shelves of the literati and the middling classes rapidly became populated with gothic novels, spy novels and sentimental novels, as well as *Fielding's Miscellanies*. That strict preachers among the Presbyterians and Calvinists such as the brothers James and David Fordyce warned young readers away from the reading of romances, that the elite English universities of Oxford and Cambridge rejected this bastard form of prose fiction – all did little to curtail the novel's appeal for the youth of the day. The students' lively curiosity and debating society discussion of the novel made it inevitable that the university academics (who were in their own private chambers and public literary societies conducting comparable discussions) would find it difficult if not impossible to place any sort of cap on the novel. Thus, although constrained to a degree by their own moderate sentiments and religious rectitude, the Scottish professors intuitively recognized not only the metropolitan London but also the increasingly cosmopolitan stamp of the novel. They actually offered but perfunctory resistance – what Robert Crawford observes (in his Introduction to this volume) as a feeble attempt to 'police students' reading habits' – to this emerging form of prose fiction and may instead be seen to have put forth a critical plan that would lead toward more formal acceptance of the novel in the nineteenth-century academies of England, India and America. My argument here is that the Scottish professors of Rhetoric began at the mid point of the eighteenth century to see that the novel provided a unique and unstoppable vehicle by which their students could observe and learn vicariously the manners of their English brethren without having to make the journey to London.

The academic discipline of Rhetoric and Belles Lettres reflected the developing practice of popular and professional literary critics, who treated all manner of prose fiction being published in rapid-fire fashion at the mid point of the century. Despite sermonic pulpit railings and warnings against the reading of romances, there appeared to have been no real move on the part of the moderate literati to turn their backs on the novel. What they did do, however, as a way of maintaining the face of moral propriety, perhaps, was to sort the good from the bad. Geoffrey Day points up how Richardson's 'dismissive reference to "such Novels and romances, as have a Tendency to inflame and corrupt" reinforces the idea . . . that he did not take kindly to the thought that his own works could be described by either of these terms, and thus aligns him very firmly alongside Fielding in this matter'.[2] Richardson, of course, thought himself to have been creating works of true virtue, probability, and natural realism – work not to be confused with the scribblers of mere fiction. Just as Richardson and Fielding took pains to distance themselves from the popular romance writers of the day, preferring to be recognized as writers of found histories, as it were, and not to be called romance writers or mere novelists, so the eighteenth-century Scottish professors and librarians attempted to allow consideration of a certain class or first-tier of fiction into their lectures and libraries.

Although Hugh Blair at Edinburgh and Adam Smith at Glasgow did not prelect upon the new prose species at any length, they did make direct reference to the novel or romance in their lectures. Blair, the Moderate Presbyterian leader, and Smith, the Oxford-trained 'impartial spectator', found no room in their lectures for detailed criticism of individual novels, in part, no doubt, because the professional literary critics of the day were churning out review after review. Blair delivered his lectures at the University of Edinburgh under the auspices of his Professorship of Rhetoric and Belles Lettres from 1762–84, yet his popular and well-attended course was not officially required as part of the degree-granting requirements at the University of Edinburgh until 1827. Smith delivered his Rhetoric and Belles Lettres lectures not during his course of Moral Philosophy at Glasgow but as supplemental, 'Saturday' lectures. Initially, as will be shown, the novel garnered academic attention not at the larger, central lowland Scottish universities, but at the smaller, more marginal universities at Aberdeen and St Andrews. Attention to the novel is noticeable particularly in the lectures of James Beattie at Aberdeen and William Barron at St Andrews.

In their turn away from a public rhetoric of eloquence, the Scottish professors of Rhetoric and Belles Lettres began to view the novel as a utilitarian work of prose fiction that could serve their need for instructive moral examples of taste, sympathy and discreet as well as indiscreet character. Their critical effort had been didactic in nature and the lessons to be drawn from the proper novels of the day served the professors' aims well. The formative discipline of Rhetoric and Belles Lettres – as it transfigured itself into the study of English Literature – did so after the Union of Parliaments in 1707 as well as during a time of increasing publication of novels and acceptance of reading as a leisure activity. Thus, the disciplinary shift from a rhetoric engaged almost exclusively with training in eloquence or oratory toward a continental integration of Rhetoric and Belles Lettres provided an institutional avenue for the reading and critical consumption of the novel. In his lectures on Rhetoric, Robert Watson spoke not for himself nor simply to his own band of young students at St Andrews when he declared the terms rhetoric and criticism interchangeable: 'By the Rules of Rhetorick or fine writing else is meant but observations concerning the particulars which render discourse excellent & useful. . . . To what follows therefore may be given either the name of Rhetorick or of Criticism; for if it deserve the name of the one it will deserve the other also.'[3] For as Robert Crawford and Neil Rhodes posit elsewhere in this present volume, Watson's critical prescience represents a turning point for the study of 'English' literature. Since hard curricular evidence or data such as reading lists, syllabi, or detailed assignments is difficult to come by, it should not be said that the novel was actually being 'taught' *per se* in the Scottish universities of the eighteenth century as there was no organized method of introducing novels or novelists; furthermore, the novel was a mixed form of prose fiction and not yet a pure genre by any means. Nevertheless, the novel found its way into the lectures on Rhetoric and Belles Lettres as the enlightened Scottish professors envisioned a literary canon broad enough to encompass all serious prose fiction, including the novel.[4]

Hugh Blair, in his published *Lectures on Rhetoric and Belles Lettres*, conservatively pointed out to his students that the new form of prose fiction was but an 'insignificant class of Writings, known by the name of Romances and Novels' (Lecture xxxvii). Nevertheless, Blair recognized the novel's entrance upon the critical stage and realized that his students had become – as had he – avid readers of the romances and novels of the day. Foresightfully, Blair acknowledged the novel's entrance upon the academic scene in terms of its potential for providing moral instruction, saying that such 'fictitious histories' . . . were useful 'for conveying instruction, for painting human life and manners, for showing the errors into which we are betrayed by our passions'. Blair pointed his students to Richardson (*Clarissa*) as 'the most moral of all our novel writers'. Similarly, Adam Smith, while acknowledging the 'newness' of the novel as a merit, largely dismissed the proclivity his students were showing for the novel as reading recreation by characterizing 'curiosity [as] the only motive which induces us to read them' (Lecture XVII). Acutely aware, however, of the influence novels were having upon his students, Smith proceeded in his lecture on historical narration (Lecture XX) to chart the evolutionary path from myth to romance to novel:

As the marvellous could no longer please authors had recourse to that which they imagind would please and interest most; that is, to represent such actions and passions as, being affecting in themselves, or displaying the delicate feelings of the Human heart, were likely to be most interesting. Thus it was that tragedy succeded the Fabulous accounts of Heroes and centaurs and different monsters, the subject of the first Romances; and thus also, Novells which unfold the tender emotions or more violent passions in the characters they bring before us succeded the Wild and extravagant Romances which were the first performances of our ancestors in Europe. (p. III)

In his lecture 'On Fable and Romance' James Beattie, Professor of Moral Philosophy and Logic at Marischal College, Aberdeen University, from 1760 to 1893 attempted without much success to provide a typology for the 'Romance', distinguishing between 'serious romances' such as Defoe's *Robinson Crusoe* and Richardson's *Clarissa* and Comick Romances such as Smollett's *Roderick Random* and *Peregrine Pickle*.[5] Beattie, despite devoting some time and effort to the cause of classifying the types, arrangement and styles of the romances, joined Blair in warning his students against over-indulging in the new species of prose fiction: 'Let not the usefulness of Romance-writing be estimated by the length of my discourse upon it. Romances are a dangerous recreation. A few, no doubt, of the best may be friendly to good taste and good morals; but far the greater part are unskilfully written . . . I would therefore caution my young reader against them' (pp. 562–74).

William Barron, while Professor of Logic, Rhetoric and Metaphysics at St Andrews from 1778 until 1804, initially linked fiction or romance to fictitious histories but then decided just to go ahead and call a spade a spade by stating that the lot of these works are called novels.[6] In his lecture (XXXIX) entitled 'Epistolary Writing – Fiction', Barron echoes Blair and Smith when he subsumes the novel as a species that falls within the genus of fictitious history: 'In the course of the preceding century a new species of fictitious history, called Novels, has been introduced, which, if properly executed, might prove an useful and entertaining school of knowledge and virtue' (p. 44). Barron also saw the need for setting forth a working definition for the romance or novel

hinged upon the rhetorical criterion of probability: 'A romance or a
novel is a history of events altogether fictitious, in which such characters are introduced, and placed in such situations, as may promote
most effectually the design of the author, to instruct or to amuse the
reader. The author is restrained by no limitation but that of probability'
(pp. 39–40).[7] Barron went on to advise his students about the proper
narrative techniques, including character portrayal, that the novelist
should employ: 'It requires that the author should paint characters and
situations with a large portion of the genius of a comic writer, that the
incidents should be probable and interesting; the characters singular,
but not unnatural; and the narrative conducted so as to engage the
attention, and to improve the manners and the heart' (p. 45).

Additional evidence of the novel's swift approach upon the Scottish
academic terrain can be gathered through an examination of the library
borrowing records at the four universities. While original eighteenth-
century library borrowing records do exist, the various registries and
receipt books are heavily scored and incomplete. Fairly clear borrowing records are available in original manuscript form at Edinburgh,
Aberdeen and St Andrews (the Glasgow University Library 'receipt
books' are few, scattered, and provide sketchy information of books
acquired and borrowed). In 1709, the Edinburgh University Library
acquired the right to a copy of every book published in England; how
many books a year the librarians actually accepted, of course, varied
considerably. Edinburgh library records of 8 November 1734 show
that 'it was recommended to Mr Stewart and Dr Pringle, to inspect
the books sent from Stationers' Hall, and to consider what of them are
worthy to be bound'. As reported in a Royal Commission report of 1826,
Sir John Leslie wrote: 'The privilege of demanding from Stationers'
Hall a copy of every new publication has not been very productive; it
has loaded our shelves with a great deal of trash, and occasioned much
unnecessary expense in binding.'[8] Certainly, acquisition records alone
would not provide any definite indication that novels acquired were
novels being taken out and read by students and professors of the day.
But a closer examination of the actual borrowing registers demonstrates
quite convincingly that almost immediately after they were acquired
by the universities' libraries, the popular novels of the day were being
borrowed, returned and borrowed again. The library borrowing registers at St Andrews, Aberdeen and Edinburgh are in relatively good shape
and provide a revealing glimpse of the popularity of the novel at the
academy.

My scan of the St Andrews University Library borrowing registers and records indicates not only that the well-known novels of the day were entering through the front library portals, but that they were circulating regularly among students and professors. Interestingly, even before Robert Watson took over at St Andrews, the retiring initial holder of the chair of Logic, Rhetoric and Metaphysics from 1747 to 1756, Henry Rymer, can be seen to have exhibited interest in the novels of the day by the way he apparently encouraged his students to take them from the library and read them. On 22 March 1749, Alexander Duncan checked out *Adventures of Joseph Andrews* (1742) on Mr Rymer's 'order', as did David Russel on 5 April 1750 and John Barclay on 20 April 1750. On 8 February 1750 Eliza Haywood's *Fortunate Foundlings* (1744) was checked from the library on Mr Rymer's order by John Barclay. Sarah Fielding's *David Simple* (1744) similarly appeared to be a steady item on the circulation list, as Henry Rymer signed check-out 'orders' for Joseph McCormick on 19 Feb. 1750 and for John Ramsay two weeks later on 4 April 1750 and then again on 25 April 1750 to James Thomson. The borrowing registry records show Rymer, himself, for example, borrowing *Pamela* (1740–41) on 27 May 1748 and *Robinson Crusoe* (1719) on 3 Feb. 1749. On 5 November 1751 *David Simple* and *Pamela* were borrowed from the library on Mr Rymer's order by an unidentified student. Smollett's *Peregrine Pickle* (1751) was borrowed from the library on Mr Rymer's order by George Munro on 29 February 1752 and John Hill's *The History of a Woman of Quality: or, the Adventures of Lady Frail*, was taken from the library on 4 May 1752. Two other novels that Rymer appeared to sign for regularly were *Gulliver's Travels* and *Tom Jones* (1749). Whether or not Rymer actually discussed the romances and novels of the day in his Logic lectures cannot, unfortunately, be determined since no copies of Rymer's lectures appear to be available in manuscript form.

During the terms of Robert Watson (1756–78) and William Barron (1778–1803) in the Chair of Logic, Rhetoric and Metaphysics at St Andrews, the list of novels circulating among the professors and students included virtually all of today's standard 'canon' – works by Fielding, Richardson and Defoe – as well as several of the more popular prose fictions of the time which are now seldom considered ordinarily in the classroom. Laurence Sterne's *Tristram Shandy* (1760) does not appear to have been among the circulating novels at St Andrews, yet it was acquired by the libraries at Aberdeen and Edinburgh. From France, Alain René LeSage's picaresque novel *Gil Blas* (1715) and Françoise de

Graffigny's *Lettres d'une Péruvienne* (1764) were both acquired and lent repeatedly. Tobias Smollett's *Roderick Random* (1748), *Peregrine Pickle* (1751) and *Humphry Clinker* (1771) were acquired by the library and borrowed frequently soon thereafter. Similarly, the Edinburgh man of letters, Henry Mackenzie's *Man of Feeling* (1771), *The Man of the World* 1773 and *Julia de Roubigné* (1777) were circulating steadily in the last decades of the century. Frances Burney's *Evelina* (1778), *Cecilia* (1782), and *Camilla* (1796) were checked out by professor and student alike. The St Andrews student borrowing registries for 1795–1800 indicate entries for Charlotte Palmer's *Female Stability* (1780), Elizabeth Todd's *Lady Caroline Rivers* (1788) and *Edmund and Eleonora* (1797) by Edmund Marshall. Although George Saintsbury in his *Short History of English Literature* (1898) dismissed Mrs Eliza Haywood as a woman of 'no very good reputation', her novels *Betsy Thoughtless* (1751) and *Jemmy and Jenny Jessamy* (1753) proved to be popular reading items at the Scottish universities. While Charlotte Lennox's *The Female Quixote* (1752) and *Henrietta* (1758) do not appear to be among the frequently circulating library list of novels, *The Ladies Miscellany . . . a Collection of Original Poems, Novels, and Other Curious Tracts* appears frequently. Anne Ward Radcliffe's multi-volume *Mysteries of Udolpho* was acquired and also began circulating quickly after it appeared in 1795. *The Fool of Quality* (1766) by the Irishman Henry Brooke seemed to be a popular novel according to the library records at St Andrews and Edinburgh.

The library acquisition and borrowing activity at Aberdeen appears to mirror that of St Andrews and Edinburgh in terms of the standard novels of Fielding, Defoe, Richardson, Burney, Mackenzie, Sarah Fielding and Eliza Haywood at the mid point of the century. By means of the Stationers' Hall Act, King's College Library at Aberdeen was well supplied by the final decades of the eighteenth century and had acquired a range of novels in its collection. Illustration of how quickly the library received romances and novels of the day can be seen in the instance of the London publication for G. Kearsly in 1780 of Sir Herbert Croft's *Love and Madness*, which was acquired by the library at Aberdeen in 1781, as well as the anonymous publication by J. Heriot of *The Sorrows of the Heart* in 1787 acquired at Aberdeen that same year. Some of the minor or non-canonical popular novels acquired by the King's College Library toward the end of the century included Clara Reeve's *The Exiles* (acq.[acquired] 1789), Charlotte Smith's *Celestina* (acq.1791) and *Banished Man* (acq.1794), Helen Maria Williams's *Julia* (acq.1790), Judith Alexander's *The Young Lady of Fortune, a Novel* (acq.1789), Jane Purbeck's

Raynsford Park (acq.1790), *Eugenia & Adelaide* (acq.1791), Mrs Ann Howell's *Georgina* (acq.1796), *Laura Valmont,* a novel 'written by a lady' (acq. 1792), Charles Dibdin's *The Younger Brother,* 3 vols. (acq.1793), and Andrew McDonald's *The Independent, a Novel* (acq.1784).

The list of novels 'received from Stationers Hall' by the library at Edinburgh University includes most of the well-known titles of the day, repeating the standard novels acquired at Aberdeen and St Andrews, including Sterne's *Tristram Shandy,* and occasionally expanding the list to include acquisition of, for example, Mrs Aphra Behn's *Love-Letters* (1684–87), Clara Reeve's *The Old English Baron* (1778) and Sophia Lee's *The Recess* (1785). Perhaps equally telling, however, are the activities of the Edinburgh Belles Lettres Society, a student society at the University of Edinburgh, which provide an additional arena of literary activity that demonstrates how the novel edged its way into the eighteenth-century academy. The Edinburgh Belles Lettres Society (BLS) met at the University of Edinburgh from 1759 to 1764 and although it had its difficulties maintaining membership and finding suitable quarters within the university to meet, it was able to attract student members such as James Boswell and honorary members that included Professors Hugh Blair and John Stevenson and Principal William Robertson. The 'Proceedings of the Belles Lettres Society' are preserved in the Advocates Library of the National Library of Scotland.[9] The literary discussions of the BLS students, particularly their discourse on the novel, demonstrate the extent to which the students at the university were influenced by the broader critical debates about the propriety of novel reading and indicate how they sought to influence the academic discussion of novels.

Professor D. B. Horn, in his *Short History of the University of Edinburgh,* comments on the role of the students: 'It would be difficult to overestimate the importance of these student societies in the life of the eighteenth-century university. They did something to give coherence to the amorphous Edinburgh undergraduate body. Judging by what students . . . wrote in after life of their student days at Edinburgh, it is quite clear that they learned as much from these student societies as from the professors in the classrooms'.[10] The goals of the Belles Lettres Society were in concert with the larger Scottish enlightenment effort to emulate the best of English culture and literature. As Alasdair MacIntyre has observed of the Scots' desire to Anglicize themselves: 'This involved a choice most obviously of what types of career to follow and where, but it also involved choices in modes of religious observance, in manners and in habits, and in how to talk and to write'.[11] Thus, the BLS charge states that the promotion of Belles Lettres as a branch of education is 'absolutely necessary'. As the novel encompassed epistolary romance, travel account, moral satire and conduct-book instruction, it began by the end of the century to be a vehicle for displaying the character not only of individuals but of nations, Smollett's *Humphry Clinker*, for example, providing students with a comparative lesson in geography as well as social and political attitudes.

On 8 April 1761, the student members of the Edinburgh Belles Lettres Society changed the wording of an earlier question that had been submitted for discussion by one of its members. The original wording of the question was: 'Should Reading & Writing of Romances be discouraged . . .?'; this question was revised to read: 'Ought the Reading and Writing of Romances to be encouraged?' Romances were seen by the students as a form of entertainment which allowed the writer to exhibit powers of narration, description and eloquence: 'By this means many are induced to read, who have no Inclination to more serious Performances . . . who does not lament the misfortunes of a *Pamela*?' Another speaker rounded off the discussion by declaring: 'I hesitate not to affirm that the names of Xenophon, Fenelon, Fielding, and Richardson will be handed down with Honour to the latest Posterity.'

In its preliminary attempt to define the 'nature' of Romances and to distinguish the romance from the novel as they are 'by our English Writers', the BLS discourse mirrors the Scottish rhetoricians' indecision about which term to employ: romance or novel. Even though Samuel Johnson's *Dictionary* provided an entry for novel and novelist: 'NOVEL: [*nouvelle*, Fr.] 1. A small tale. NOVELIST: 1. An innovator; assertor of novelty', there was no agreement either inside or outside the academy as to the difference between a 'novel' and a 'romance', and the terms continued to be used almost interchangeably.[12] In his published *Lectures*, Hugh Blair refers to the 'romance' as a generic category or 'species' of fictitious prose composition, and, at the same time, acknowledges the familiar 'novel' as a type or 'form' of the general species (Lecture XXXVII). Adam Smith had characterized the novel as a successor to earlier forms of narrative romance. In his *Lectures on Belles Lettres and Logic*, Willam Barron, Professor of Logic, Rhetoric and Metaphysics at St Andrews University, refers at one point to 'Fiction or Romance', yet proceeds also to acknowledge the novel: 'In the course of the preceding century a new species of fictitious history, called Novels, has been introduced, which, if properly executed, might prove an useful and entertaining school of knowledge and virtue' (Lecture XXXIX).[13]

The BLS members also appeared to be aware of and sensitive to the moral charges against the novel or romance as inflamer of passions. The BLS members responded to skeptical positions about the novel or romance by voicing what was becoming a familiar moderate, moral argument resting upon virtue and natural beauty that attempts to connect the romance with all literary compositions: 'The virtuous Principles are attended with an innate Beauty which embellish and adorn every Species of Composition . . . The Influence then of Romance ought no more to be feared than a Captive whom superior Force has loaded with Chains.' The BLS discourse advanced arguments in favour of the romance or novel based upon its ability to represent national character and to promote virtue: 'By Degrees, [romances/novels] came to relate Events more common and natural, and more adapted to a civilized and polished State. . . . Our own Days stile shows us many Characters similar to a Joseph Andrews. . . . I cannot help thinking that this very Circumstance may be urged as an Argument in Favour of Romance.' When the discourse argues: 'In a well wrote Romance We have an opportunity of becoming acquainted with Characters of every kind, & we are enabled to distinguish the fine Shades which enter into the Composition', we may be reminded readily of Fielding's observations in his preface to *Joseph Andrews*: 'As to the Character of *Adams,* as it is the most glaring in the whole, so I conceive it is not to be found in any Book now extant. It is designed a Character of perfect Simplicity; and as the Goodness of his Heart will recommend him to the Good-natur'd; so I hope it will excuse me to the Gentlemen of his Cloth . . . since no other Office could have given him so many Opportunities of displaying his worthy Inclinations'. The BLS students pointed out the novel's capacity for providing imaginative pleasure and moral instruction:

Here, if any where, the agreeable and usefull, are blended together . . . The writer of Romance has in his Power to paint every Scene which can delight the Mind. He may mingle with his Narration the most beautiful Descriptions, and all the Charms of native Eloquence. Here we may justly expect what is easy, natural & picturesque. . . . Thus [through Romances] We are taught in the most agreeable Manner how We Ourselves ought to behave. Advice is thus conveyed to Us with out that Air of Authority which disgusts.

The BLS students' arguments in favour of the novel repeated what they were reading in the reviews of the day and certainly offered no startling basis for advancement of the romance or novel. Nonetheless, the fact that they were, in an extra-mural activity, taking measure of, reading, and registering the popularity and influence of the novel demonstrates their eagerness to acquire a certain cosmopolitan demeanor and to improve themselves by enlarging the range of their approved academic reading.

The entrance of the novel into the eighteenth-century universities in Scotland was indirect, tentative, yet clearly noticeable. Evidence of the novel's stamp upon the curriculum, as has been shown here, can be seen most directly through the references to the romance or novel in the student lecture notes and published lectures of Hugh Blair at Edinburgh, Adam Smith at Glasgow, James Beattie at Aberdeen and William Barron at St Andrews. The literary debate in the outside critical world about the suitability of novels as fit reading material for the youth of Scottish society persisted into the nineteenth century, as Francis Jeffrey provided witness, for example, in *The Edinburgh Review* of 1842: '[novels] were rated very low with us – scarcely allowed to pass as part of a nation's permanent literature – and generally deemed altogether unworthy of any grave critical notice'. Nevertheless, the Scottish university libraries began acquiring the standard novels of the day shortly after they were published in London, and the borrowing records indicate that they were circulating repeatedly amoung the students and professors. Student literary societies, such as the Edinburgh Belles Lettres Society, took up the debate over the novel as proper reading material and thereby issued a ripple-effect upon their entrance into the classroom. There appeared to have been a tacit awareness and agreement on the part of the students and professors by the 1750s that the novel was indeed important, that although it was an unsettled 'genre' it had the potential for representing and conveying what Edward Said today refers to as the cultural significance of the English [sic] novel in the British nineteenth century, making claims for the novel as a cultural agent, an ideological force, an encyclopedic absorber, an historical narrative and preserver of values.[14] The critical discussion of the novel is not a latecomer to the field of university English; instead, it is a limited yet recognizable part of its foundation.

NOTES

1 J. Paul Hunter, in his essay 'The Novel and Social/Cultural History' must be referring to eighteenth-century England primarily and not Scotland when he observes: 'Still, however, education at the highest (university) level remained scandalously poor in quality and, of course, severely limited to the privileged few, and literacy had actually begun to slip in the new industrial parts of the nation' (p. 29). Hunter, in fact, reminds us that

'Literacy was higher in some regions of Britain than others: highest in Scotland, the Southeast of England, and (especially) London' (p. 20). In *The Cambridge Companion To The Eighteenth-Century Novel*, ed. John Richetti (Cambridge University Press, 1996), pp. 9–40.

2 Geoffrey Day, *From Fiction to The Novel* (London: Routledge & Kegan Paul, 1987), p. 133.

3 Robert Watson P., 'Heads of Lectures on Rhetoric and Belles Lettres' (1764. MS Dc. 6.50/2. University of Edinburgh Library). Similarly, Hugh Blair begins his *Lectures*: 'Some [students and general readers] may have the view of being employed in composition, or in public speaking. Others, without any prospect of this kind, may wish only to improve their taste with respect to writing and discourse, and to acquire principles which will enable them to judge for themselves in that part of literature called the Belles Lettres' (vol. I, pp. 4–5). References to Blair's *Lectures* in this essay are to the edition by Harold F. Harding (Carbondale: Southern Illinois University Press, 1965). References to Adam Smith's *Lectures on Rhetoric and Belles Lettres* are to the edition by J. C. Bryce (Oxford: Clarendon Press, 1983).

4 My discussion of the novel's place at the university here is extended further in 'Rhetoric and the Novel in the Eighteenth Century British University Curriculum', *Eighteenth-Century Studies* (forthcoming Winter 1996–97).

5 'On Fable and Romance,' by James Beattie, which was published in Beattie's *Dissertations Moral and Critical* in London in 1783 and, importantly, which we can safely say was delivered by Beattie at Marischal College, Aberdeen University, while Beattie was Professor of Moral Philosophy and Logic from 1760 to 1803. See E. H. King, 'James Beattie And The Eighteenth-Century University', *Aberdeen University Review* 44 (1972), 174–85.

6 William Barron, *Lectures On Belles Lettres And Logic*, 2 vols. (London: Longman, Hurst, Rees, & Orme; and Bell & Bradfute, Edinburgh, 1806). (Subsequent parenthetical text references to Barron's *Lectures* refer to this edition.)

7 Barron continues: 'If he keep within this boundary, he is perfectly at liberty to feign characters and situations; he must not, however, transcend probability, otherwise he demolishes his own charm, he shocks the faith of the reader, and prevents the operation of that deceit, by means of which alone he either can interest or improve' (pp. 39–40).

8 *Evidence*, Royal Commission of 1826, p. 156.

9 Advocates Library, National Library of Scotland Adv.MS 23.3.4. contains: 'Proceedings of the Belles Lettres Society' from 12 January 1759 through 29 May 1761; Adv.MS 5.1.6. contains: 'Proceedings of the Belles Lettres Society' from 9 December 1761 through 7 December 1764; Adv.MS 22.3.8. 'Belles Lettres Society Notes and Speeches on Questions Debated'. Permission to quote from the Advocates Library Manuscripts was kindly granted by the Trustees of the National Library of Scotland. For fuller discussion, see Paul Bator, 'The University of Edinburgh Belles Lettres Society (1759–64) and the Rhetoric of the Novel', *Rhetoric Review* 14 (Spring 1996), 280–98.

10 D. B. Horn *Short History of the University of Edinburgh* (Edinburgh University Press, 1967), p. 93.

11 Alasdair MacIntyre, *Whose Justice? Which Rationality?* (Notre Dame University Press, 1988), p. 111.

12 Samuel Johnson, *Dictionary* (I consulted a Dublin 1763 version), NOVEL: [*nouvelle*, Fr.] 1. A small tale. *Dryden.* 2 A law annexed to the code. *Ayl.* NOVELIST: 1. An innovator; assertor of novelty. *Bacon.* 2. A writer of novels. Note also: No entries for 'genre'; there are for genus and species.

13 In her 1785 dialogue entitled *The Progress of Romance*, Clara Reeve attempted to 'mark the distinguishing characters of the Romance and the Novel, to point out the boundaries of both', and in so doing, took up her task more directly and explicitly than most of the periodical reviewers of her day were wont to do. Clara Reeve, *The Progress of Romance* (New York: The Facsimile Text Society; Series 1: Literature and Language volume 4, 1930, vi. Reproduced from the Colchester Edition of 1785, with a bibliographical note by Esther M. McGill). In her preface, interestingly, Reeve makes a point of stating that while she was aware of James Beattie's *Dissertation on Fable and Romance* and Mr Warton's *History of English Poetry*, she had read neither work prior to finishing her own dialogue on the subject. Reeve's critical assessment of authors included Aphra Behn, Mrs Haywood, Mrs Manly, Henry and Sarah Fielding, Richardson, Charlotte Lennox, Smollett, Defoe, Sterne and Henry MacKenzie.

14 Edward H. Said, *Culture and Imperialism* (New York: Alfred K. Knopf, 1993).

CHAPTER 6

William Greenfield: gender and the transmission
of literary culture

Martin Moonie

Mr Greenfield is of a superior order. The bleedings of humanity,
the generous resolve, a manly regard of the paltry subjects of
vanity, virgin modesty, the truest taste, and a very sound judgement, characterize him . . . He certainly possesses no small share
of poetic abilities; he is a steady and most disinterested friend,
without the affectation of seeming so; and as a companion, his
good sense, his joyous hilarity, his sweetness of manners and
modesty, are most engagingly charming.

[Robert Burns][1]

Like most of his contemporaries and successors in eighteenth- and
nineteenth-century Scottish academia, Hugh Blair in his *Lectures on Rhetoric and Belles Lettres* pays little attention to Scottish literature. However, as
Robert Burns and others recognized, Blair's successor, William Greenfield, was more sympathetic to important aspects of Scottish writing. At
the same time, Greenfield's career serves to emphasize what Neil Rhodes
(in an earlier chapter of this book) and Adam Potkay (in his study of
eloquence in the age of Hume)[2] have pointed out – the importance of
gender in the academic construction of Belles Lettres. That Greenfield's
name is now almost completely forgotten is no accident of history. On
the contrary, the record of Greenfield's career has been actively suppressed. And in order to understand the climate in which English literary
studies first developed within Scotland, it is necessary to re-examine
both Greenfield and his writings, paying particular attention to the
scandal that caused him to be removed from the historical record.

On the evening of the 19 July 1822, the 58-year-old Bishop of Clogher
and a 22-year-old soldier were attacked in the back rooms of a London
pub.[3] Repeatedly beaten and dragged naked through the streets by an
outraged mob, the couple found themselves on trial the following day
for homosexual offences. Prior to his unfortunate outing, the Bishop
had been a noted member of the Society for the Suppression of Vice,

and a respected dignitary within the Church. The ensuing scandal
brought with it a carnival of pamphlets, broadsides and poems:

> The Devil to prove that the Church was a farce
> Went out for to seek for a bugger,
> He baited his hook with a soldier's arse
> And pulled out the Bishop of Clogher.[4]

In a collection of these pamphlets and poems, held in the British
Library, a single undated broadside yokes the Clogher scandal of 1822
to the crisis that removed William Greenfield from Edinburgh in 1798.
For more than a dozen verses, *The Lion in Tears: Or, the Church's lament for
Dr Greenfield*, rages against both Greenfield and the Church of Scotland,
the poem's savagery all the more stunning since it describes events that
took place more than twenty years before the Clogher scandal. The
broadside is a crucial document in any discussion of the history and
interpretation of Greenfield's career, since it is the only contemporary
source to explicitly identify his crime:[5]

> [Greenfield] was the Church's prop and stay,
>   Penn'd a' her sage addresses,
> But yet forsook God's holy way,
>   And f-d in barbers a-s.
>
> O! may we never hear at hame,
>   A tale so very shockin',
> While there's a c-t in Christendom,
>   For man to put a c-ck in.
>
> But he who heavenly c-t forsakes,
>   A fellow's a-se to kiss,
> Should be entomb'd beneath a' jakes,
>   Or drown'd in women's piss.[6]

Greenfield virtually vanished as a result of the scandal: physically exiled
to England, but also disappearing from contemporary biographies and
official records, his surviving historical traces obscured by his own
need for anonymity, and the fear, among his contemporaries, of being
known to associate with him. Lockhart voids Greenfield's name under
a string of asterisks in his *Like of Walter Scott*,[7] and the earliest biography
of Hugh Blair, Greenfield's closest colleague, refuses to acknowledge
that Greenfield existed.[8]

Nevertheless, Greenfield's early career was meteoric. Graduating from
the University of Edinburgh in 1778,[9] he was immediately nominated
for a professorship in Mathematics at Marischal College, Aberdeen.

Robert Arbuthnot, the man who had been responsible for James Beattie's appointment to the Chair of Moral Philosophy in 1760,[10] wrote to support Greenfield's application with the claim that 'he is so much estem'd here at present, that were there any vacancy in the College [Edinburgh University] I know of no body who would have a better chance to supply it'. Although the position did not become vacant that year, the recommendation clearly demonstrates that Greenfield was establishing a formidable reputation.[11]

Rather than going to Aberdeen, Greenfield was ordained in 1781. He became a parish minister in Wemys in Fife for the next three years, before returning to Edinburgh to become the inaugural minister of the New Town's church of St Andrews. He remained there for a further three years, before joining Hugh Blair both as a minister in St Giles, the principal church in Scotland, and as a university professor in Rhetoric and Belles Lettres. Within the university, Greenfield rose to become Dean of the Faculty of Arts. In 1797 he was elected to his church's most senior ecclesiastical position and became Moderator of the Church of Scotland.[12] Two of his sermons survive from this period.[13] In his spare time, Greenfield wrote for Henry Mackenzie's journal, *The Mirror*,[14] produced an essay 'On the Use of Negative Quantities in the Solution of Algebraic Equations' for the Royal Society of Edinburgh[15] and delivered an additional course of lectures on Natural Philosophy.[16] He married in 1786 and had five children.[17]

More than any other contemporary writer, it is Burns who gives the clearest impression of Greenfield's position within Edinburgh society in the 1780s: his poems, letters and memoirs repeatedly showing Greenfield at the centre of the capital's literary life. In a letter dated December 1786, Burns claims to have 'warm friends among the literati, Professors Stewart, Blair, Greenfield, and Mr Mckenzie the Man of feeling'.[18] In the comic poem 'To William Creech (Willie's Awa)', Burns celebrates his publisher's influence by naming the leading literary figures about town, and joking that Creech's departure to London, and more importantly the closure of his book shop, traumatizes them by depriving them of a meeting place:

> Nae mair we see his levee door
> Philosophers and Poets pour,
> And toothy Critics by the score
>   In bloody raw;
> The Adjutant of a' the core
>   Willie's awa.-

> Now worthy Greg'ry's latin face,
> Tytler's and Greenfield's modest grace,
> McKenzie, Stuart, such a brace
>   As Rome ne'er saw;
> They a' maun meet some ither place,
>   Willie's awa. –[19]

The above evidence, taken in conjunction with Greenfield's impressive list of appointments, should suggest that he was far from being an insignificant figure in the public life of Edinburgh – particularly when it is remembered that Professor Greenfield would only have been in his late twenties when Burns visited the capital. This is reinforced by in a letter, perhaps the most intimate that Burns wrote to any of the literati, in which Burns effectively claims that he will be remembered, if at all, as a footnote in Greenfield's biography.

Revd Sir,
On raking the recesses of my memory the other day, I stumbled on two Songs which I here inclose to you as a kind of curiosity to a Professor of the Belle lettres de la Nature; which, allow me to say, I look upon as an additional merit of yours; a kind of bye Professorship, not always to be found among the Fathers and Brothers of scientific Criticism – They were the work of Bards such as I lately was; and such as, I believe, I had better still have been – ...

I mention this to you, once and for all, merely, in the Confessor style, to disburthen my conscience, and that – 'When proud fortune's ebbing tide recedes' – you may bear me witness, when my buble of fame was at the highest, I stood, unintoxicated, with the inebriating cup in my hand, looking forward, with rueful resolve, to the hastening time when the stroke of envious Calumny, with all the eagerness of vengeful triumph, should dash it to the ground.[20]

The contrast with Burns's remarks on Hugh Blair could not be more striking:

Dr Blair is merely an astonishing proof of what industry and application can do. Natural parts like his are frequently to be met with; his vanity is proverbially known among his acquaintances; but he is justly at the head of what may be called fine writing; and a Critic of the first, the very first rank in Prose; even a good Bard of Nature's making can only take the pas of him.[21]

Unlike Burns ('a good Bard of Nature's making') and Greenfield ('Professor of the Belles Lettres de la Nature'), literary critics and especially Blair are represented as being radically un-Natural (stretched by 'industry and application', and engaged in 'scientific Criticism'). Burns grudgingly recognizes that this criticism is important, but simultaneously casts doubt on its legitimacy with the phrase 'what may be called fine writing'.

In sharp contrast, Greenfield is credited with 'the truest taste, [and] . . . poetic abilities'[22] together with a 'kind of bye Professorship . . . [which is] an additional merit'. For Burns, this clearly marked Greenfield as a better critic than Blair since he was able to operate within the spheres of both science and 'Nature'. More significantly, Burns may also be offering a gendered account of literary discourse; contrasting masculine criticism (the 'scientific' preserve of 'Fathers and Brothers') with a feminine poetics of Nature and the sentiments – more of which later.

Twelve years later, proceedings against Greenfield's unmanly behaviour were initiated within his own Kirk Session. Having heard a number of very flagrant reports about their minister's conduct, their worst suspicions were confirmed when they received a note from Greenfield saying that he was leaving Edinburgh and resigning from his ministerial duties. By the end of the meeting Greenfield was excommunicated for 'a Sin particularly heinous and offensive in its nature . . . [which] it would be highly inexpedient to mention in the Record of their proceedings . . . the Sin of which he is accused by the voice of the public'.[23] The Kirk Session then contacted the Town Council and the University of Edinburgh, who stripped him of his degrees and stopped him from teaching. Greenfield went into exile in England where, ten years later, he produced an abbreviated version of his university lectures under the title *Essays on the Sources of the Pleasures received from Literary Compositions* (London, 1809). The anonymous *Essays* have been erroneously attributed to Edward Mangin.[24]

At this point Greenfield briefly reappears, in the letters of Walter Scott. Writing to John Murray in 1809, Scott excitedly announces:

An idea of great importance has occurd to me which if you can follow out with success it will be of immense use to your Review . . . You cannot but have heard of that very unfortunate man Dr Greenshields [sic] who for a dishonourable or rather infamous cause was obliged to leave Edinburgh where he was long beloved and admired by every human being. He is I believe in London writing for bread and certainly would be [from a] literary point of view a most important addition to our strength. His principles as to politics are with us and he would in fact be the best or only match whom we could bring against Playfair on articles of general philosophy. But could his assistance be obtained it would be of the last importance to contain it.[25]

Through Scott's agency Greenfield subsequently contributed a number of pieces to the *Quarterly Review*,[26] and in the following decade he was believed to be the author of the Waverley Novels – a rumour that Scott himself seems to have briefly encouraged.[27] He died in 1827, while still living in exile in England, under the assumed name of Rutherford. Having given a summary of Greenfield's career, it is now possible to turn to his position in the history of English Studies.

In 1783, after publishing his *Lectures on Rhetoric and Belles Lettres*, Hugh Blair retired from the active duties of his professorship, leaving William Greenfield in charge of the course. Until recently it was assumed that no student notes had survived from Greenfield's professorship, and that his lectures were largely the same as those given by his predecessor. However, an extensive and detailed set is to be found in the archives of the University of Aberdeen, which demonstrates that Greenfield radically altered the size and structure of the Edinburgh course.[28]

The transcript is dated 1785–6, and is part of a collection of lecture notes that belonged to Robert Eden Scott, Professor of Rhetoric in King's College, Aberdeen, from 1801. Scott published a short guide to his own Rhetoric course in 1802 and enough similarities exist between Scott's *Elements of Rhetoric* and Greenfield's lectures to suggest that the scandal did not wholly prevent Greenfield from influencing the future development of English literary studies within Scotland.[29] In order to say more about Greenfield's course it will be necessary to outline the ways in which Blair's university lectures relate to the form in which they were published.

Surviving student notes from Blair's lectures, of which the latest accurately dated set is held by Glasgow University Library, indicate that the course comprised of around thirty-nine lectures and was divided into five distinct sections.[30] In their published form the *Lectures* amount to forty-seven chapters, largely resulting from two types of editorial revision. Firstly, Blair added a number of 'Critical Examinations', and secondly, he occasionally divided individual lectures so that they became two chapters. The table 7.1 should give a general idea of this editorial process.

Although incomplete, the Aberdeen manuscript of Greenfield's course runs to more than fifty lectures, and does not follow Blair's chapter divisions. In place of Blair's second section, Greenfield was to tell his students:

Altho the consideration of the origin & progress of languages be a very curious subject – & may be considered as part of the business of this course – & accordingly is excellently treated of by Dr Blair – yet we shall not here enter upon it . . . because it is rather an appendage than a part of this course[31]

Greenfield also dropped Blair's fourth section discussing practical rhetorical skills in favour of more general comments on forms of writing appropriate to different literary genres. With this in mind, Greenfield's

Table 7.1. *Blair's lectures: the transition to print*

Glasgow University Library, MS Murray 1	Published form of *Lectures on Rhetoric* (1783)
Section One. Introduction, and general discussion of Taste, Beauty, Sublimity and Genius (Lectures 1–5)	Chapters 1–5
Section Two. Origin and progress of language and writing (Lectures 6–9)	Chapters 6–9
Section Three. Discussion of elements of style; Sentences, Metaphor, and Figurative Writing (Lectures 10–19)	Chapters 10–19
Single 'Critical Examination' of section from *The Spectator* (Lecture 20)	Chapters 20–24 'Critical Examinations'
Section Four. Discussion of rhetoric and oratory; the eloquence of popular assemblies, the bar, and the pulpit (Lectures 21–28)	Chapters 25–34
Section Five. Discussion of literary compositions; Historical writing, poetry, tragedy, etc. (Lectures 29–39)	Chapters 35–47

course can be seen to confirm Adam Potkay's suggestion in *The Fate of Eloquence in the Age of Hume* that in the course of the eighteenth century an enthusiasm for public eloquence gave way to a concern to cultivate a polite written style.[32] However, it should be emphasized that Greenfield's lectures contain comments on a particularly wide range of literary genres, and as such they also strengthen Rajit Dosanjh's account of the ways in which the Edinburgh course on Rhetoric evolved to allow students to maximize their acquired liberal knowledge (see chapter 4 of this volume). Greenfield, though, displays a far broader conception of what the liberal arts represent than does his predecessor – perhaps as the result of his own interest in science and mathematics. In a section devoted to 'those compositions which convey instruction' Greenfield concentrates much of his attention to a discussion of textbooks on Astronomy, Geometry and Natural Philosophy, using them as examples of works which often alienate their readers by assuming unreasonable levels of knowledge.[33] This is not to say that Greenfield was not concerned to give his students guidance in practical oratory skills, but it serves, once again, to suggest that there are extensive differences between his approach and that of Hugh Blair.

Greenfield also substantially revised the subject matter of the lectures to include texts that had previously received damning remarks from Blair. The inclusion of Thomas Otway's sentimental tragedy *Venice Preserved* is perhaps the most obvious of these changes. Greenfield repeatedly uses the play and its dramatist as a prime example of great tragic writing.

Whoever has seen the representation of *Venice Preserved* must have been struck with the effect which the tolling of the bell for the execution of the conspirators had upon him the force of this is much increased by the tender & compassionate temper the mind is in occasioned by the most affecting parting scene between Jaffier & Belvidera immediately preceding –[34]

Blair thought quite the reverse:

[Otway] is a writer, doubtless, of genius and strong passion; but, at the same time, exceedingly gross and indelicate. No tragedies are less moral than those of Otway. There are no generous sentiments in them; but a licentious spirit discovers itself. He . . . has contrived to introduce obscenity and indecent allusions, into the midst of deep tragedy.[35]

In particular, Greenfield was attracted to a set of texts in which women play leading roles; Marmontel's *The Shepherdess of the Alps*, Southerne's *Isabella*, Home's *Douglas* (which is as much the story of Lady Randolph as it is the tragedy of her son, Douglas), and Otway's *Venice Preserved*. The texts share a number of common themes: transgressive desire, unwanted marriages, secrecy and death. At their most extreme points they show characters torn between roles and values closely associated with masculine and feminine spheres of action. They also seem to suggest that the tragedy itself grows out of this confusion of gender identity. Typically, the narratives involve protagonists whose love for each other is in some sense unlawful; opposed either by the patriarchal dictates of the Church or their families, and further complicated by the male partner's involvement in the masculine sphere of warfare or rebellion. The male partner is then killed or removed, leaving his widow destitute and alienated from her family. She is forced to marry a rival for whom she has no real affection and the relationship generally ends with prolonged suffering and suicide. Certainly such an emphasis in Greenfield's lectures shows how strong considerations of gender were in the early evolution of the study of English in the universities.

While the above recipe does not produce particularly exciting stories, it does provide ample opportunities for speeches celebrating forbidden love. It also repeatedly shows men whose patriarchal duties (to their troops, their fellow conspirators, or their family) stand in the way of their desire for sexual and romantic fulfilment. Elements of this may have more than a passing similarity with the situation in which Greenfield found himself in eighteenth-century Scotland and a biographical reading of his canon may go some way towards suggesting why the professor was repeatedly drawn to texts where illegitimate desire, unwanted marriage and secrecy were balanced against suicide and death.

Edinburgh had, of course, virtually given birth to both sentimental writing in the form of Henry Mackenzie's *The Man of Feeling* and the spectral romanticism of James Macpherson's Ossianic poetry – a poetry, moreover, that repeatedly problematizes a binary opposition between the imperatives of heroic masculinity and the feminine sphere of tender sentiments, compassion and love. The new texts that Greenfield introduced to the course are, perhaps then, not wholly unexpected. They are, however, also symptomatic of far more radical changes that he initiated. Towards the end of his second lecture, the notes read:

The Ends of all composition are reduced by Dr Campbell to four, to enlighten the understanding, to please the imaginations, to excite the emotions, & to engage the will – He says that each of these is preparatory to the subsequent, & that every following one depends on the forgoing – Mr G[reenfield]. reduces them to three viz.: to enlighten the understanding – to excite the emotions, & to engage the will.[36]

The emotions, then, become the key concept in Greenfield's aesthetics, and works that raise the sentiments of pity, terror and melancholy are given a central role in his new canon of gothic fiction, sentimental prose and pathetic tragedies. *Essays on the Sources of the Pleasures Received from Literary Compositions* are an extended version of the first twenty lectures in the Aberdeen manuscript, and include chapters on terror, pity, melancholy and the sublime. Since the Aberdeen notes date from 1785–6, two years after Greenfield took over the Edinburgh course, it is possible that the *Essays*, published in 1809, actually reflect the subsequent development of the lectures. Sentimentalism is, however, only one aspect of the *Essays*, which range freely through epic to gothic writing, Shakespeare, pathetic drama, Scottish poetry and novels.

Fielding and Swift both receive reasonably detailed attention in a chapter on ludicrous composition, whose primary focus is Butler's *Hudibras*, but which nonetheless demonstrates Greenfield's appreciation of the novel.

Few serious discourses are so well calculated as the Voyage to Liliput, for reminding us how often the most contemptible trifles are wrought up by human folly into objects of the most serious importance; and for checking that low pride and selfish ambition, which are so apt to corrupt the powerful, and which, in all nations, and under all forms of government, have sometimes led them to the most atrocious as well as the vilest crimes.[37]

Similarly, his chapter on terror, although never explicitly discussing gothic novels, demonstrates that Greenfield had a keen awareness of the genre and its elements.

It was a good observation of an exquisite artist, that he could conceive a picture in which no human figure, nor action, nor any object very terrible in itself was represented, which yet should raise a high degree of horror. Such, he imagined, would be the effect of a picture representing a bedchamber, with a lady's slipper and a bloody dagger on the floor; and at the door, the foot of a man as just leaving the room.[38]

If Greenfield's interest in sentimental fiction may be related to Mackenzie's *The Man of Feeling* and Macpherson's *Ossian*, it should additionally be noted that his lectures, and particularly the *Essays*, give far more attention to Scottish writing than had been the case with Blair. The poetry of both James Beattie and James Thomson is discussed, and Home's *Douglas* is frequently cited as a prime example of sentimental tragedy. Greenfield also makes extensive use of Scottish criticism in the lectures; Lord Kames, Lord Monboddo, Alexander Gerrard and George Campbell are frequently cited, and an entire section is given over to a discussion of Adam Smith's *Theory of Moral Sentiments*. His attention to Scottish writing becomes even more pronounced in the *Essays*, where, once again, the poems and plays of Beattie, Thomson and Home are discussed. Here, however, they are joined by writers such as Buchanan, Burns and Scott, and Greenfield's range of Scottish theorists extends to include Alison's association of ideas, Hutcheson's reflections on laughter, and Beattie's essays on ludicrous composition, poetry and music. His remarks about Walter Scott are particularly revealing:

But since these translations were printed, the author of them, Walter Scott, Esquire, has acquired great and deserved celebrity by his original compositions, ... [where] a minute acquaintance with the history and antiquities of *his country* is happily united to a poetical genius of the highest order.[39] (emphasis mine)

Here, addressing British readers, Greenfield emphasizes not only that Scotland exists as a 'country' in its own right (earlier figures of the Scottish Enlightenment had preferred to talk about 'North Britain') but also stresses the cultural difference of its 'history and antiquities'. His remarks about Burns, 'our poet of Nature' are similarly surprising – particularly when addressed to a British audience, and especially so when Greenfield continues by quoting a poem, not in English, but in vernacular Scots:

In many calamities, which wring the heart with severest anguish, and afford the tragic poet the most affecting subjects, the sufferer has not to complain that he is destitute of blessings. If he could only forget what he has been, or might have been; if he could only forget what he once enjoyed or once aspired to, he would find himself in a situation, where he might still have all the happiness which this life can afford. The hearts of the miserable are broken by the cruel contrasts which haunt their imagination, and which they are but too much disposed to brood over and encourage. This state of mind is well expressed by Burns, our poet of nature, in his words to the pathetic air of 'The Banks of Doon'.

> Thou'lt break my heart, thou little bird,
> That warblest from yon blooming thorn;
> Thou'lt mind'st me of departed joys,
> Departed never to return.

It is evident, then, how much an author may heighten our pity, by availing himself of the opportunities which the subject may naturally suggest, to represent, in a striking view, not only the former happiness, which the sufferer actually enjoyed, but also the blessings to which he was entitled to aspire, or which have fallen to others, whose pretensions were not superior to his own, or which but for some cruel event he would now be possessing.[40]

By the time that the *Essays* were published Greenfield had been in exile for over ten years and Burns was dead. With the disconcerting phrase 'Burns, our poet of nature', Greenfield seems to echo Burns's tribute to the professor of Belles Lettres de la Nature, and hark back to happier days in Edinburgh. It is almost impossible to read the above passage as anything other than autobiography.

From the above account of Greenfield's lectures and his *Essays*, it should be clear that his work is marked by an unusual and refreshing concern for both gender and Scottish writing. It should, however, finally be noted that his criticism also exhibits forms of oppression typical of his time. More than once he refers to 'peasants' as a sort of *untermensch*, beneath contempt, and certainly unable to receive any pleasure from the refined objects of taste. And in a section where he discusses beauty with reference to optics, he tells a story about a boy, blind from birth, who, having regained the sight of his eyes was 'struck with the utmost horror and could not be reconciled to the sight . . . [of a] negro woman'.[41] Nevertheless, his inclusion in the narrative of the university origins of English Studies is valuable, since it demonstrates how much struggles involving gender, sexuality and the articulation of Scottish identity were bound up with the part played by the development of university English in the transmission of literary culture.

NOTES

1 William Wallace, *The Life and Works of Robert Burns edited by Robert Chambers, revised by William Wallace* (London: W. & R. Chambers Limited, 1896), vol. II, pp. 86–7.
2 Adam Potkay, *The Fate of Eloquence in the Age of Hume* (Ithaca: Cornell University Press, 1994).
3 Rictor Norton, *Mother Clapp's Molly House: the Gay Subculture in England 1700–1830* (London: Gay Men's Press, 1992), pp. 216–21.
4 *Ibid.*, p. 218.
5 Other accounts are far more guarded and ambiguous: *The Scots Magazine* 60 (1798), 863; Adam Ferguson, to Alexander Carlyle, 25 December 1798, Edinburgh University Library, MS Dc. 4.41/58; Edinburgh University Senatus, Minutes, 31 December 1798, Edinburgh University Library, MS Da 31.5.
6 Anonymous broadside, *The Lion in Tears; or, the Church's Lament for Dr Greenfield* [? 1822], British Library, Cup.363.ggg.31(4).
7 John Gibson Lockhart, *Memoirs of the Life of Sir Walter Scott, Bart.* (Edinburgh: Ballantyne and Co., 1837), vol. I, p. 241.
8 John Hill, *An Account of the Life and Writings of Hugh Blair* (Edinburgh: J. Ballantyne and Co., 1807).
9 Hew Scott, *Fasti Ecclesiae Scotticanae* (Edinburgh: Oliver & Boyd, 1915), vol. I, pp. 60–1, 88.
10 Margaret Forbes, *Beattie and his Friends* (Westminster: Archibald Constable & Co., 1904), pp. 15–16.
11 Robert Arbuthnot to James Beattie, 10 April 1778, Aberdeen University Library MS 30.C304.
12 See Scott, *Fasti*, pp. 60–1; Alexander Grant, *The Story of the University of Edinburgh During its First Three Hundred Years* (London: Longman, Greens and Co., 1884), pp. 358–9.
13 William Greenfield, *Address delivered to the congregation of the High Church of Edinburgh, on Thursday 9th March 1797* . . . (Edinburgh, 1797) & *Sermon, preached in the High-Church of Edinburgh, before his grace the Earl of Leven and Melville . . . on Thursday the 18th May 1797, at the opening of the General Assembly of the Church of Scotland . . .* (Edinburgh, 1797).
14 Horst W. Drescher, *Themen und Formen des periodishen Essays im spaten 18. Jahrhundert* (Frankfurt a. M.: Athenaum Verlag, 1971), p. 25.
15 William Greenfield, 'On the Use of Negative Quantities in the Solution of Algebraic Equations', *Transactions of the Royal Society of Edinburgh* 1 (1788), 131–45.
16 William Greenfield, *Lectures on Natural Philosophy*, 1794–5, Edinburgh, New College Library, MS. GRE.

17 Scott, *Fasti*, pp. 60–1.
18 J. De Lancey Ferguson, *The Letters of Robert Burns* (Oxford: Clarendon Press, 1931), p. 56.
19 James Kinsley (ed.), *The Poems and Songs of Robert Burns* (Oxford, 1968), vol. 1, p. 334.
20 Ferguson, *Burns*, 59.
21 Wallace, *Burns*, vol. 11, pp. 86–7.
22 *Ibid.*, vol. 11, pp. 86–7.
23 Edinburgh University Senatus, *Minutes*, 31 December 1798, Edinburgh University Library, MS. D.A. 31.5.
24 In many places the *Essays* follow AUL MS 189/1 (discussed later in the chapter) word for word, but both the *Dictionary of National Biography* and the British Library attribute them to Edward Mangin.
25 Herbert Grierson, *The Letters of Sir Walter Scott 1808–1811* (London: Constable & Co. Ltd., 1932), pp. 178–9.
26 D. Cook, 'Murray's Mysterious Contributor: Unpublished Letters of Sir Walter Scott' *The Nineteenth Century* 101 (1927), 605–13.
27 Herbert Grierson, *The Letters of Sir Walter Scott 1815–1817* (London: Constable & Co. Ltd., 1933), p. 341.
28 William Greenfield, *Lectures on Rhetoric and Belles Lettres*, 1785–6, Aberdeen University Library, MS 189/1.
29 Robert Eden Scott, *Elements of Rhetoric, for the use of students of King's College, Aberdeen* (Aberdeen, 1802).
30 Hugh Blair, *Lectures on Rhetoric and Belles Lettres*, 1777, Glasgow University Library, MS. Murray 1.
31 Greenfield, *Lectures*, lecture 24.
32 Potkay, *The Fate of Eloquence in the Age of Hume*.
33 Greenfield, *Lectures*, lectures 47–8.
34 *Ibid.*, lecture 4.
35 Blair, *Lectures on Rhetoric and Belles Lettres* (London: 1783), vol. 11, p. 525.
36 Greenfield, *Lectures*, lecture 2.
37 William Greenfield, *Essays on the Sources of the Pleasures Received from Literary Compositions* (London, 1809), p. 371.
38 *Ibid.*, p. 102.
39 *Ibid.*, p. 111.
40 *Ibid.*, pp. 158–9.
41 Greenfield, *Lectures*, lecture 7.

CHAPTER 7

An evolutionary microcosm: the teaching of Literature and aesthetics at Aberdeen

Joan H. Pittock

> In the good old days we love to praise
>   Our Profs were a home-grown lot,
> With homely ways and a Doric phrase,
>   For each was a sturdy Scot.
> They came from the shafts
>   Of the rustic plough
> From diverse crofts
>   And a country knowe.[1]

Perhaps more strikingly than any of the other Scottish universities, Aberdeen demonstrates how the university subject of Rhetoric and Belles Lettres developed into the modern subject of English. Because the intellectual genealogy within Aberdeen is so clearly continuous, Aberdeen functions as an evolutionary microcosm in the history of English Studies. Its reliance on home-grown talent may be unusual, but the uninterrupted succession of professors there makes transparent the way the new university discipline was founded, and how its early development underpinned the shifting subject of English right up to the twentieth century. So, remarkably and illuminatingly, from the mid-eighteenth-century David Fordyce to the early-twentieth-century Herbert Grierson, each Aberdeen professor of the subject whose eventual name was English Literature had been taught by his predecessor. To examine the professorial line of succession in Aberdeen is to trace the growth of the university subject of English from its Scottish origins to its modern position in university curricula worldwide.

The strong regional identity of Aberdeen and the northeast of Scotland was due to its geographical barriers. It was distanced, too, from the cultural and social climates of Edinburgh and Glasgow by the events and controversies of the 1680s to the Jacobite Rebellion of 1745. In Aberdeen the rivalry of two such university institutions as King's College and Marischal College gave an edge to their largely shared interests. The region and the city, remote from the southern belt, developed an independence and self-respect. The universities had a special role in the communities of Old and New Aberdeen. In 1495 Pope Alexander the Sixth had proposed the erection of the University of Aberdeen to educate men

separated by the arms of the sea and very high mountains . . . ignorant of letters and almost barbarous . . . who, on account of the over great distance from the places in which universities flourish and the dangerous passage to such places, cannot have leisure for the study of letters . . . [and] are so ignorant . . . that suitable men cannot be found not only for preaching the word of God . . . but even for administering the sacraments of the church.[2]

Marischal was founded by the Earl Marischal in the town for similarly practical ends. The universities had a clear remit to educate the student intake for professions in church and school, law and medicine so that they might serve the community. The art of educating has always been the keenest concern of their professors, a close and practical interest in the students at the heart of their tradition.[3] No Jude need have stayed obscure, had he been persistent enough in Aberdeen.

The calibre of the professors and regents affected the standing of their institutions. Literary annals were as yet in their infancy. Pope's draft of a History of Poetry was sent to Warton by Gray in the 1760s when Warton was embarking on his four-volume *History of English Poetry*. Standards of criticism were increasingly probed at all levels from the university to Grub Street. Literary canons were charted in magazines, established by publishers and journalists but, more important, increasingly complicated by usage. As a source of learning through illustration ancient and modern examples were used indiscriminately in dictionaries and in works on Rhetoric and Belles Lettres as well as to illustrate propositions in Logic and styles in Rhetoric.

The pervasive French cultural insistence on the impact of the *je ne scay quoi* in imaginative writing was firmly grounded in (high-culture) reader-response. In chapter 2 of this volume Neil Rhodes writes of Rollin's *De la manière d'enseigner et d'étudier les belles lettres*, a popular text in Aberdeen, whose university library holds copies or part copies of six editions and several of Rollin's works in French and in translation – his history of ancient Egypt for example: the antiquarian and the literary going hand in hand.[4] Belles Lettres no longer functions as a critical tool: it was in the eighteenth century an essential part of breeding and politeness to have good taste in the belles lettres, whether innate or educated.

In the writings of the Scottish Enlightenment it was at the core of reader response – exploring the relationship between reader and text. But the nature of the response was a matter for scientific enquiry into self-analysis encouraged by new understanding of and preoccupation with the nervous system. This was integral to the recognition of the social and educational importance of standards of taste. Following Shaftesbury and Hutcheson, the Aberdeen academic community in their new Philosophical Society or Wise Club deliberated among other issues the questions of taste. At the same time Rhetoric became, as Adam Smith had shown, a newly flexible medium to meet the needs of a society under rapid and pressurized change. It was seized on as such by the societies of the Enlightenment in Scotland.[5]

Literature as a storehouse of recorded values, as learning, knowledge (*literae humaniores, scientia*), as a canon for standardizing taste, as a vehicle for entertainment and instruction, and through imagination offering access to philosophy, is part of the long humanist tradition described by Neil Rhodes in his chapter. It is increasingly a source of illustration for logical proposition, communication and composition. The work of two early-eighteenth-century professors implies the strength of the humanist tradition and the special differences of the region and its past.

The first of these is David Fordyce (1711–51) – drowned on a voyage from Turkey whilst returning from leave of absence – Marischal Professor of Moral Philosophy and Logic from 1742, author of *Dialogues Concerning Education* (2 volumes, 1745–8), and *The Elements of Moral Philosophy* which first appeared in Dodsley's *Preceptor*.[6] In the Aberdeen University Library MS M 184 'Concerning Reading', Fordyce makes his views clear: poetry is a source of wisdom. He advises his students that:

The Poets Orpheus, Linus and Hesiod are amongst the earliest Philosophers of Greece; for the Philosophic Poetic and often legislative characters were joined in the same persons; there being as yet no separation of the Sciences . . .

Fordyce has no concern with the harmful effects of imaginative reading: the fancies of poets are not a problem, for 'The knowledge of Truth is the knowledge of Fact.' The end of all reading and learning is 'to be Wise, good & useful Creatures . . . no man can be a good Creature who is not Religious, nor a lover of God as well as a friend to men'.

In all your reading search for truth, & seek knowledge, not for shew or mere talk, but for use; the improvement of your own mind, & the advantage of others . . .

It is another world from the contemporary concerns of Adam Smith on efficacy of communication in his Glasgow lectures and from David Hume's leaving the question of a standard of taste to a small group of well-educated men. The good of society as a whole and an awareness of the generality of mankind is Fordyce's concern.

Thomas Blackwell the younger (1701–57), related by marriage to Fordyce, was Principal of Marischal as his father had been before him. Blackwell had been Professor of Greek since 1723. He was a friend of Bishop Berkeley, who suggested Blackwell for a chair in the projected university in the Bermudas. Blackwell published his *Enquiry into the Life and Writings of Homer* anonymously in 1735, exploring the conditions and scenery in which Homer wrote. This went into a second (acknowledged) edition in 1736. *The Enquiry* sets out to look at 'Homer in his Poetical Capacity – how did the Tenour of his Life serve to raise him to be "the Prince of his Profession"?'

In this Search, we must remember that *young Minds* are apt to receive such strong Impressions from the Circumstances of the Country where they are born and bred, that they contract a mutual kind of likeness to those Circumstances, and bear the Mark of the Course of Life thro'which they have passed.[7]

Blackwell in anti-Enlightenment vein writes that Poetry and Criticism may go together, but that the most moving emotions defy analysis:

What may be the Appearances or Aspects of Things natural or divine, which have the virtues thus to shake our Frame and raise such a Commotion in the Soul, I will not so much as enquire. The Search, I should suspect, would be fruitless, if not irreverent. It would be like prying into the Author of Fairy-Favours, which deprives the curious Enquirer of his present Enjoyment, while the courted Phantom mocks his eager Grasp, or presents him with a Turf, a Stone, instead of a Goddess. The Objects . . . cannot bear to be stared at, and far less to be criticized and taken to pieces: It is unlawful to doubt of their Charms, and the ready way to elude their Force, and rob ourselves of the delightful Astonishment . . . the original Cause of this Passion must be some wondrous sublime thing, since it produces such admired Effects; Its Dictates, in many places, are received with profound Submission, and the Persons touched with it are held in high veneration. (pp. 159–60)

This might seem over-fanciful to his contemporaries, but there are complex undertows here – Longinian sublimity surfaces as belief in bardic gifts, folklore and superstition are material evidence; readers may be transported: there is the very essence of *je ne scai quoi* without the social veneer. The germ of Wordsworth's 'Leechgatherer' lurks and the phenomenon of Macpherson's epics becomes more intelligible. Homer 'took his plan from Nature. His Work is the great Drama of Life acted in our View.'

In 1748 appeared Blackwell's *Letters Concerning Mythology* and not so very long after this James (Ossian) Macpherson was a student in Marischal. The synthesis of taste, feeling, scenery and association became a potent brew. *Ossian* (1760) and his tribe affected Goethe and the entire Romantic era of writers. Macpherson's contemporary, the Marischal Professor of Moral Philosophy, was James Beattie, whose most famous poem *The Minstrel* (1762–74) further fuelled Gray's interest in the poetic promise of Highland superstition and inspired and influenced both Cowper and Wordsworth.[8]

Meantime in Oxford the Poetry Professors gave their lectures – but in Latin – a medium which limited their choice of illustration and efficacy of communication. It seemed appropriate, however, in the self-consciously academic community of which they were a part. Joseph Trapp lectured on Poetry and Rhetoric, Joseph Spence on classical sculpture and mythology; Robert Lowth on the sacred poetry of the Hebrews; and William Hawkins on Shakespeare. Thomas Warton, shortly to commence compiling the first *History of English Poetry* and already the commentator on Spenser and editor of Theocritus, lectured on the poetry of the Greeks. Within the universities of Aberdeen, however, Latin as a vehicle of instruction had been abandoned by the 1740s. After the Act of Union (1707) Scottish universities had special linguistic problems, especially so in the northeast, where the speech of Buchan is still at times unintelligible to Aberdonians.

On the report of the Commissioners of 1690 the arts curriculum in the first year was a Philosophy course: Hebrew, Greek and Latin; in the second year Logic and methods of reasoning are taught: 'both conform to the principle of old and new Philosophie'. The several exercises are explained each morning and examined each night and 'in the close of the week are examined of ane sacred lessone, and upon Sabath dayes after sermon do give ane account of God's Word preached unto them'. In the third year General Physics and the Principles of Natural Philosophy; in the fourth Metaphysics and Physiology as well as Astrology are taught. Public theses are to be individually defended 'in the presence of all the Doctors, Professors and learned men of the University. And thereafter, after they have solemnly bound themselves by oath to the Protestant Religion, and to be gratefull to the Alma Mater, they doe conforme to their severall qualifications, receive the degree of Master of Arts.' (Aberdeen was the last university to forsake the oath, in the 1880s.)[9]

By the mid century changes were necessary. In 1753 the Senate of Marischal asked Alexander Gerard to devise an amended curriculum. He published his proposals in 1755 as *A Plan of Education* to explain the new policy to 'the public, which is interested in every thing that relates to education'. The old scholasticism in Philosophy and Logic is opaque and mechanical. The new philosophy is based 'on the reality of Nature'. There is a new science of human nature, and a methodology by which it may be analysed:

The natural history of the human understanding must be known, and its phenomena discovered; for without this the exertions of the intellectual faculties, and their application to the various subjects of science will be unintelligible.[10]

Gerard proceeds:

the displacement of Logic results in the implication by analogy that the literary reading experience is educationally of central importance in developing the mind and sensibility in this new science of human nature . . . [it] . . . is precisely the same to Philosophy, that works of criticism are to Poetry. The rules of criticism are formed by an accurate scrutiny and examination of the best works of poetry . . . If one peruses the best poetical performances, he will acquire some degree of taste, tho' he has never professedly studied the rules of criticism; and he will, at the same time, lay in materials, and obtain a stock of examples, which may render these rules intelligible to him, and enable him to judge whether they are just or not. And by afterwards studying these rules, he improves, refines and corrects his taste, perceives the principles on which he has founded all his judgments, tho' he did not in the mean time, think of them, and gains additional security against his judging wrong. (p. 12 my italics)

Literature as a discipline is within reach.

The arts students at Marischal in mid century were now to study Greek in their first (bajan) year, in their second year (demi) Greek with Maths, Natural History, Geography; Civil History and Natural Philosophy in their third (tertian) and in their fourth (magistrand) dedicate their studies to 'the Philosophy of the Human Mind and the Sciences that depend upon it'. Thomas Reid (1710–96), regent at King's, encouraged the adoption of the changes and comments:

By the Philosophy of the Mind is understood an Account of the Constitution of the Human Mind and of all its Powers and Faculties, whether Sensitive, Intellectual, or Moral; the Improvements these are capable of, and the Means of their Improvement; of the Mutual Influences of Body and Mind on each other; and the Knowledge we may acquire of other Minds, and particularly of the Supreme Mind. And the Sciences Depending on the Philosophy of the Mind are understood to be Logic, Rhetoric, the Laws of Nature and Nations, Oeconomicks, the fine Arts, and Natural Religion.[11]

In 1756 Thomas Reid of King's and John Gregory, the 'midiciner' of Marischal, founded the Philosophical Society or 'Wise Club' for both academic communities. The new philosophy of human nature was discussed in twice weekly meetings with refreshments. The society continued to meet until the early 1770s. In its meetings the professors of both universities, Reid, Campbell, Gerard and Beattie among others deliberated questions of Poetry, Beauty, Imitation, Genius, Metrical Composition and, of course, the Standard of Taste. Challenged by Hume's *Treatise on Human Nature* (1739) ideas were aired and elaborated which were later to be published: by Reid in his *Inquiry into the Human Mind on the Principles of Common Sense* (1764); by George Campbell, Principal of Marischal College and Professor of Divinity (1719–96), in his *Philosophy of Rhetoric* (1776); by Alexander Gerard, Professor of Philosophy at Marischal and later of Divinity at Marischal and then at King's, in the *Essay on Taste* (1759) and the *Essay on Genius* (1774); and James Beattie, Professor of Moral Philosophy (1735–1803), in the surprisingly popular *Essay on Truth* (1770). There may not be a 'hot-bed of genius' here, but it is an impressive concentration of interest in an area of educational cultivation with its articulated priorities. It presents a tougher tradition than that of the belles lettristes: a discourse modelled on the methodological precision of scientific analysis in the interests of the development of virtue and good taste.

With his son, Gerard later wrote *A Compendious View of the Evidences of Natural and Revealed Religion; Being the Substance of Lectures Read in the University and King's College of Aberdeen* (printed 1828) where they continue to insist on the importance of cultivating the mind:

As man, even when innocent, is, from his nature, in danger of becoming vicious, he is plainly intended for moral discipline and culture, and stands in need of it for preserving his innocence and virtue . . . Virtuous education is the application of all the means of Moral Culture, – and that at a time when the mind is most pliable and susceptible; and is, therefore, of very great importance for forming the character. (pp. 136, 411)

The essence of human nature was the moral faculty innate in man: perception of this was to be cultivated in young minds. The analysis of the nature of Taste which had earned Gerard the award for the best

essay on the subject from the Edinburgh Society for the encouragement of arts, sciences and manufacturers, and agriculture in 1756
related aesthetic emotions of Beauty, Grandeur, Terror, Sublimity to
the Philosophy of Taste. It moved towards the identification of Beauty
with Truth. Shaftesbury had implied their identity: the pedagogic tradition and the moral ethos of the northeast developed it with scrupulous
and dedicated energy. In the 1759 edition Gerard's essay is bound in
with the essays on taste of the French philosophes: Montesquieu,
D'Alembert and Diderot. Taste is a focal topic of the Enlightenment
as Rhetoric is its flexible expression.

Taste consists chiefly in the improvement of those principles, which are
commonly called the powers of imagination, including the senses of novelty,
sublimity, beauty, imitation, harmony, ridicule and virtue.[12]

Gerard's definition of taste establishes an aesthetic position in literature: his elaboration of its properties carries it forward into criticism.
He is one of many writing on the subject: the community of scholars
he belongs to is idiosyncratic in its adherence to this interpretation,
and Reid, Campbell and Beattie share common ground. Lecturing on
the Institutes of Moral Philosophy James Dunbar of King's reiterates
the theme: 'Man's nature evidences that he is designed to rise: for he
alone is capable of progress, and all his faculties are found susceptible
of high improvement, and without culture liable to proportionable
degeneracy.'[13]

Standards of taste in education, teaching, establishing canons, are
still the cultural issue. For any English graduate from what may have
been the hey-day of the discipline, the first number of *Scrutiny* insisted
on the discrimination which standards of taste involve: 'The general
dissolution of standards is a commonplace . . . Those who are aware
of the situation will be concerned to cultivate awareness and will be
actively concerned for standards . . . We take it as axiomatic that concern for standards of living imples concern for standards in the arts.'[14]
Even today taste acts as a ghost in the cultural machine.

For over thirty years James Beattie (1735–1803) dedicated himself
to the chair of Moral Philosophy, to educating students to cultivate
their minds in accordance with the precepts of religion and morality.
The sheer length of his service and loyalty to his ideals and to his
community reinforced the respect and admiration with which he was
regarded by Johnson, Reynolds and other of his contemporaries, hon-
oured by his King and by Oxford University. He is the exemplar of

virtuous discourse and the opponent of cynicism and worldliness. It was probably Beattie's artless fidelity to Truth and Virtue (he was a country lad of humble origin) that prompted his mentor Gregory to write dissuading him from moving to a post in Edinburgh. Urban culture and fashionable taste were not for him. The small city bordered so nearly by coast and country districts and dotted with small towns was familiar and sure of its own standards and values: it was a regional culture, like that of Burns: it had a sense of identity lacking in the heterogeneous mixing of population and class in the fashion-conscious bigger cities.

Beattie's simple and meticulous application to duty is perhaps best illustrated by his Day Book entry for the close of the session 1779–80. The number of meetings he had taught in the session so far was 281. In the last two weeks of March he taught at 8 am, 11 am, 1 pm and 3 or, alternately, 4 pm the use and abuse of tropes and figures; good style; historical prose; characters of historians; scotticisms in writing (to be added to the printed pamphlet); fabulous prose; origin and progress of prose; feudal government; chivalry; old and new Romances; common and rhetorical prose . . . Thirty-two meetings in all; twelve of them lectures. For over thirty years every teaching hour was accounted for.[15] Three sets of Beattie's lecture notes to the fourth-year students are held in Aberdeen University archives for the years 1760–93 in lectures meticulously revised, dictates carefully corrected.[16] His tribute to Gregory serves as the conclusion to the second book of *The Minstrel*, relating the Imagination to Philosophy:

> Her bounty, unimproved, is deadly bane:
> Dark woods and rankling wilds, from shore to shore,
> Stretch their enormous gloom; which to explore
> Even Fancy trembles, in her sprightliest mood;
> For there, each eyeball gleams with lust of gore,
> Nestles each murderous and each monstrous brood,
> Plague lurks in every shade, and steams from every flood.
>   . . .
> 'Twas from Philosophy man learn'd to tame
> The soil by plenty to intemperance fed.
> Lo, from the echoing ax and thundering flame,
> Poison and plague and yelling rage are fled . . .
>
> Adieu, ye lays, that Fancy's flowers adorn,
> The soft amusement of the vacant mind![17]

Beattie's practical if conventional good sense in his respect for intelligibility and polite discourse were not incompatible with his work on

Scottish song and the beginning of his co-operation with Burns. In Literature however, the struggle between the classics and the vernacular was coming to a head in Beattie's time: there he retained a strong sense of tradition. So, we learn from his 'Remarks on the Utility of Classical Learning' in his *Essays* (1770) that the ancients and moderns conflict has raised its head:

It seemed to be allowed in general that the study of the Classic Authors was a necessary part of polite education. This, however, has of late been not only questioned, but denied: and it has been said, that every thing worth preserving of ancient literature might be more easily transmitted, both to us and to posterity, through the channel of the modern languages, than through that of the Greek and Latin.

He starts a mock defence of this position 'For who, that is an adept in the philosophy of Locke and Newton, can have any need of Aristotle?'

The young student should . . . read his authors, first as a grammarian, secondly as a philosopher, and lastly as a critic, and all this he may do without difficulty, and with delight as well as profit, if care is taken to proportion his task to his years and capacity . . . the rules for applying the elegancies of language, being founded in the science of human nature, must gradually lead the young rhetorician to attend to what passes in his own mind, which of all the scenes of human observation is the most important, and in the early part of life the least attended to.

'I agree with Rousseau', he concludes, 'that the aim of education should be, to teach us rather how to think, than what to think; rather to improve our minds so as to enable us to think for ourselves, than to load the memory with the insights of other men.'[18]

In King's Robert Eden Scott, Professor of Moral Philosophy from 1801, defined criticism as a 'scientific investigation' made possible by the new philosophy of human nature.[19] In his 1798 Graduation address he recommends literature to the departing students as a 'very important accessory source of sublunary happiness'.[20] Scott based his view of human nature on the foundation he believed had been established so scientifically by Thomas Reid and, like Beattie, he defended the role of the classics in the formation of character.

In the early nineteenth century Beattie's assistant, William Glennie, taught the Rhetoric and Belles Lettres class in Marischal, using his master's old notes. According to Alexander Bain (1818–1903) who would later be appointed to an Aberdeen chair of Logic and Rhetoric (later Logic and English Literature) in 1860, and who had attended Glennie's classes, the elderly Glennie ('the Venerable Goose') so bored the students

that every class went prepared with 'the alternative employments
which students can so readily devise'.[21] This state of affairs made it
impossible for Bain to follow instructions and simply repeat Glennie's
notes as he was supposed to do. Bain was discontinued at the end of
his third year.

The degree provisions in Aberdeen universities had been left un-
disturbed by Parliamentary Commissions for over a hundred years. In
1827, however, there was a Visitation. Professor Glennie described his
Rhetoric course for the fourth-year class:

To Rhetoric is referred the theory of language, introduced in the early part
of the course; the difference between ancient and modern criticism, as far as
the latter is denominated philosophical; the nature of poetical composition, as
distinguished from prose; the nature and use of tropes and figures, and the
rules for the structure of the various sorts of periods and sentences.[22]

A writer in *The Scotsman* in 1848 points out the extreme youth of some
of the students and deplores the lack of chairs in Rhetoric and Belles
Lettres in Scottish universities 'a pure deficiency [in] ... the most
important, and what might be made also the most popular, class in the
academic curriculum'. He reminds his readers that the professoriat of
the northern universities have recommended to Peel's Commission the
establishment of chairs in Rhetoric.[23]

From the mid nineteenth century in literary and debating societies
the students showed an enthusiasm for literary effort of all kinds. The
student newspaper became a regular and handsome publication as
Alma Mater in the 1880s. A daily newspaper had flourished in Aberdeen
from 1746, begun by an ancestor of the founder of the English chair.
The currents of journalism, strong and vital in essay, debate, comment
and criticism, were important in the careers of the succeeding professors Bain, Minto and Grierson.

Alexander Bain was awarded his degree at Marischal, but only after
a long apprenticeship in self-education. His early occupation as a weaver
led him to the Mechanics' Institute. There were several organizations
influencing the development of adult education outside the universities
and there was some bursary provision for university education in
Aberdeen. Bain won prizes and a bursary to pay for his classes. Bain's
career illustrates the importance of the number of institutions now
developing to broaden the appetite and the provision for education. In
a dauntingly terse 'Preliminary Note of Explanation' to his *Autobiography*
Bain states his reason for writing:

especially to indicate the stages of mental growth, under the circumstances of the time. Institutions and varying influences had here to be reckoned with, and not individuals solely.

From the nature of the case, the institutions most dwelt upon are educational – schools, colleges and universities. *The changes that have taken place in all that relates to teaching are so numerous and so great, that a historic, not to say antiquarian, interest attaches to many of these details.* (my italics)

Bain's scrupulous chronicling of his membership of examining boards, school boards, university reform committees, competitions and societies for educational reform over nearly seventy unremittingly active years clearly shows the new role of English in education and of education in English. This above all guaranteed the adoption by universities of English as an attractive and essential discipline. Bain judged the study of literature for its own sake a leisure pursuit rather than a discipline. His progress in a career was impeded by his refusal to conform to the Church of Scotland. His early excellence in Mathematics and Physiology and his strong practical and analytical mind drew his concern with teaching English towards Psychology. Bain's pursuit of knowledge is in terms not so much of a science of man as of a philosophy of mind: education as a science, rhetoric in terms of intellect and emotion.

Unsuccessful in Aberdeen he went to London where he spent the greater part of the next twenty years working as a contributor to the *Westminster Gazette*, lecturing to Mechanics Institutes, working in public health with Edwin Chadwick, collaborating with John Stuart Mill (of whom he wrote a memoir and with Herbert Spencer, Henry Sidgwick, Darwin, Huxley and other members of the group of radical pragmatists to which he belonged. Minto's manuscript diary relates Bain's acount of this circle at which G. H. Lewes and George Eliot made their appearance.[24] He was involved as an examiner with David Masson's University College, London, courses described in a later chapter of the present volume by Linda Ferriera Buckley. When he was appointed Professor of Logic and Rhetoric in the newly constituted University of Aberdeen in 1860 he did not follow Masson's example in providing a survey of literature. His remit was with written expression, with English Language and with the processes of the mind which literature engaged and its effect on them. He is quoted: 'I could not vote to tax the nation for coaching Hamlet and Macbeth ... I hold that an English Poet that has not of himself sufficient attractions to be read, understood and relished, without the prelections of a University professor is by that very fact a failure.'[25]

Like his predecessors Bain viewed Rhetoric and English Grammar scientifically and the effects of literature as physiological. His reaction to Shakespeare, however, was not merely analytic, but helped him to 'psychological results, both intellectual and emotional'.[26] His conscientiousness and efficiency, and the sheer polish and precision of his teaching went with a wholehearted commitment to educating. In connection with his teaching and his own incessant self-improvement he published textbooks which, completed to his satisfaction (and the editions were always to be corrected and updated as far as possible), left him free to go on to new work. His *Mind and Body* remained on the University of Sydney Philosophy list of recommended reading until the 1960s. He established the journal *Mind*, with his student Croom-Robertson as editor, in 1876. In answer to the protests against the examination system he wrote 'The Pressure of Examinations' for *Mind* in 1889, recommending that every curriculum of liberal study should by its width secure an amount of culture far beyond the individual likings of the very best pupils.

I have not traced any link between Bain and I. A. Richards, but the resemblances between their work are striking. The phrase used by Richards in his introduction to *Mencius on the Mind* 'information about thinking', describes Bain's approach.[27] There Richards attempts to unravel the problem of a hermeneutic for historic texts – which may help to account for the disappearance of ways of learning and losses of reputation which are only – if at all – retrieved with difficulty.

In *Science and Poetry*, Richards wrote:

Neither the professional psychologist, whose interest in poetry is frequently not intense, nor the man of letters, who as a rule has no adequate ideas of the mind as a whole, has been equipped for the investigation [of the high place of poetry in human affairs]. Both a passionate knowledge of poetry and a capacity for dispassionate psychological analysis are required if it is to be satisfactorily presented.[28]

'The study of the mind had now become with me recurrent and overmastering' Bain wrote in his *Autobiography*.[29]

The precision of his analyses of short passages of literature is grammatical, rhetorical, intellectual and emotional. To modern readers it may appear to resemble Richards's use of Sense, Tone, Feeling and Intention in his *Practical Criticism*, just as Bain's approach to analysis has some resemblance to that in *Interpretation and Teaching*. The importance of Rhetoric was yielding to that of Language and Grammar in Bain's work, perhaps because of the clear need for expansion and reform in education.

William Minto, his successor, was also a polymath, graduating in 1865 with honours in classics, mathematics and philosophy. He spent a year at Merton College, Oxford, then assisted Bain before leaving to become a London journalist and the editor of *The Examiner*. An account of his introductory lecture to first-year students decribes his face vivified and lit up with persuading his hearers of the force of literature in bringing us nearer the True, the Good and the Beautiful, and of the mingled profit and pleasure of its pursuit. The Aberdeen University periodical *Alma Mater* records in 1891 the 'strong magnetic influence between teacher and disciple'.[30] His manuscript diary of the early 1870s, when he was assisting Bain, is interesting. Minto was not only concerned with the literary heritage of his students, but with comparative literature and periodization – in the 'Literature of the Georgian Era' he writes 'there is a certain interest in seeing how literature prospered when it was no longer sunned by royal countenances, and when new influences came in to compensate the loss'.[31] The new influences in English were at all levels, with a series of commissions and visitations; the Commissioners' Report of 1878 recommended new degrees in the arts:

We think it of great importance that the field of study should be so enlarged as to make it more suitable and attractive to different classes of students than at present, and this object can, in our opinion, be best attained by allowing, after a certain foundation of general culture, a tolerably free choice along certain distinct lines of study adapted to various bents of mind, and having relation to different professional pursuits. We believe that, by the opportunities which such a freedom of selection would present, many students would be induced to take a larger share than they do now in University study, and the advantages of the culture which the University affords would be extended.

The business of educating has changed and English language and literature is its focus. The post-Arnoldian concern with the foundation of a general culture tended to be elbowed out by aestheticism and in the universities by the administrative difficulties of the new MA.[32]

In the *Senatus Document Book for 1893* the Heads of Proposals for the Foundation of a Chair of English Literature following the bequest of John Gray Chalmers recommend that Honours in English Literature as a separate department should be the same as for Classical Literature. That the chief subject shall be the History and Criticism of English Literature in both Prose and Verse, including that portion of it known as Lowland Scotch and that instruction on the Principles of English Style and Composition, Precis and Essay Writing and the Principles of

Rhetoric be included as well as the Philology of the English Language; and that instruction in Anglo-Saxon be made available. Of interest is an extra mural provision that the Professor give 'a separate course in Marischal College, which course might be of a more popular character and open to non-matriculated students . . .' There had always been a considerable addition of voluntary numbers to the English Literature classes, as Bain noted in his time and this continued: Minto's interest in the Extension Course movement was one of the reasons his loss was so deeply mourned in the special number of *Alma Mater* devoted to his memory.

Minto's successor, the young Shetlander Herbert Grierson, had worked as Minto's assistant in the year of the latter's death. Grierson was presented with the problem of teaching the degree in English after experiencing himself only some lectures in Rhetoric and in early English Literature. He saw his taste in poetry as 'unsophisticated . . . so that even in Donne it is the note of passion which has made fascinating his subtle and far-fetched wit'.[33] His remit was to teach Linguistics (he went to Leipzig to get some idea of philology), Rhetoric and Composition and Literature. Anglo-Saxon was from the beginning a minority interest.[34] Grierson's twenty-one years at Aberdeen 'were years of unflagging and infectious enthusiasm for literature, as a discipline and as a delight, and as a constant pursuit of the best that was known and thought in times past and present, in Britain and on the Continent.'[35] A special kind of professor had developed a special kind of discipline, but within a long and dedicated tradition.

The development of the Honours degree (first offered in 1898: Grierson successfully campaigned for the required History chair) was accelerated by the gifted students whose need for such a course of study was evident. Grierson's pride in the intelligence and insights of the poetess Rachel Annand Taylor, a student training for teaching, is recorded in his manuscript autobiography.[36] Before going to Edinburgh in 1915 Grierson wrote a part of a survey of European Literature, completed his edition of the poems of John Donne, compiled *The English Parnassus* with Macneile Dixon and began the selection of metaphysical poets which stimulated students well into the 1950s. It is not common for the work of a critic and scholar to foreshadow the same creative concerns as those of the major creative writers of the day. It is clear from his connection with Richards and his correspondence with Eliot that Grierson's work fed the new streams of intellect and sensibility developing in the study of English, helping to rechannel the philosophically nurtured Aberdonian tradition of literary education in a way that was picked up by the philosophically alert English and American avatars of modernist poetry and criticism. Remote yet alert and seminal, Aberdeen exemplifies over three centuries ways in which the Scottish university study of vernacular literature grew from a locally inflected pedagogic development to a subject of global currency. In the article he wrote for the *Aberdeen University Review* on the development of English, Grierson refers to his one-time assistants 'Mr John Purves, (now Professor of English in the Transvaal University) . . . and Mr Wallace (now Professor of English in the University of Melbourne).'[37] These proud parentheses are telling instances of the way in which, as the following chapters demonstrate more fully, English Literature became a Scottish intellectual export.

NOTES

For their assistance with this piece I wish to thank my Aberdeen colleagues Dr Donald Withrington and Mr Colin McLaren, as well as Mrs Myrtle Anderson-Smith and her staff in the Special Collections department of Aberdeen University Library.

1 J. M. Bulloch, quoted in Nan Shepherd, 'Professors and Students' in W. Douglas Simpson, ed., *The Fusion of 1860: A Record of the Centenary Celebrations and a History of the United University of Aberdeen, 1860–1960*, Aberdeen University Studies 146 (Edinburgh: Oliver and Boyd, 1963), p. 141.

2 For a fuller account of the Papal Bull and the foundation see Robert Sangster Rait, *The Universities of Aberdeen: A History* (Aberdeen: James Gordon Bisset, 1895), pp. 21–40.

3 Reverend Dr Glennie in *Evidence Oral and Documentary taken and recorded by the Commissioners appointed by his Majesty George IV July 23 1826 and reappointed by his Majesty William IV October 12 1830 for Visiting the Universities of Scotland, Volume IV, University of Aberdeen* (London: W. Clowes and Son for H. M. Stationery Office, 1837), p. 108.

4 Aberdeen University Library holds the translation of Rollin's Rhetoric lectures in six editions, from the first in 1734 to the sixth in 1798: the first edition, 1734 (volumes 1 and 4 – the other two volumes presumably lost), 1737, 1749 (volumes 2 and 4), 1769 (volume 3), 1773 and 1798 editions.

5 See Murray G. H. Pittock, 'Staff and Student: the Teaching of Rhetoric', *Scottish Literary Journal* 23 (1996), 33–41.

6 Robert Dodsley, *The Preceptor, containing a General Course of Education* (1748), rev. edn of 1754, ed. John Valdimir Price, 2 vols. (Bristol: Thoemmes Press, 1990), vol. II, pp. 241–379. In his *Scienza Nuova* (1725–30) Fordyce's contemporary, Vico, had distinguished between poetic logic as opposed to intellectual logic, the poetic form being anterior to the reasoning form.

On Vico's influence on the teaching of Rhetoric see Michael Mooney, *Vico in the Tradition of Rhetoric* (Princeton University Press, 1985).

7 Thomas Blackwell, *An Enquiry into the Life and Writings of Homer* (London, 1735), p. 11. Further references in the text are to this edition.

8 See J. H. Pittock, 'James Beattie: A Friend to All' in D. S. Hewitt and M. R. G. Spiller, eds., *Literature of the North* (Aberdeen University Press, 1983), pp. 55–69.

9 Alexander Bain, *Autobiography* (London: Longman's Green & Co., 1904), p. 381.

10 Alexander Gerard, *A Plan of Education* (Aberdeen, 1755), p. 9. Further references in the text are to this edition.

11 Thomas Reid, quoted in Robert Rait, *The Universities of Aberdeen* (Aberdeen: J. G. Bisset, 1895), p. 203.

12 Alexander Gerard, *An Essay on Taste* (1758; 3rd edn, London and Edinburgh, 1759), p. 10.

13 James Dunbar, *Institutes of Philosophy (1789–1794)*, edited from the Aberdeen University MS K 3107/5/2/6 by Hiroshi Mizuta, Centre for Historical Social Science Literature, Study Series Number 35 (Hitotshubashi, Japan: Hitotshubashi University, 1996), p. 29.

14 L. C. Knights and Donald Culver, 'Scrutiny: A Manifesto', *Scrutiny* 1 (1932), 2.

15 James Beattie, 'Day Book', Aberdeen University Library MS M 30/16.

16 Aberdeen University Library MS M 185.

17 James Beattie, *The Minstrel; or The Progress of Genius. A Poem. The Second Book* (London and Edinburgh: Dilly and Creech, 1774), pp. 25, 26, 31 (stanzas xlix, l, lxi).

18 James Beattie, *Essays on Poetry and Musick as they affect the Mind, on Laughter, and Ludicrous Composition; and on the Usefulness of Classical Learning* (1770; 2nd edn, Edinburgh: W. Creech and E. & C. Dilly, 1777), pp. 497–503.

19 See J. H. Pittock, 'The Criticism of the Scottish Enlightenment' in Barry Nisbet and Claude Rawson, eds., *The New Cambridge History of Criticism*, vol. 4 (Cambridge University Press, 1997), pp. 546–59 and 866–8.

20 Aberdeen University Library MS K 182.

21 Bain, *Autobiography*, p. 119.

22 Glennie in *Evidence Oral and Documentary*, 105.

23 David Kilgour, 'University Reform' in *Aberdeen University Pamphlets*, 2 (8 articles reprinted from *The Scotsman*) (Edinburgh, 1848), pp. 34–9.

24 William Minto, 'Diary', Aberdeen University Library MS 2487/1–2.

25 Andrew Rutherford, 'The Teaching of Literature', *Aberdeen University Review* 43 (1969), 211–12.

26 Bain, *Autobiography*, p. 77.

27 I. A. Richards, *Mencius on the Mind: Experiments in Multiple Definition* (1930; rpt., London: Hyperion, 1989), p. xiii.

28 I. A. Richards, *Science and Poetry* (1926; 2nd edn, Cambridge: R. I. Severs, 1936), p. 15.

29 Bain, *Autobiography*, p. 49.

30 Anon. note, *Alma Mater*, VIII (1891), 129.

31 Minto, 'Diary', vol. I, p. 4.

32 Simpson, *The Fusion of 1860*, p. 33.

33 H. J. C. Grierson, 'Vita mea', Aberdeen University Library MS 2478/2/1. The quotation is from p. 32. Later references to the text are to this manuscript.

34 *Ibid.*, ch. 11.

35 Minutes of Meeting of the Senatus Academicus of the University of Edinburgh, 14 November 1935, in Aberdeen University Library, H. J. C. Grierson Miscellaneous Manuscripts, MS 2478/5.

36 'Vita mea', pp. 188 ff.

37 H. J. C. Grierson, 'The Development of English Teaching at Aberdeen', *Aberdeen University Review* I (1913), 52.

CHAPTER 8

The early impact of Scottish literary teaching in North America

Franklin E. Court

The formative impact of Scotland, the Scottish rhetorical tradition and Scottish moral philosophy on the history of English literary studies in North America extended from the early eighteenth century to the mid nineteenth century. From the mid nineteenth century onwards, other influences, particularly from continental Europe, were paramount. During the early colonial years, however, the Scottish educational system, owing to reforms that favoured the separation of education from government control, was more in tune with life, as lived and idealized in North America, than any other European educational system, including England's. Eighteenth-century Scottish universities had also encouraged expanding the curriculum in an effort to make it appeal across class barriers and to include, among other innovative studies, the teaching of vernacular languages.

Theoretically, the earliest difference between the old and the new rested on whether or not the focus of higher education should be 'classical', with a traditional concentration on the study of Greek and Latin, or what was termed at the time, 'philosophical'. The term, 'philosophical', carried a meaning that eighteenth-century scholars associated with ancient school texts such as Cicero's *De Oratore* where the word was used specifically to suggest the mastery of all knowledge, either 'by scientific investigation or by the methods of dialectic', as Cicero informed Quintus. 'For indeed,' Cicero advised, ' "philosophy [is] the creator and mother, as it were, of all the reputable arts." '[1]

As this study argues, in the history of the development of vernacular literary study in the United States, the term is most appropriate since expanding interest in the formal study of moral philosophy combined frequently with courses in Rhetoric, from approximately the decade of the 1740s onward, provided the foundation from which English and American literary study as autonomous disciplines eventually would emerge. Course offerings in moral philosophy, as we shall see, encouraged and augmented training in the art of oratory which, in turn, produced the first academic effort in North America to combine general principles of an all-inclusive literary criticism with an appreciation of vernacular literature, English and American.[2]

In 1725, the Scottish philosopher, Francis Hutcheson, published *An Inquiry into the Origin of our Ideas of Beauty and Virtue; in Two Treatises.* The book, cited recently by Ian Ross as the first work to be published in Britain that dealt specifically with aesthetics,[3] promoted the claim that humans have an innate sense of beauty that is analogous to a moral sense. As Ross suggests, the idea formed the basis of a developing set of arguments that linked aesthetics directly to morals, by specifying an '"Author of Nature"' who had blessed us with '"strong Affections to be the Springs of each virtuous Action."'[4] The idea of a benevolent 'Author of Nature' behind virtuous human actions appealed to the sensibilities of many eighteenth-century writers, rhetoricians as well as philosophers, including Adam Smith, who, according to Ross, explored the idea in his *Theory of Moral Sentiments.* The value of virtuous actions was also at the heart of the desire to work for the common good and became an essential part of utilitarian thought, summed up in Hutcheson's famous phrase from the *Inquiry* that the 'best' action is that 'which accomplishes the *greatest happiness* for the *greatest Numbers*'.[5] Hutcheson's role as a precursor of utilitarianism is important in the context of the history of literary study in North America for embedded in the connection between the desire for virtuous actions and utilitarianism is the desire to be a good citizen as well as a virtuous person. To be socially useful, then, was also to be virtuous. Education, it was believed, could enhance the process by teaching individuals to understand that in acting for the common good they were also promoting personal good.

For Hutcheson, who was also a Presbyterian minister, the moral sense was intimately related to the sense of beauty. Although Hutcheson distinguished several internal senses to explain various human experiences, he, like Lord Kames, Adam Smith, Thomas Reid, Hugh Blair, George Turnbull, William Barron and the other influential eighteenth-century Scottish men of letters who followed him, building on the basic premise of an intimate connection between beauty and virtue, promoted, consequently, in their writings their individual conceptions of just how ethics actually complemented aesthetics.

Interest in combining ethics with aesthetics lead naturally to a pre-occupation with the 'moral-sense theory', represented, first, in Scotland by Hutcheson and, to a lesser degree, by Adam Smith who, while a student at Glasgow University, attended Hutcheson's classes in moral philosophy from 1738 to 1740. Hutcheson was Glasgow's Professor of Moral Philosophy from 1730 to 1746. Against Thomas Hobbes's contention that humans acted fundamentally from motives of selfishness and egotism, Scottish 'moral-sense' theorists, following Hutcheson and, to some extent, David Hume, argued that the 'moral sense' disposed us to the approvals and disapprovals, the pleasures and pains, that we feel. They maintained that humans comprehend moral values and virtue through this innate 'sense' or sentiment, and they insisted on the importance of the 'social nature' of humanity as one normal way to experience approval. Accordingly, the presence of a 'moral sense', therefore, depended more on feelings than on reason.[6]

Hutcheson's courses at Glasgow University extended the scope of the study of moral philosophy to include contemporary social and cultural issues. Hutcheson was particularly keen on teaching the works of Cicero, particularly Cicero's *De Officiis*, from which he borrowed heavily for the *Inquiry*. He promoted, consequently, a rather predictable brand of Ciceronian humanism that linked a variety of academic subjects, including the study of Rhetoric and Belles Lettres, with practical social concerns.[7] Since Ciceronian humanism traditionally emphasized civic responsibility and the value of civic discourse, it encouraged the formation of debating societies and increased the classroom practice of disputation. The practice, in turn, was at the center of what literary historians call the 'oratorical tradition', a naggingly unclear academic and critical phenomenon that helped shape the development of language study in late-eighteenth- and early-nineteenth-century America.

As ill-defined as the 'oratorical tradition' is, one thing is clear and that is that a trend developed in North American colleges near the end of the eighteenth century that was characterized by the increased use of vernacular literature as a tool for teaching oratory and disputation. The actual course focus was on the teaching of what many professors at the time literally called 'criticism', which, in essence, was what we now understand as 'literary criticism'. Since English, rather than Latin or Greek, was the language of disputation, the use of literary criticism in the process presupposed the ready availability of literary selections written in English. The selections, as we shall see, were not always works that are customarily classified as 'literature', but they were all written in English and were primarily British in origin. 'Literature', we need to remember, was understood at the time and for many years afterwards in the pre-Romantic sense as anything of value written well. Generally speaking, classroom selections that were belletristic in content were English in origin, a development that in time would lead to the equating of refined and polished writing with a canon represented almost exclusively by predominantly English authorship.

In the early colonial years of exploration and experimentation with English language study in the US, however, readings in disputation and literary criticism extended well beyond English cultural imperialism and the academic literary canon as it would be conceived by the end of the nineteenth century. Hence, pedagogical and philosophical writings by David Hume, Adam Smith, Hugh Blair, Lord Kames, Dugald Stewart, Thomas Reid, George Campbell, the Scottish historian, A. F. Tytler (Lord Woodhouselee), and even Hutcheson himself, in those early years, although not usually considered as examples of canonical belles lettres, nevertheless, were taught. Generally, they were taught under the category of 'criticism' and were included in courses in moral philosophy or rhetoric or, oftentimes, courses that were labelled, 'Rhetoric and Belles-lettres'. By the 1820s, a significant number of actual courses labelled either wholly or partly as 'Criticism' began to appear, attesting to the growing importance in the advancement of English literary study of what, for want of any other designation, we might call the 'oratorical tradition'.

Philosophical and social themes that Hutcheson promoted, that were at the centre of eighteenth-century Scottish moral-sense theory, also were at the centre of efforts in the North American colonies to add a deeper moral and social dimension to education. Scottish immigrants to North America were largely responsible for the eventual dissemination of Hutcheson's teachings as well as the teachings of other prominent Scottish Enlightenment figures. Eventually, as extant college reading lists make clear, the writings of the Scottish moral-sense theorists formed the basis for programmes of study not only in moral philosophy but also in rhetoric, belles lettres, oratory and criticism.

Scottish immigration to the North American colonies increased considerably after 1700. Most of the immigrants were, like Hutcheson himself, Scots-Irish from Ulster.[8] The Scots-Irish carried two very important principles with them when they left Ulster: one was an insatiable desire for independence, especially from exploitive government control; the other was a traditional concern for community education embodied in the figures of their Presbyterian ministers, most of whom were graduates of Scotland's universities.[9]

Traditionally, in Presbyterian communities, the minister was the intellectual and cultural source of knowledge. Most of the Ulster-born ministers who immigrated were the products themselves of education first in academies similar to Francis Hutcheson's Dublin academy, one usually run by the resident minister. Later, the usual course of action was to attend a Scottish university. Douglas Sloan notes that of the twenty-six ministers on record with the Presbytery of Philadelphia before 1717, twelve had finished their education at Glasgow University, four at Edinburgh.[10] The Presbytery of Philadelphia early in the eighteenth century also decided that young men from the colonies who desired to become ministers should have proper educational opportunities available to them in the colonies and should, in all areas of study, measure up to the level of competence demanded by the Scottish and Scots-Irish examining boards. A show of competence in theology and in the liberal arts was of particular concern.

The first date of consequence in the actual history of English literary study in North America is 1742, the date when the Rev. Francis Alison, a Scots-Irish Presbyterian minister, appears on record as combining the teaching of English grammar, composition and literature at his academy at New London, Maryland, in an effort to preserve 'Old Side' Presbyterianism.[11] Old Side Presbyterians were opposed to a growing revivalist faction in the colonial American Presbyterian church that was promoting a type of 'born-again' Evangelicalism that encouraged tent revivals, fire and brimstone pulpit oratory, and other highly emotional public displays of religious fervor. The revivalists were called 'New Siders'. Old Siders accused them of being anti-intellectual and of promoting religious fanaticism. New Siders, most of whom were New England based and listed Jonathan Edwards and George Whitefield among their supporters, promoted an open, freer ecclesiastical organization than the Old Siders, one that would enable ministers to capitalize on highly emotional religious conversions and the appeal to inner 'lights' wherever and whenever the opportunity arose.

Presbyterian New Siders were opposed to what they deemed a 'dead church' and to a moribund classical educational system that they believed supported it. They wanted reform. So they proposed the establishment of a series of colleges throughout North America dedicated to the propogation of new revivalist theology. These new schools were to be called 'Log Colleges', after William Tennent's famous 'Log College' which opened in 1735 at Neshaminy, north of Philadelphia. Tennent, a New Sider, was an outspoken Scot, a 1695 graduate of Edinburgh University, who was at first a Presbyterian minister but became an ordained Anglican minister in 1704. After he immigrated to America in 1718, he denounced his Anglicanism and was reinstated in the Presbyterian ministry. His Log College was increasingly viewed as offensive to the more conservative Old Siders, most of whom were recent Scots-Irish immigrants from Ulster who feared a deterioration of doctrine and central discipline if the New Siders gained ecclesiastical control. The very idea of a series of Log Colleges scattered around the land dedicated to the education of revivalist ministers repulsed and threatened them.[12]

Records suggest that Alison, an Old Sider, who was educated in Scotland, graduating from Edinburgh University in 1732, came under the influence of Francis Hutcheson at some crucial point in his youth. His friendship with Hutcheson was close enough to enable Alison in 1746 to write freely to Hutcheson for advice on the course of study and on books that he could use in the New London Academy. As a result of his progressive educational designs, Alison devised a curriculum that went well beyond the Log College's concentration on divinity studies. For one thing, he taught composition and critically examined student themes. He also adopted Hutcheson's practice of requiring his students to make abstracts and abridgements of essays from various English literary sources. He particularly liked to have his students in his moral philosophy course make English abridgements of Hutcheson's *Short Introduction to Moral Philosophy*. Consequently, one must conclude that since Alison's students were involved in studied critical readings of essays with accompanying classroom written exercises based on the readings, and since those written exercises were in turn evaluated by the instructor, that his classes were involved, however elementarily, in the critical study of English literature.

Alison also used a technique borrowed from John Stevenson, Professor of Logic and Metaphysics at Edinburgh, who may have been the first to introduce young Alison to the critical study of modern literature. The technique involved comparing classical authors with modern French and English authors. Alison also taught, as Matthew Wilson, one of his students, recalled, 'a *course of philosophy, instrumental, natural* and *moral*'.[13] Alison's moral philosophy course was indebted to Hutcheson from whom he drew the principle that philosophical teaching of any kind should concentrate more on feelings than on a priori reason as a guide to ethical conduct.[14] He also, from Hutcheson, acquired the belief that recognition of the virtuous affections is akin to a sense of taste. Like Hutcheson, Alison also promoted a civic humanism that envisioned society and the bonds of social commitment as a learning stage for the observation of proper human conduct. Sloan contends that Alison actually was responsible for introducing Hutcheson's theories to America.[15] Alison's moral philosophy course was essentially the first of a long history of similar courses that would remain at the core of the liberal arts curriculum of Presbyterian dominated colleges in both the US and Canada until well into the early half of the nineteenth century.

When Alison left New London for the Philadelphia Academy in 1752, he took his curriculum with him. In 1756 the Philadelphia Academy became the College of Philadelphia, later to be known as the University of Pennsylvania. There another Scottish immigrant to the colonies, William Smith, would be Provost; Alison, of Scots-Irish descent, would be Vice Provost. Although the new college had no official church connection, Alison continued to promote his Old Side Presbyterianism. Smith, an Anglican, worked to have an Anglican bishop seated in the colonies, a prospect that Alison translated into the dreaded possiblity that the College of Philadelphia could eventually become an Anglican institution, a possibility which Alison found unacceptable.

From 1743 to 1747, while Alison had been overseeing the New London Academy, William Smith had been enrolled as a student at Aberdeen's King's College. By 1753, Smith was in America and had published a pamphlet about an imaginary college entitled, *General Idea of the College of Mirania*. The pamphlet generated so much interest that on 31 May 1754, an advertisement appeared in the *New York Gazette* outlining a course of study planned for the newly conceived King's College, later, Columbia, which was based on Smith's pamphlet. The course of study was never realized at Columbia, but it would be at the centre of the College of Philadelphia's curriculum.

Smith's course of study was designed to realize the philosophical principle at the centre of Scottish common-sense education, a design intended, as Smith observed in the pamphlet, to produce '"a succession of sober, virtuous, industrious citizens"'.[16] Louis Franklin Snow, in his study of early curricula in American colleges, calls the pamphlet the 'first comprehensive plan of a college course developed logically' in the North American colonies.[17] In the pamphlet, Smith addressed the issue of offering courses in English literary study. He argued that the study of polite literature not only taught students to write well and rendered ' "life comfortable" ', but also contributed ' "highly to the cement of society and the tranquillity of the state" '. The argument was based on the belief that a college education should be a preparation for citizenship, an argument that was also a primary tenet of Scottish Enlightenment thinking.

The imaginary Miranians, the pamphlet continued, ' "greatly condemn the practice of neglecting the mother tongue, and embarassing a young student, by obliging him to speak or compose in a dead language" '.[18] Significantly, the works on moral philosophy of Francis Hutcheson were recommended for study in the third year. In the fourth year, students were to link their previous studies to the actual business of life, with an emphasis on ' "writing and speaking well" ', Since ' "nothing contributes so much as being capable to relish what has been well written or spoken by others" '. Hence, Smith observed, ' "the proper studies of this class are rhetoric and poetry, from which arise criticism and composition" '.[19]

Smith was a practically minded educator, a product of Scottish empiricism, and, like Alison, an educational visionary for his time. Shortly after *The College of Mirania* appeared, he had an opportunity to test his ideal course of study in a real college. In the early 1750s, Smith had aligned himself with Alison at the academy in Philadelphia. Together they proposed to the academy's Board of Trustees that a College of Philadelphia be established that could grant degrees. In 1755, a college charter was drafted.[20]

Smith's and Alison's proposed course of study was designed with utilitarian objectives in mind. Consequently, the course subordinated the study of the classical languages to more practical concerns, and it eliminated ' "any special aim toward theology as a profession" '.[21] The course design covered three years; moral philosophy was introduced in the second year. Moral philosophy continued into the third year with afternoons set aside for composition and declamation on moral and ethical topics. As Smith noted in the outline of his programme, ' "composition . . . cannot well be begun at an earlier period in the plan. The knowledge of Mathematics is not more necessary, as an introduction to natural philosophy, than an acquaintance with the best ancient and modern writers, especially the critics, is to just composition; and besides this," ' he added, ' "the topics or materials are to be supplied, in a good measure from moral and natural philosophy." '[22]

For private study during 'Private Hours', Smith included in the course outline a lengthy list of authors with instructions that the ideal students in his ideal college would ' "neither at college, nor afterwards, rest satisfied with a general knowledge, as is to be acquired from the public lectures and exercises" '. The hope was that ' "for the acquisition of solid wisdom" ', they would, randomly during the three years, ' "accomplish themselves still further" ' through private study. As a guide to their private reading, he included in a separate section in his outline a wide ' "choice of approved writers in the various branches of literature" '. These books, he added, were not intended to be consulted only occasionally; they were to be read in order to accomplish the completion of ' "the whole" ' of their education.

The list included, among a broad selection of religious, classical and scientific titles and authors, popular offerings from English literature but, mainly, English literary criticism. Specifically, he listed essays from Addison's and Steele's *Spectator* and Johnson's *Rambler* (' "for improvement of style and knowledge of life" '), Dryden's *Essays and Prefaces* and Joseph Spence's *Essay on Pope's Odyssey*. The list also included the dramatic works of Sir William Davenant, poet laureate from 1638 to 1668. The students were also advised to read Hutcheson's *Works*, Locke's *Essay on Human Understanding*, Hooker's *Ecclesiastical Polity*, and the works of Sir Francis Bacon.[23] In essence, the course outline that Smith laid before the Board of Trustees of the College of Philadelphia in 1756 may well have been the first in colonial North America to include authors and titles that later would be considered standard reading in surveys of English literary criticism.

Charles Janeway Stille, who later would also serve as Provost at the University of Pennsylvania, writing in 1869 in his biography of Smith claimed that Smith's curriculum actually formed the basis of the 'present American College System', and that 'it may be safely affirmed that in 1756 no such comprehensive scheme of education existed in any college in the American colonies'.[24] Beyond his formative role in the creation of the College of Philadelphia, Smith's influence on the development of early American college courses remains problematic. Indisputable, however, is the fact that his ideal course of study bore distinctly Scottish roots. His pedagogical vision owed much to his years as a student at Aberdeen. In fact, his ideal course outline, as some historians have suggested, is strikingly similar to a revised course of study introduced at Aberdeen in 1753 by Alexander Gerard.[25]

In 1795, the course of study at Pennsylvania for the second year, quite notably, included in what was now technically termed the 'Moral Philosophy Department', the study of ethics, economics, politics, logic and rhetoric. Required reading included Cicero's *Offices* and Longinus's *On the Sublime*. Within fifteen years, in 1811, the duties of the Professor of Moral Philosophy at the University of Pennsylvania included, along with teaching logic and moral philosophy, instruction in belles lettres and the ' "English language generally" '. During the sophomore year, the Moral Philosophy Professor taught rhetoric, grammar, logic and declamation in English. The required texts were Longinus, Quintilian, Cicero's *De Oratore* and Horace's *Art of Poetry*. The teaching focus was on literary criticism. All of the required texts, the class notes advised, were to be taught ' "critically" '.[26] By 1820, sophomores were also studying Hugh Blair's *Lectures* and Homer's *Iliad*. By 1826, the Moral Philosophy Professor was charged with instructing sophomores in English composition and in what was now labelled distinctly, 'Rhetoric and Criticism'. The professor taught juniors logic, grammar, composition, moral philosophy and forensics. He taught seniors natural and political law, metaphysics and 'Composition and Forensics'.

The University of Pennsylvania, by the 1820s, had established a pattern for the development of English language study that would be copied by other American universities. One college in particular that followed the University of Pennsylvania's lead was Columbia. Established in 1754 as King's College, by 1785, it offered a course of study that included many of the reforms that originally had appeared in William Smith's 1754 pamphlet on *The College of Mirania*. Regularly scheduled lectures were offered in English composition and in subjects appearing for the first time in a North American college, specifically, courses in 'Universal Grammar', 'The Rise and Progress of Language', and, a course, particularly relevant to this essay's focus, in the 'Rise and Progress of the Written Character and Criticism'. The subjects, appropriately, were under the direction of the Professor of Rhetoric and Moral Philosophy. Seniors concentrated on moral philosophy with lectures three times a week. The senior courses on 'The Rise and Progress of Language' and on the 'Rise and Progress of the Written Character and Criticism' required the reading of Cicero's *De Oratore*, Quintilian (likely the *Institutio Oratoria*), Longinus's *On the Sublime* and other relevant titles in literary criticism chosen by the Professors of Rhetoric and Moral Philosophy.

By 1811, Columbia was making allowances strictly for the study of literary criticism. Although its freshmen and sophomores were still studying rhetoric, grammar and composition under the rubric 'Rhetoric and Belles Lettres', using Holmes's and Sterling's rhetoric and Blair's *Lectures*, both juniors and seniors were studying courses designated specifically as 'criticism', using, as Snow points out, a variety of selected classical and modern literary works. By 1821 Columbia's course for juniors would be called 'Principles of Taste and Criticism'. It was described as a 'course of criticism – including the classical works – ancient and modern' and was taught in conjunction with the 'Theory and Practice of English Composition'. Columbia's juniors in 1821 also had the option of studying a general history of European literature and a 'Critical History of English Literature'. The senior class of 1821 concentrated on philosophy, moral philosophy and political economy.[27]

The influence of Scottish educational principles was also felt at William and Mary College during the colonial era. Initially, William and Mary was an Episcopalian institution founded by James Blair, a Scot, who was educated at Marischal College, Aberdeen. Blair emigrated to the colonies in 1685. In 1691 he went to England to petition for a college in Virginia that was chartered in 1693 as William and Mary College. Blair was named president for life and, until his death in 1743, the curriculum at William and Mary remained largely classical and traditionally Episcopalian. By 1776, however, William and Mary had adopted a curriculum similar to William Smith's earlier course of study at the College of Philadelphia. Exactly how influential William Smith was in the development of William and Mary's curriculum, however, remains unclear.[28] There is also the possibility that Thomas Jefferson, who first proposed the use of the elective system of courses, may have been the primary agent behind the college's curricular reforms. If so, Jefferson's reforms also bear a distinct Scottish connection since they were probably inspired by his earlier association, while a student at William and Mary, with a progressive Scottish professor named William Small, who, like James Blair, was also a graduate, but in 1755, of Aberdeen's Marischal College. Small taught mathematics and natural philosophy. Jefferson studied with him from 1760 to 1762. According to Jefferson, Small was ' "the first who ever gave . . . regular lectures in Ethics, Rhetoric, and Belles Lettres" ' at William and Mary.[29] The extent to which William Small's rather than William Smith's influence shaped Jefferson's reforms at William and Mary in 1779, which included designating one particular professor to teach the course that now combined ethics with belles lettres, can only be conjectured. As Sloan observes, however, 'Jefferson's proposals', regardless of where they originated, were similar to programmes in other North American colleges at the time 'that had similar links to the Scottish universities'.[30]

In 1752, the year when Francis Alison left New London to head the Philadelphia Academy and William Smith was in the final stages of drafting *The General Idea of the College of Mirania*, Samuel Davies, a practising Scottish Presbyterian minister, living in Virginia, acknowledged in popular print the important educational link that he envisioned between literary study, civic morality, and public service in the colonies. Davies, who at the time was a poet of religious verse of some slight renown, valued good reading and desired to share the benefits of fine literature with his congregation. The congregation was poor, and so Davies wrote to his friends abroad requesting books. When they arrived, they were circulated among the church-goers. Davies commented in a collection of verse that he published in 1752 entitled, *Miscellaneous Poems Chiefly on Divine Subjects . . .*,[31] on the promising potential for the use of literature as a teaching tool to impart lessons to the masses and to improve public morality.[32]

What Davies, a Presbyterian New Sider, was addressing in 1752 was the romantic conception of using literature, especially poetry, to assist people to understand what New Side revivalists, inspired by the Hutchesonian defence of emotion rather than reason as a guide to truth, promoted as the rational, eminently sensible nature of the conversion experience. Good literature was respectable and could appeal to the masses on the level of emotions and feelings without seeming excessive. Samuel Blair, a New Side leader, observed that he had made a special effort to try to convince his congregation that the conversion experience did not involve just 'visions, dreams, or immediate inspirations', but a rational comprehension of the value of emotions and feelings in the acceptance of religious ideals.[33] The argument, of course, in all respects, was essentially Hutchesonian.

Davies recognized how literature could be used publicly to teach ethics and morality. The objective – raising the public moral consciousness – complemented the New Side revivalist conception of Presbyterianism. Literature, according to this vision, should be read for more than just improving one's taste and writing or one's declamatory style. New Side ministers, consequently, felt just as comfortable alluding to Pope, Addison, Whitefield and Thomas Prince in their sermons as they did to Horace, Plato, Tacitus and Cicero. According to Sloan, they were always prepared 'to abandon classical and genteel literary canons of taste when the occasion demanded'. Consequently, the psychology of conversion developed by New Side Presbyterians was deliberately related to other avenues of learning.[34] For Davies and other New Side ministers, farmers and common folk were not only fully able to enjoy the excitement of literature as an avenue of learning but also entitled to it by nature.

For a period from 1759 to 1761, Davies was the President of the infant College of New Jersey, later, in 1896, to be officially known as Princeton. The College had been originally founded in 1746 on the model of Tennent's Log College by a small group of New England Presbyterian clergymen who felt the need for a college in the middle colonies which would train evangelical ministers to accommodate the increasing influx of settlers and immigrants, mostly Scots-Irish, to the area.[35] Although not initially, the College of New Jersey eventually did become the experimental college model for the trying out of Presbyterian New Side educational principles, just as Old Side Presbyterian principles prevailed for the most part, in spite of its claim of non-sectarianism, at the College of Philadelphia. Aaron Burr, a New Sider, served as head of the College of New Jersey from 1748 to 1757. Jonathan Edwards, his successor, and a New Side sympathizer, died a brief six weeks after following Burr in the position. Edward's successor, none other than Samuel Davies, was President for two years, dying of tuberculosis in 1761. In 1761, Samuel Finley left his position as head of the Nottingham Academy in Pennsylvania in order to assume the presidency of the new college. Finley was a Scots-Irish Presbyterian minister who had emigrated to Philadelphia in 1743 and in 1744 founded the Nottingham Academy on the Pennsylvania–Maryland border.[36]

At Nottingham, in addition to the usual fare of Greek and Latin, Finley had put special emphasis on the study of English and had encouraged as much instruction in belles lettres as was reasonably possible. Once at the helm of the College of New Jersey, Finley revised the curriculum, perhaps feeling the influence of Francis Alison at the College of Philadelphia, in order to give greater importance to English and English literature. Students read Shakespeare, Addison, Milton and other modern writers. During their last two years, students were required to take part in public disputations in both Latin and English. In 1763, Finley established an English department designed to teach 'young lads to write well, to cipher, and to pronounce and read the

English tongue with accuracy and precision'. Eventually, however, the English department was deemed an 'inconvenience' and classes were ordered held outside the college.[37]

Finley's successor in 1768 was the Rev. John Witherspoon. David Daiches calls Witherspoon 'the single most influential educator in America in his time'.[38] Witherspoon was also a Scottish Presbyterian minister. Although committed to neither New Side nor Old Side factions in the American church, he was the favorite choice of the New Siders for the position. While a student at Edinburgh University, Witherspoon, along with Hugh Blair, had studied literary criticism, classical and modern, with John Stevenson, Professor of Logic and Metaphysics. Stevenson had included in his classes the reading of Cicero and Quintilian, as primary classical sources in literary criticism, but he also included modern selections, Bacon and Locke, particularly. Witherspoon was predisposed toward Ciceronian humanism. He believed that good citizens automatically promote the common interest.[39] But Witherspoon also felt the influence of Hutcheson's teachings while a student in Scotland. With Hutcheson, he promoted the belief in the existence of an innate moral sense and in the essential goodness and 'good sense' of ordinary citizens. Consequently, he was a staunch supporter of the rights of the commonality and in 1776 was the only prominent colonial academic to sign the Declaration of Independence.[40]

Witherspoon left Scotland in 1768 to take up the presidency of the College of New Jersey. From the outset, like Finley before him, he insisted on the educational value of English studies. Before he had left Scotland, he arranged for over three hundred books to be sent to the College's library. Included among the books were works by Hutcheson, Hume, Adam Ferguson, Adam Smith and other contemporary Scottish authors.[41] His *Lectures on Moral Philosophy*, published posthumously in 1800–1801, were actually his class lecture notes. In his classes, he used a teaching technique reminiscent of both John Stevenson and Hutcheson that involved a comparative reading of classic and modern authors. Since he systematically incorporated into his classroom analysis works by Shakespeare, Addison, Johnson, Pope, Swift and Hume, among others, an argument can be made, apropos of Daiches's claim, that Witherspoon actually was the first North American professor to teach a course that concentrated on English literary study, even though there was no course at the time labelled exclusively, 'English Literature'.[42]

During his administration, the freshman year remained elementary and basically classical, but the sophomore year involved the study of the classics, mathematics, geography and Witherspoon's own addition, the study of English grammar and composition. With this addition, as Varnum Collins suggests, Witherspoon's emphasis on English expression commenced. The junior year was devoted chiefly to science but was augmented by Witherspoon's lectures on history and 'Eloquence'. The lectures on 'Eloquence' included the study of rhetoric, advanced English composition, style and literary criticism. Seniors reviewed the classics, studied logic and natural philosophy, and heard lectures on ethics, politics and government, which were delivered under the rubric, 'moral philosophy'. Public oratory was always one of Witherspoon's major concerns; consequently, as Collins notes, his 'insistence on the serious study of written and spoken English was plainly discernible in the public style of his graduates'.[43]

Witherspoon had learned much from Hutcheson and from Thomas Reid whom he knew personally. He is often credited with introducing Reid's theories on 'philosophical realism' into North America. Reid was Adam Smith's successor to the chair of moral philosophy at Glasgow. Following Reid, Witherspoon believed that the object of formal university study should be directed at learning more about the nature of mankind. Moral philosophy, for instance, benefited more from the direct study of human nature itself than from the study of general principles. Hence, along with Hutcheson, he valued the usefulness, the utility, of academic subjects as they addressed and enhanced the common experience of all people. The test of utility, therefore, was applied to the college curriculum as an exercise in 'common sense'. Witherspoon also posited, after both Hutcheson and Adam Smith, the ideal of the bourgeois gentleman – Smith's economic man – as a desired standard of conduct for his graduates. According to Sloan, Witherspoon's gentleman was 'the man who, not by birth, but by virtue of his prudence, industry, and learning could provide leadership to a burgeoning and aggressive middle class'.[44]

In 1762, six years before Witherspoon left Scotland for the College of New Jersey, James Manning proposed that a college be established in Warren, Rhode Island. His efforts were successful, and in 1764 a charter for Rhode Island College was obtained from the colonial legislature. In 1804 it would be renamed Brown College, later, Brown University. When it opened in 1765, Manning was the obvious choice for President.

He was also officially appointed Professor of Languages.[45] In 1770 the college, whose enrollment until then had not exceeded thirty students, was relocated at Providence, a larger town. Manning remained President until his death in 1791.

By 1783, first-year students at Rhode Island College were studying Latin and Greek classical authors and the New Testament in Greek. Second-year students studied Cicero's *De Oratore*, Caesar's *Commentaries*, Homer's *Iliad*, and Longinus's *On the Sublime*. They also studied geography, Robert Lowth's *Grammar* and *Rhetoric*, Ward's *Oratory*, Sheridan's *Lectures on Elocution*, Lord Kame's *Elements of Criticism*, and Watts's and Duncan's *Logic*. Hutcheson's *Moral Philosophy* was taught in the third year, along with astronomy, mathematics and Martins's *Philosophia Britannica*. Fourth-year students studied history, Locke's *Essay Concerning Human Understanding* and Kennedy's *Chronology*.[46]

The 1783 Rhode Island College curriculum was Manning's design. What is particularly noteworthy is the limited number of assigned works in Latin and Greek when compared with assigned works written in English. Throughout the four years, students were also urged to compose their themes in English rather than in Latin. Manning's 1783 Rhode Island curriculum was also a harbinger of the increasing influence of the oratorical tradition in United States colleges, a direction in language study that would eventually link the study of oratory with experimental exercises in literary criticism, thus paving the way for full-term college courses in English Literature.

Manning promoted the study of English by combining instruction in rhetoric, composition, and public speaking, but it was Jonathan Maxcy, Manning's successor as college president in 1792, who actually combined the teaching of oratory with belles lettres at Rhode Island College. From 1787 to 1791, Maxcy had served the college as a tutor. He remained as Rhode Island's president until 1802 when he was named the first president of the newly established South Carolina College in Columbia, eventually to be known as the University of South Carolina. In 1793 at Rhode Island College, under Maxcy's direction, Kames's *Elements of Criticism* was moved from the second to the third year, Sheridan's *Lectures on Elocution* was moved to the freshman year to be studied as a prerequisite for more advanced courses in oratory, and a separate subject called simply 'criticism' was instituted. During Maxcy's eight-year administration, Rhode Island acquired a reputation as a centre for the study of oratory, belles lettres, literary criticism and moral philosophy.

Maxcy's efforts to promote oratory and Literature at Rhode Island
bore tangible fruit in 1804, two years after he left, with the institution
of a formal Chair of Oratory and Belles Lettres. It was the first endowed
chair at the newly designated Brown College. By 1823, the course of
study at Brown included, among the list of usual classical selections,
Blair's *Lectures*, Kames's *Criticism*, Hedge's *Logic*, Paley's *Moral Philosophy*
and his *Evidences*, Campbell's *Philosophy of Rhetoric*, Dugald Stewart's
Philosophy of the Human Mind and Butler's *Analogy*.

By 1827, the oratorical tradition was fully entrenched at Brown. The
freshmen continued to read Sheridan's *Lectures on Elocution* as a prerequisite to more advanced courses in oratory. Sophomores read Cicero's
De Oratore and Longinus's *On the Sublime*, but now combined with both
Blair's *Lectures* and Kames's *Elements of Criticism*. Juniors studied Paley's
Moral Philosophy and *Natural Theology*, but now with Campbell's *Philosophy
of Rhetoric*. 'Criticism' continued to be listed as a separate and distinct
subject assigned to the professor who taught natural philosophy.[47]

When Jonathan Maxcy assumed the presidency at South Carolina
College in 1804, he implemented a course of study designed, as Patrick
Scott observed, 'to emphasize esthetics as an element of general philosophy, in the style of Kames or Campbell and the Scottish school, rather
than occupy himself with rhetoric as it traditionally had been taught'.[48]
The movement away from traditional rhetoric was not unusual at this
time. Other colleges in the US were also beginning to experiment with
directions in language study that veered away from traditional classical
rhetoric courses toward courses that promised to be more practical
and sociological in scope. Maxcy all along had envisioned 'rhetoric' as
embodying a combination of oratory and criticism.[49]

By 1800, oratory was emerging in the US as the primary vehicle
through which English studies would progress through the first half of
the nineteenth century. In his last commencement address at Rhode
Island College in 1802, Maxcy recognized Hugh Blair on the importance of language study and then went on to attest to the value of the
study of criticism itself as a ' "rational science" ' that ' "occupies a middle
status between the higher senses and the intellect" '.[50] In a clear recognition of the relationship between criticism and the Hutchesonian
emphasis on feeling and emotions as a check on reason in the act of
critical evaluation, he added that the virtue of ' "criticism" ' is that it
' "unites sentiment and reason; enlivens and improves both" '.[51]

The impact of Maxcy on the progress of the oratorical tradition in
the early nineteenth century, one that envisioned 'criticism' as an ideal

synthesis of rhetoric, philosophy, public speaking and literary study, was significant. Criticism, or more to the point, 'philosophical criticism', for Maxcy, involved the 'application of scientific principles to the productions of art and genius, with a view to ascertain the beauties and defects of the latter, and to adjust their intrinsic and comparative merits'.[52] The study of criticism, he argued, which he linked directly to understanding the nature of mankind, provided students with valuable self knowledge. Criticism, in other words, improved character. The argument recalls the line of thought advocated by Adam Smith and other Scottish moral philosophers and rhetoricians on the study of rhetoric and belles lettres as ultimately a means for the improvement of character. For Maxcy, like the Scottish moralists, combining the study of philosophy with literature enlarged one's 'knowledge of mind'. As he put it, to study language, 'as a philosopher does', is to study 'the powers, laws, and operations of the mind'.[53]

The idea of combining the study of philosophy with oratory and literary criticism directly influenced the design of Maxcy's curriculum at South Carolina, but the idea was also very much in the air at the time and helped to promote curricular changes in language study in US colleges that eventually would make formal courses in the critical study of English literature a reality. To the degree with which Maxcy envisioned the value of connecting philosophy, oratory and literary criticism, as Scott observes, his curriculum was indeed 'absolutely representative of its period'.[54]

Maxcy died in 1820, too soon to realize just how influential the oratorical tradition would become in American higher education. By the 1820s, Yale and Harvard had shifted academic priorities away from the old preoccupation with divinity and had begun to offer subjects that covered a much wider spectrum of learning. One important innovation was the gradual introduction of 'criticism', an extension of both oratory and moral philosophy, as a separate discipline.[55]

Yale, founded originally in 1701 to promote 'the Arts and Sciences', envisioned its mission as twofold: first, was the education of the ministry; but second was an acknowledged commitment to preparing its students 'for Publick employment'.[56] Late-eighteenth- and early-nineteenth-century efforts of Ezra Stiles, Timothy Dwight, James L. Kingsley and other early promoters of English studies at Yale, finally succeeded in 1828 in gaining a formal public acknowledgement of the link between the critical reading of English literature and the study of oratory. In

1828, then President Jeremiah Day claimed in the famous Yale Report of 1828 to the Connecticut General Assembly, part two of which was authored by Professor Kingsley, that by reading English authors, the Yale students were learning '"the powers of the language"' in which they '"speak and write"'. By reading English authors, students were also learning, Day added, '"that eloquence and solid learning should go together; that he who has accumulated the richest treasures of thought, should possess the highest powers of oratory"'.[57] The Yale Report was a timely statement attesting to a developing trend in higher education in the US that, by 1828, was encouraging the use of both English and American literary selections in the teaching of ethics and conduct under the rubric of the study of moral philosophy. The effort remained visibly indebted to the work of earlier Scottish moral philosophers and rhetoricians. Oratory, public declamation, and criticism were being taught at the time either as rhetoric or eloquence or both. In 1824 in a course labelled, 'Rhetoric and Oratory', Yale's students read Cicero's *De Oratore* in combination with Homer's *Iliad* for the first term. Seniors read Blair's *Rhetoric* during the first term and Dugald Stewart's *Philosophy of the Mind* in the second term, along with Paley's *Natural Theology*. Paley's *Moral Philosophy* was required of seniors during the third term. Worth noting is that the texts read by the seniors were all written in English.

The importance attached to the combination of rhetoric and criticism in the study of oratory also helps to explain developments in English studies at Harvard during the first few decades of the nineteenth century. In 1819, Edward Tyrell Channing assumed Harvard's Boylston Chair of Rhetoric and Oratory, a position he held for thirty-two years.[58] As Myron Tuman has suggested, with Channing, we begin to see the study of oratory concentrating increasingly on classroom assignments in literary criticism.[59]

Scattered throughout Channing's lectures and articles on literary criticism is abundant evidence of the impact of Thomas Reid and other Scottish philosophers on his teaching. He fully accepted Reid's commonsense belief that the study of human nature should form the basis for the study of criticism. In his lectures on literary criticism and principles of oratorical declamation he emphasized Hutchesonian civic humanism by concentrating on social institutions and various social circumstances where speech and language were evidently instrumental in the formation of judgments and decisions. Yet, though he believed that the best eloquence grew naturally out of its close connections with the institutions and the temper of the times, he warned constantly of the foolishness of thinking that contemporary oratory should do little more than simply replicate classical oratory. Channing also was a serious reader of Adam Smith, and, like Smith, envisioned the patriot as basically a public servant, one of the multitude bound in sympathy to devote himself to public service.

In his courses, Channing assigned poetry in English as well as prose readings because he believed that rhetoric, generally, should encompass all forms of discourse – poetry as well as oratory, expository writing and oral declamations. In the final analysis, what Channing was teaching after 1827, regardless of what the course was called, was literary criticism. He responded to the general temper of the age which, building on a new awareness of what the study of oratory could effect in the development of English Studies, began to blur the distinction between oratory as simple speech-making and other forms of writing.[60] Owing to his predisposition toward the value of combining oral and written recitations on English literature, he decided, like Timothy Dwight had done earlier at Yale, to make the study of English literature available on a voluntary basis in the evenings either to examine ' "some established Authors" ' or to read ' "some of the early English poets" '.[61] Also, the title of his journal articles and reviews, all exercises in literary criticism, attest to his consuming interest in English and American literary study. Consider, for example, his ongoing *North American Review* articles, written over a thirty-year period, on such topics as 'On Models in Literature' (July 1816), 'Cowper's Memoir of His Early Life' (May 1817), 'Moore's Lalla Rookh' (November 1817), 'Dunlap's Charles Brockden Brown' (June 1819), 'Montgomery's Poems' (September 1819), 'Periodical Literature of the Age of Anne' (April 1838), and 'The Works of Lord Chesterfield' (April 1840), to cite but a few.

His students wrote expository and persuasive themes on literary subjects. In his oratory classes, his students read aloud poetry and prose of their own choosing.[62] He assigned theme topics that demanded critical analysis, all done in the interest of improving the student's critical reading abilities. Among the topics for declamation listed by Anderson and Braden are the following:

Evidences of the Moral and Literary influence of Shakespeare.
[The] Stability of Literary Fame.
Irving's Foreign Compared with his Domestic Titles.
The alleged want of variety in Scott's Chivalrous Characters.

What distinguishes a Play from any other composition?

Gray's 'Elegy' and Bryant's 'Thanatopsis' – View of Death.

The English Poets as advocates of Liberty.

Describe the kind of character of Orations, which may be properly called a part of Literature. Name some of the Eminent Orator-Authors.

A Novel, designed to exhibit and enforce certain opinions in Theology, Politics, or Education – distinct from what are called Historical Novels.

'The Orator and His Times' was the title of Channing's inauguration lecture, delivered on 8 December 1819. In it he observed that the task before Harvard's educators was 'to determine the kind of eloquence' which suited the times. He added, 'there never was a time when the disposition was stronger to make classical literature practically useful; to take it from the sophist, the disputant, the overloaded slumbering scholar, and place it in the hand of the philosopher, the soldier, the physician, the divine, the jurist, and the statesman.' The pressing need, accordingly, he thought, was to 'raise the moral character' of the state; public conduct, he maintained, should be the 'result of settled principles, and not of vague, transient impulse'.[63]

Channing was a transitional figure at Harvard. Before his retirement in 1851, he succeeded in transforming the study of oratory into the study of oratory and literary criticism; done, I might add, with an eye toward both oral and written presentations of topics based often on critical readings in English literature that he assigned. He was a remarkable and highly influential teacher who placed great emphasis on the 'interaction' between society and the individual and who ground his revolutionary teaching, as Anderson and Braden remind us, 'firmly in Scottish philosophy'.[64] His ongoing debt to Scottish moral philosophy also prompted William Charvat, in his study of *The Origins of American Critical Thought 1810–1835*, to single him out as 'perhaps the most important individual of his time' in the dissemination of Scottish aesthetics in North America.[65]

In Canada, although developments, mostly post-1800, came later than in the US, the role played by early religious zealots in the establishment of colleges and the promotion of English literary study was similar. One significant difference, however, between the two countries, was that religious lines in Canada were more clearly drawn, especially between the Presbyterians, most of whom traced their roots to Scotland or Ireland,

and the predominantly English Anglicans. Like their counterparts in the US, however, Canadian Presbyterians were at the forefront of the promotion of vernacular literary study, but with more of a concentration eventually on the promotion of English literary history as a record of English cultural supremacy than on either English oratory or rhetoric. Hence, the oratorical tradition that so largely influenced developments in English literary study in the US appears to have had much less of an impact in Canada.

Since Scottish settlers, mainly Presbyterian, were excluded from Anglican colleges by statutes and social pressures that required students to belong to the Church of England, they founded their own colleges, or, as in the case of Dalhousie College in Halifax, and to some extent, McGill College in Montreal, they eventually managed to take control of major non-sectarian institutions supported by Canadian government funds. The programmes of study instituted in these colleges were derived mainly from the universities of Scotland. These Scottish-influenced universities generally adopted an approach to education that stressed moral philosophy and the study of the humanities in contrast to the classically centred Anglican-based Canadian universities. Hence, the desire in the Scottish-based universities increasingly to relate the teaching of rhetoric to the thematic and ideological concerns of English literature.[66]

The earliest attempt to teach English in Canada likely occurred in Nova Scotia in the Scottish settlement of Pictou. A Presbyterian minister from Glasgow named Thomas McCulloch spent the winter of 1803 in Nova Scotia at the request of the Pictou Scots.[67] Because of severe educational restrictions on Presbyterians imposed by Church of England authorities in Nova Scotia, admission to King's College in Windsor was restricted to Anglicans. Consequently, Pictou's Scottish Presbyterians, in a fashion similar to what their American counterparts had done in earlier years, decided to establish their own academy with McCulloch in charge. McCulloch, who had been educated in Glasgow, was a student of moral philosophy who believed with the Scottish common-sense philosophers that education should promote utilitarian objectives, civic humanism and moral improvement. Henry A. Hubert cites lines from McCulloch's *Nature and Uses of a Liberal Education* that promoted a conception of the benefits of imitation and good models in the training of youth that recalls particularly Adam Smith's earlier promotion of similar points in *The Theory of Moral Sentiments* and in his lectures on belles lettres.[68] At one point, McCulloch observed, for instance, that '"everything tending to depravity of disposition"' must be replaced by '"whatever appear[ed] to be good and useful and calculated to encourage imitation"'. Echoing Hutcheson, McCulloch also believed that a proper liberal education should promote civic humanism, for '"the existence of a social state produce[d] a variety of offices and duties, which, by promoting the safety and comfort of the individual parts of society, ultimately tend[ed] to the benefit of the whole"'.[69]

In 1809, McCulloch opened the Pictou Academy. Owing to political objections from the Anglicans, the academy was prohibited from granting degrees. Consequently, graduates had to travel to the US or Scotland for degrees. One of them was J. W. Dawson, a geologist and graduate of Edinburgh University, who later, in 1855, as President of McGill instituted a programme of study in English literature that was taught by the Rev. W. T. Leach. Leach brought to the position a background in rhetoric and belles lettres learned while a student at Edinburgh University. Dawson's approach to English Studies was philosophical and philological rather than belletristic or rhetorical. He was more interested in using English literature to promote British cultural and ethical concerns that he believed would help to determine Britain's history than he was in using English literature to promote the study of the language per se. He attached '"paramount importance"', as he noted in his inaugural address in 1855, to '"the philosophical study of [English] grammar and philological relations, the principles of style and composition, the critical examination of its highest literary productions, and the history of its literature"'.[70] In 1858, the Molson chair in English Language and Literature was established at McGill; Leach was the first to hold the chair.

Dawson's public recognition in 1855 of the cultural and political value of the study of English literary history strikes the note that most informed the progress of English literary study in Canadian universities in the nineteenth century. Dawson's perception of the patriotic value of teaching English literary history mirrored developments that had occurred two years earlier in 1853 at the University of Toronto, when Daniel Wilson, the famous Scottish patriot and antiquarian, assumed Toronto's professorship of History and English Literature, a position he occupied for thirty-five years.[71] A chair of History and English Literature had been proposed as early as 1851, but Wilson in 1853 was the first to hold it. Fascinated with the past, he was particularly proud of his Celtic Scottish heritage. In 1851, he had published *Archaeology and Prehistoric Annals of Scotland*, which was the first comprehensive survey of

Scottish archaeological history. The book's thesis, which ties in directly with Wilson's interest in the promotion of a historically based programme of study in British literature and culture, challenged the assumption that the history of western civilization was traceable exclusively to the Greeks and Romans, with later advancements being made by the Scandinavians, and that the early Celts, by contrast, had been rude and primitive until raised out of barbarism by the Roman invasions. Wilson's self-appointed task was to rescue Scottish or Celtic archaeology from those who at the time dismissed it as primitive. The study of English or British literature, especially British literary history, was advanced by Wilson as another way to reassess the past.

At Toronto, during Wilson's tenure, the English programme was based squarely on Scottish curricular models. Using literary selections as models for writing was de-emphasized in favor of the study of English literary history. In the first year students studied composition, language and English literary history up to the end of the Elizabethan age. In the second year, the literary history section covered the period from Elizabeth to Queen Anne. English was not required in the third year. In the fourth year, literary history included the study of selected works and authors from the eighteenth century to the period of Wilson's 'present', the mid nineteenth century.

The core text for the literary history courses, not surprisingly, was William Spalding's *A History of English Literature* which was originally published in Edinburgh in 1853, the same year Wilson emigrated to Toronto.[72] Spalding, a Scot, was Professor of Rhetoric at Edinburgh University in 1840. In 1845 he gave up the Edinburgh chair to become Professor of Logic, Rhetoric, and Metaphysics at St Andrews. Alistair Tilson in a 1991 article on Spalding refers to the *History* as 'the principal text used for English studies in Canadian universities in 1860'. Tilson also notes that the text remained popular and in use until the late 1880s.[73] Spalding's *History* was also required reading for Leach's literature courses at McGill. By 1865, Leach was teaching a major British authors course. By 1870, the programme at McGill included courses in English Literature for the first three years. In all of the courses, as Hubert notes, the core texts were literary histories.[74] Spalding's *History* was preferred, supplemented at times by G. L. Craik's 1844 publication of *Sketches of the History of Literature and Learning in England*.

The emphasis on English history in the English programmes at both Toronto and McGill also may account for the use in the English language courses at both schools of Robert Gordon Latham's *Handbook of the English Language,* originally published in 1851. Latham was a prominent ethnologist and linguistic philologist who succeeded, while at London's University College in the 1840s, in shifting the emphasis of the English programme from rhetoric and etymology to a concentration on cultural morphology. Latham had introduced into the institutional debate over the credibility of English Studies that was waging in England at the time, the ethnological argument for the use of literary study as evidence of experiential structures that determined what Latham believed was the character of a race.[75] The interest in combining language study with the study of cultural or racial history that Latham advanced complemented the efforts of both Leach and Wilson in Canada to promote an historically based programme of study that advocated the ideological superiority of British literature and culture. The effort helps to explain the wide popularity and use of Latham's *Handbook* in Canada. The same cannot be said for its popularity and use in US colleges and universities at the time since, as I have argued, the concentration on English literary study in the US through mid century was mainly critical rather than racially ideological or historical. The Canadian concentration, in contrast, remained almost uniformly ideological and historical from the mid 1850s until the 1890s. As Hubert points out, by the late nineteenth century, the emphasis in Canadian universities was squarely on the promotion of an ideological cultural vision represented by canonical British authors. 'This idealism,' he suggests, 'derived from roots deep in British religious and educational traditions, both Scottish and English, although the two differed considerably from each other.'[76]

There had been efforts prior to Wilson's at Toronto and Dawson's and Leach's at McGill to teach English Literature in Canada. According to Robin Harris, in 1842–43 a tutor named Crowley who held an appointment at Victoria College, supposedly offered a course in English studies, but nothing is known of him, including his first name.[77] Egerton Ryerson who was Victoria's first president when it opened in 1842 also appealed for the inclusion of a programme of study in English. He had in mind principally, however, the study of grammar and composition rather than Literature.[78] In 1846 Andrew McNabb began teaching Rhetoric and Belles Lettres at Victoria; he was succeeded by S. S. Nelles who continued to teach at Victoria until his death in 1887. Harris notes that Nelles was lecturing on English Literature as early as 1852 and that by 1857 English Literature was a required fourth-year course at Victoria.[79] Yet, efforts at Victoria to implement a programme of English literary study seem to have had little influence nationally. The direction that English literary study in Canadian colleges and universities generally took in the nineteenth century was best represented by the efforts of Wilson at Toronto and Dawson and Leach at McGill to combine English literary study with the promotion of a fundamentally ideological conception of British cultural history.

There appears to have been little change in the progress of higher education in Canada between the 1860s and the 1880s. By the 1880s, as Harris notes, enrollment was on the rise; by 1890 'there were professors of English language and literature firmly in place at McGill, Toronto, Dalhousie, Queen's, and Mount Allison'.[80] By the 1890s, as well, English literary study in Canada was promoting British cultural history and, subsequently, British culture. The Scottish influence had been subsumed into a nationalistic tradition that now promoted the superiority of a racial and cultural ideal that was associated mainly with life south of the Tweed. Yet, the legacy, throughout North America, of the early Scottish influence on both English literary study and, later, American literary study lived on in the work of teachers and critics who continued to advocate the philosophical and utilitarian value of English literature as a pedagogical and critical tool for promoting social responsibility, civic humanism and moral improvement.

NOTES

1 *De Oratore*, trans. E. W. Sutton (Cambridge, MA: Harvard University Press, 1942), p. 9.
2 The present study suggests that the oratorical culture began to influence the development of English studies in the United States much earlier than the period suggested by Gerald Graff in *Professing Literature: An Institutional History* (University of Chicago Press, 1987), pp. 35, 36–44. See also, Kermit Vanderbilt, *American Literature and the Academy: The Roots, Growth, and Maturity of a Profession* (University of Pennsylvania Press, 1986), esp., pp. 29–48; Richard Ohmann, *English in America: A Radical View of the Profession* (New York: Oxford University Press, 1976); Andrew Hook, *Scotland and America, 1750–1835* (Glasgow: Blackie, 1975); and Robert Crawford, *Devolving English Literature* (Oxford: Clarendon Press, 1992), esp. the chapter on 'Anthologizing America', pp. 176–215.
3 *The Life of Adam Smith* (Oxford: Clarendon Press, 1995), p. 50. Ross's chapter 4 on '*The Never to be Forgotten Hutcheson*' has been of singular value to me in preparing this study.
4 Ibid., pp. 50–1. The quote is from Hutcheson's 'Preface' to the *Inquiry*.
5 *Inquiry*: Treatise II: 164, *Works* (Glasgow, 1772). Cited in Ross, p. 51.

6 Frederick Copleston, SJ, *Modern Philosophy: From Descartes to Leibniz, A History of Philosophy*, vol. 4 (Garden City, NY: Image Books, 1963), pp. 48f.

7 For more on this point see Copleston, *Modern Philosophy: The British Philosophers from Hobbes to Hume, A History of Philosophy*, vol. 5 (New York: Image Books, 1994), pp. 178–84; see also Thomas P. Miller, 'John Witherspoon', *Eighteenth-Century British and American Rhetorics and Rhetoricians*, ed. Michael G. Moran (Westport, CT: Greenwood Press, 1994), p. 269.

8 James G. Leyburn, *The Scotch-Irish* (Chapel Hill: University of North Carolina Press, 1962), p. 180. Leyburn estimates that over 200,000 Scots-Irish left Ulster for America between 1700 and 1776. See also, Ian Graham, *Colonists from Scotland* (Ithaca: Cornell University Press, 1956), esp. p. 189.

9 Douglas Sloan, *The Scottish Enlightenment and the American College Ideal* (New York: Teachers College Press, 1971), p. 37.

10 Ibid., p. 41.

11 Ibid., p. 75.

12 Ibid., pp. 42–60.

13 'Obituary of Alison', *Pennsylvania Journal*, 19 April 1780; cited in Charles Coleman Sellers, *Dickinson College: A History* (Middletown, CT: Wesleyan University Press, 1973), pp. 20–1.

14 See David Fare Norton, 'Francis Hutcheson in America', *Studies on Voltaire and the Eighteenth Century* 154 (1976), 1562–5.

15 Sloan, *Scottish Enlightenment*, p. 88.

16 Cited in Louis Franklin Snow, *The College Curriculum in the United States* (Printed for the Author, 1907), p. 60.

17 Ibid., p. 60.

18 Ibid., p. 64.

19 Cited in ibid., p. 63.

20 Sloan, *Scottish Enlightenment*, pp. 82–3.

21 Cited in Snow, *College Curriculum*, p. 72.

22 Ibid., p. 72, fn. 1.

23 Ibid., pp. 70–1.

24 *Memoir of Rev. William Smith* (Philadelphia: Moore & Sons, 1869).

25 See John Malcolm Bulloch, *A History of the University of Aberdeen, 1495–1895* (London: Hodder and Stoughton, 1895).

26 Snow, *College Curriculum*, pp. 136–7.

27 Ibid., pp. 93–108.

28 Smith's great-grandson, Horace Wemyss Smith, in the *Life and Correspondence of Rev. William Smith, D. D.* (Philadelphia: Jacobs, 1880), observed that James Madison, an older cousin of the American President of the same name, who in 1776 was President of William and Mary, chose Smith's course of study for use in the college. Thomas Harrison Montgomery in his *History of the University of Pennsylvania . . . to 1770 . . .* (Philadelphia: Jacobs, 1900), however, disputes the accuracy of the claim (p. 263).

29 Cited in Sloan, *Scottish Enlightenment*, p. 246.

30 Ibid., p. 247.

31 The full title is *Miscellaneous Poems Chiefly on Divine Subjects; In Two Books; Published for the Religious Entertainment of Christians in General* (Williamsburg: William Hunter, 1752).

32 Cited in Sloan, *Scottish Enlightenment*, p. 54.

33 Cited in Leonard J. Trinterud, *Forming of an American Tradition* (Philadelphia: Westminster Press, 1949), pp. 79f.

34 Sloan, *Scottish Enlightenment*, pp. 50–1.

35 See Varnum Lansing Collins, *Princeton* (New York: Oxford University Press, 1914), pp. 3–5.

36 Wayland F. Dunaway, *Scotch-Irish of Colonial Pennsylvania* (Chapel Hill: University of North Carolina Press, 1944), pp. 222–3.

37 Collins, *Princeton*, pp. 60–1.

38 'John Witherspoon, James Wilson and the Influence of Scottish Rhetoric in America', *Eighteenth-Century Life* 15 (1991), 167.

39 For a helpful summary perspective on this point see Thomas P. Miller, 'John Witherspoon', in *Eighteenth-Century British and American Rhetorics and Rhetoricians* pp. 268–9; see also Miller's essay on 'Witherspoon, Blair and the Rhetoric of Civic Humanism', in *Scotland and America in the Age of the Enlightenment*, ed. Richard B. Sher and Jeffrey R. Smitten (Edinburgh University Press, 1990), pp. 100–14.

40 See Peter J. Diamond, 'Witherspoon, William Smith and the Scottish Philosophy', in *Scotland and America in the Age of the Enlightenment*, pp. 115–32.

41 Sloan, *Scottish Enlightenment*, pp. 110–11.

42 For more on Witherspoon's interest in English literary study and his strong preparation in literary criticism, see his lecture on 'Eloquence' in *Works*, 7 (London: Dilly, 1765–1815).

43 Collins, *Princeton*, p. 301.

44 Sloan, *Scottish Enlightenment*, p. 137.

45 For a fuller account of Manning's presidency and early efforts to promote literary study at Rhode Island College, see Romeo Elton, *Memoir of [Jonathan Maxcy's] Life* in *The Literary Remains of the Rev. Jonathan Maxcy, D. D.* (New York: A. V. Blake, 1844).

46 Walter C. Bronson, *The History of Brown University* (Providence: Brown University Press, 1914); rpt. (New York: Arno Press, 1971), p. 103.

47 Snow, *College Curriculum*, p. 122.

48 'Jonathan Maxcy and the Aims of Early Nineteenth-Century Rhetorical Teaching', *College English* 45 (January 1983), 23.

49 See 'Introductory Lecture, to a Course on the Philosophical Principles of Rhetoric and Criticism; Designed for the Senior Class of the South Carolina College . . .' in Elton's *Literary Remains*, p. 397.

50 In light of J. Tarver's recent article on abridgements of Blair's *Lectures* originating in the US at Harvard in 1802 with Eliphalet Pearson's popular abridged edition of the *Lectures*, one must assume that Maxcy's Rhode Island College programme in English required the reading of an earlier version that probably contained the full lectures. See Tarver's 'Abridged

Editions of Blair's *Lectures on Rhetoric and Belles Lettres* in America: what nineteenth-century college students really learned about Blair on rhetoric,' *The Bibliotheck: A Journal of Scottish Bibliography* 21 (1996), 54–67.

51 Cited in Elton, *Literary Remains*, pp. 333–5.

52 Ibid., pp. 398–9.

53 Ibid., p. 401.

54 'Jonathan Maxcy and the Aims of Early Nineteenth-Century Rhetorical Teaching', p. 23.

55 Snow, *College Curriculum*, pp. 119–23.

56 Brooks Mather Kelly, *Yale: A History* (New Haven: Yale University Press, 1974), p. 8.

57 Ibid., p. 163.

58 For some informative insights into the history of Harvard's Boylston chair of Rhetoric and Oratory, see Tarver, 'Abridged Editions', p. 59.

59 'From Astor Place to Kenyon Road,' *College English* 48 (April 1986), 344.

60 See Channing's *Lectures Read to the Seniors*, ed. Dorothy I. Anderson and Waldo Braden, Foreword by David Potter (Edwardsville: Southern Illinois University Press, 1968), p. xxxiv.

61 *Lectures*, p. xxxv.

62 *Lectures*, p. xli.

63 *Lectures*, p. 20.

64 *Lectures*, p. li.

65 (Philadelphia: University of Pennsylvania Press, 1936), p. 186.

66 For more on this point, see Robin S. Harris, *English Studies at Toronto: A History* (University of Toronto Press, 1988), p. 7. See also Harris's earlier *A History of Higher Education in Canada* (University of Toronto Press, 1976); and Henry A. Hubert, *Harmonious Perfection: The Development of English Studies in Nineteenth-Century Anglo-Canadian Colleges* (East Lansing: Michigan State University Press, 1994).

67 Hubert, *Harmonious Perfection*, pp. 28–30.

68 For more on Adam Smith on the value of good models, see Franklin E. Court, *Institutionalizing English Literature: The Culture and Politics of Literary Study, 1750–1900* (Stanford University Press, 1992), pp. 17–30.

69 Cited in Hubert, *Harmonious Perfection*, p. 29.

70 Cited in ibid., p. 102.

71 Carl Berger, 'Daniel Wilson,' *Dictionary of Canadian Biography*, vol. 12 (1990).

72 Spalding's *History of English Literature: with an Outline of the Origin and Growth of the English Language*, originally published in Edinburgh by Oliver and Boyd, was presumably based on Spalding's Edinburgh lectures.

73 'Who Now Reads *Spalding*?' *English Studies in Canada* 17 (December 1991), 469.

74 Hubert, *Harmonious Perfection*, p. 103.

75 Court, *Institutionalizing English Literature*, pp. 77–84.

76 Hubert, 4.

77 *English Studies at Toronto*, p. 6.

78 In 1860, Daniel Wilson responded critically to Ryerson's claim that history and English Literature should not be taught in college since they were taught in grammar school. Their differences were aired in a public debate in 1860 before the Parliamentary Committee on the Toronto University Endowment. Ryerson wanted the English courses to concentrate on composition and grammar. Wilson, an historian–ethnologist, was interested more in the significance of literary history in the promotion of cultural concerns. In his response, Wilson openly endorsed the Scottish model of higher education with its concentration on a broad base of study and on courses that prepared students for the professions. See his response in John Langton's *University Question. The Statements of John Langton . . . and Professor Daniel Wilson* (Toronto: Rowsell & Ellis, 1860).

79 *English Studies at Toronto*, p. 6.

80 *English Studies at Toronto*, p. 19.

CHAPTER 9

Scottish academia and the invention of
American Studies

Andrew Hook

The volume in which this essay appears is itself part of a wider scholarly endeavour which in recent years has been attempting to clarify and redefine Scotland's distinctive intellectual and cultural development from the eighteenth century to the present. Centrally involved is the assertion that the term 'British' – and sometimes even 'English' – serves only to disguise or conceal what in, say, the history of ideas, should be more accurately described as 'Scottish'. Focusing on the furore in the USA occasioned by the appearance of Garry Wills's book *Inventing America* (1979), I have already made a contribution to this process of Scottish cultural redefinition. Wills's central argument, which proved so contentious particularly among American scholars, was that Thomas Jefferson, in his drafting of the American Declaration of Independence, owed a good deal more to the thinkers of the Scottish Enlightenment than to John Locke. Wills's book, that is, attempted to overturn one of the most established orthodoxies of American historiography, and as such inevitably provoked furious criticism. Writing in the 1990s, however, and defending Wills from the often scandalous attacks upon him, I had no hesitation, bearing in mind his book's perfectly plausible central contention, in calling my own essay 'The Scottish Invention of the USA'.[1]

Of course one recognizes that there will continue to be those who will remain scornfully dismissive of the notion that Scotland could in any sense whatsoever have been a contributor to the 'invention' of the USA. Where does that leave the idea that the Scots were major contributors to the 'invention' of American Studies? Final proof, perhaps, that Scottish cultural nationalism is fast developing into Scottish cultural imperialism? Certainly on the face of it the suggestion that Scottish academia invented American Studies is absurd. American Studies, as an academic discipline, did not really begin to emerge even in American universities until after the Second World War. The formal study and teaching of American Literature had begun only a decade or two earlier. In 1921 the president of the Modern Languages Association of America was the Chaucerian scholar J. M. Manly, and it was Manly who reorganized the association into a series of separate groups for cooperative research and specialized meetings. A small American Literature group managed to emerge as a subdivision of the English Language section. There can be no doubting, however, that this tiny band of MLA members were the founding fathers of the vast enterprise that the academic study of American Literature has become; and in due course the exact kind of study of American Literature they originally promoted became profoundly important in the context of the emergence of the new American Studies discipline in general.

Thus both American Literature and American Studies are relatively recent American creations as subjects available for academic study. How then can the Scots be seen as contributing in any way to their invention? The obvious answer is to refer to the now widely held view that the origins of what was to become literary study in the modern sense are to be found in the lecture courses in Rhetoric and Belles Lettres which became part of the curriculum of the eighteenth-century Scottish universities. If this view is accepted in the context of Britain – and I am not aware that it has been seriously challenged – then it is equally applicable to the development of literary studies in the United States. The Scottish rhetoricians, Blair, Kames and Campbell, that is, by the end of the eighteenth century and through the early decades of the nineteenth, were as standard a part of the American university and college curriculum as was the case in Scotland itself. The essay in this volume by Franklin Court demonstrates the crucial importance of this Scottish rhetorical tradition, with its emphasis both on utility – how to speak and write well – and on moral improvement – the link between literature and moral persuasion – in the development of English as an academic subject both in the USA and Canada.[2]

However, while there is indeed a general relevance of this Scottish background to the eventual emergence of American Literature as a subject for academic study, it is not this Scottish tradition that provides the basis for the argument that Scotland may be seen as inventing American Studies. Given its links to moderation in the Church of Scotland, its frequent association with the Scottish common sense school of philosophy, designed above all to refute Humean scepticism, and given too its crucial general contribution to the emergence of modern Scottish civic society, correct, polished, and anglicized, the Scottish

rhetorical tradition was broadly conservative in its social and political impact. The Scottish tradition directly relevant to the eventual
emergence of American Studies was rather more radical in its nature.
In question here is support within Scotland for social and political
reform towards the end of the eighteenth century. The 1780s and
1790s in Scotland saw the emergence of pressure groups demanding
change in the existing power-structure, and pursuing causes likely to
bring about reform in society and politics. But it is in the American
Revolution, rather than the French Revolution, that the origins of this
Scottish movement for political reform are to be located. Thus when
the Scottish Whigs famously established a national voice by creating
in 1802 the soon powerful *Edinburgh Review*, one of the causes they
consistently supported was that of America. For all those concerned
to defend and uphold the *anciens régimes* of Europe at the end of the
eighteenth, and early in the nineteenth century, the existence of the USA
was a thorn in the flesh. For British 'Church and King' Tories, American republicanism, American democracy and America's rejection
of a national church, were personal affronts: they longed for the failure
of the American experiment. For the Scottish Whigs, on the other
hand, American success was proof that major social and political change
was in no way incompatible with stability and progress. Thus, from
the beginning, the *Edinburgh Review* tended to defend America from its
European detractors and, despite the furore occasioned by Sydney
Smith's notorious 'Who reads an American book?' remark, to look
favourably on the new society and culture arising in the United States.
It is out of this Scottish Whig tradition of sympathy for America that,
as I hope to show, the Scottish invention of American Studies eventually emerges.

The earliest evidence of Scottish academic interest in American literature occurs in William Spalding's *A History of English Literature* originally published in Edinburgh in 1853. Born in 1809, Spalding was an
Aberdonian who studied at both Marischal College, Aberdeen, and
the University of Edinburgh. A lawyer, he came to know Francis
Jeffrey and published articles on Shakespeare and other literary topics
in the *Edinburgh Review*. Largely as a result of Jeffrey's influence he was
appointed to the Chair of Rhetoric and Belles Lettres in Edinburgh
which he held from 1840 to 1845. In 1845 he moved to the Chair of
Logic, Rhetoric and Metaphysics at St Andrews which he occupied
until his death in 1859.[3]

Spalding's *History* is presented very much as a textbook 'for the Use of Schools and Private Students'; as such it was eminently successful appearing in no less than fifteen editions, many of them published in the years after the author's early death. Striking is the appearance in the early editions of a section entitled 'Contemporary American Literature'. In some half-a-dozen pages, at the end of his volume, Spalding offers a general account of American literature, focusing almost exclusively on the nineteenth century, and noting that nearly all the important American writers are still alive. Warmly praised are Poe and Hawthorne, while Robert Bird's novel *Nick of the Woods* is preferred to the work of Fenimore Cooper. General comment includes the suggestion that 'In respect of those circumstances which affect style, the position of Americans is much like that of Scotsmen; and the results have not been very dissimilar.'[4] Tantalizingly, the comment is not expanded upon. In the later editions of Spalding's *History*, published after the author's death, the treatment of American literature is more perfunctory: the in-house editors distribute brief comments on American writers across a range of chapters; are on the whole more dismissive of America's literary achievements; and even overturn Spalding's critical judgments. Thus in the revised fourteenth edition of 1877, we are told that Poe's 'weird' stories 'confer upon him a distinction not merited by the unrestrained sensuality of his life'.[5] Despite these posthumous changes, Spalding's own interest in American literature is significant: his is the earliest treatment of American authors in a literary-historical context by a British academic, and his influence must explain why, as early as 1874, English students at St Andrews were being invited in their examination to 'give some account of American literature'.[6] How had his interest originated? In my view in all probability through Francis Jeffrey's *Edinburgh Review* and the positive view of American culture which the Scottish Whig tradition it supported tended to adopt.

The relevance of the same tradition to the life and career of the second Scottish academic I wish to discuss is, as we shall see, self-evident. John Nichol was the first occupant of the new Chair in English Literature at Glasgow University created in 1862 in response to the recommendations of the Universities Commission of 1858. Nichol held the chair until 1889, but it would be quite erroneous to believe that it was only with Nichol's appointment that forms of literary study became part of the Glasgow curriculum. Adam Smith had lectured on Rhetoric and Belles Lettres in Glasgow in the 1750s and 1760s, and

Smith's pupils such as George Jardine, Archibald Arthur and William Richardson, ensured that the tradition of literary and rhetorical study at Glasgow continued to flourish on into the nineteenth century. Nichol's appointment, that is, accorded a new authority and status to a subject which had existed previously, as it were, in between more established disciplines. More significantly still, Nichol's appointment was to make possible the Scottish invention of American Studies.

Nichol, himself a Glasgow graduate, grew up in a family context that was at once strongly academic and strongly politicized. His father, J. P. Nichol, had been appointed to the Chair of Astronomy in Glasgow in 1837. Famous as a public speaker and lecturer, Nichol senior was a Victorian of a powerfully liberal persuasion. His son described him as 'a temperate radical' and he was well known as a campaigner against slavery, and as a friend in Scotland of Kossuth and Mazzini. As a student friend of the young John Nichol put it:

Dr Nichol was known to be a friend of Kossuth and Mazzini; his sympathies and those of Mrs Nichol were strongly with the Anti-Slavery party in the United States. He did not repress, he encouraged, our zeal for those who in Hungary and Austria, and France and Italy, and America, were for personal freedom . . .[7]

The Mrs Nichol referred to here was Nichol senior's second wife. His first wife – John Nichol's mother – having died in 1851, in 1853 he married Elizabeth Pease of Darlington. She and her father, Joseph Pease, the first Quaker MP, were prominent members of the British Anti-Slavery Society. It is then not surprising that Nichol senior should have had many American friends and correspondents, including Longfellow and the leading New England abolitionist, William Lloyd Garrison – nor that in 1847–48 he should have undertaken a lecture tour in America. That tour was destined to be of crucial importance – as we shall see – in influencing the direction of his son's major research and scholarship after becoming Glasgow's first professor of English. More immediately, J. P. Nichol's politics permanently influenced those of his son. At least until the closing years of his life, Professor Nichol's political feelings were even more radical than those of his father. In 1891, three years before his death, looking back on his student days in Glasgow in the early 1850s, he wrote: 'We were all, or thought ourselves to be, keen "Radicals"; believing in the "people", "progress", "free education", "wider suffrage", "rights of man", "rights of women", etc., etc.'[8] Thirty years earlier Nichol had written an account of his early years for his wife's benefit. In this short autobiographical account, Nichol emerges as a fairly typical middle-class radical of the mid nineteenth century. In his description of his response to the events of the years 1848–9, there is no hint of the ironies present in 1891:

I have been, of later years, thrown much into the society of men younger than myself, and found it difficult to make them realize the breathless interest with which the friends of liberty in Europe watched every phase of that momentous struggle.

Like his father, Nichol came to know both Kossuth and Mazzini personally. 'My feeling regarding the wars,' he went on, 'remains as it was when I ran every morning through the woods to the village, to catch the first tidings from the East.'[9]

In 1855 the twenty-one-year-old Nichol left Glasgow University for Balliol College, Oxford. Benjamin Jowett, Master of Balliol, became a lifelong friend, but perhaps the most significant event of his Oxford career was the founding of 'Old Mortality', an essay-writing and discussion society. The list of original members of this society makes impressive reading: Swinburne, T. H. Green, G. R. Luke, A. V. Dicey, G. B. Hill, and, most interesting of all in this context, another Glasgow graduate, James Bryce. The society may have owed its name to Walter Scott, but the members did not share that author's Tory politics. Their sympathies rather were firmly on the side of radicalism. Dicey later wrote that by virtue of the strength of their views on such questions as University Tests, Italian nationalism, the policies of Louis Napoleon and restrictions of any kind on the free expression of opinion – questions which, he says, 'were the subject of daily, I might almost say of hourly, discussion' – 'we considered ourselves advanced Radicals, not to say Republicans'.[10]

Some members of the Old Mortality society, however, were soon preoccupied by a new issue, a new challenge to the liberal principles they endorsed: the impending struggle between North and South in the United States. Edward Caird, Jowett's successor at Balliol, recalled that Nichol and T. H. Green were from the first aware of the significance of what was at stake:

The great contest of North and South in the United States was then beginning, and Nichol and Green showed themselves from the first well-informed as to the nature of the struggle, and zealously maintained the justice of the Northern cause.[11]

Like Green, Nichol remained a powerful advocate for the North
throughout the course of the American Civil War. Back in Glasgow
for most of the war's duration as the new professor of English, he was
undeterred by the fact that established opinion in Glasgow, as elsewhere in the United Kingdom, often tended to side with the South: on
the public platform and in the newspapers, he energetically supported
the Northern cause.

Soon after the close of the Civil War Nichol, like his father before
him, made an extended visit to the United States. In the autumn of
1865 he travelled through the New England states and as far south
as Virginia. In the course of his trip he visited and was entertained by
a range of New England's cultural leaders: Emerson, Longfellow,
Oliver Wendell Holmes, Wendell Phillips and William Lloyd Garrison.
Nichol found America enthralling. Experience of the country and its
society confirmed all his expectations: the positive view of the new
republic, always present in the Scottish Whig tradition represented
by the *Edinburgh Review*, proved to be amply justified. 'America,' he
told his wife, 'is far better than I dreamt of in almost every respect,
especially Boston.' Indeed Boston struck him as much superior to
Glasgow: 'I would give my left hand to leave Glasgow and come here,
but at present there is no opening.' From what he says here, one may
reasonably guess that Nichol had talked to his Boston friends about
the possibility of exchanging his Glasgow chair for a Harvard one:
'I must publish a book in England,' he writes, 'and get it made known
here.' And he concludes with another ringing endorsement of American
cultural life:

Every one I meet in society is sympathetic, literary or metaphysical, refined
beyond the refinement of Englishmen, not to say of Scotchmen, and in the
van of the world, not tugging at the rear.[12]

Nichol's dream of becoming a pioneer of the transatlantic brain-
drain was not destined to be realized. He never did return to America,
but his Boston letter does hint at the direction his scholarly career was
going to take. Back in 1848 his father had brought home from America,
after his lecture tour, a mass of books including the works of Hawthorne,
Longfellow, Bryant and James Russell Lowell. These were the books
which first fired the enthusiasm of the young John Nichol, still a schoolboy in Kelso, for American literature. That enthusiasm he was never
to lose. As early as 1861 he was lecturing on American poetry in
Edinburgh. In 1867 he published articles in the *North British Review* on

American poetry and Emerson. In 1875 he contributed the article on American literature in the *Encyclopaedia Britannica*. In 1879 he lectured on American literature in Cheltenham, and in 1880 on the American novel in Edinburgh. For a senior British academic such as Nichol to chose to specialize in American writing at this time is quite simply extraordinary. Back in 1866, Henry Yates Thompson of Liverpool had offered to endow a lectureship at Cambridge in the 'History, Literature, and Institutions of the United States'; but for a combination of political, ecclesiastical and academic reasons, Cambridge spurned this offer to appoint a lecturer in American Studies as a dangerous novelty. As I indicated at the beginning of this essay, the formal study of American literature did not begin even in American universities until the 1920s; and in Britain it would be the 1950s and 1960s before courses in American Literature begin to appear in university departments of English Literature. Yet in 1882, in Edinburgh, Professor John Nichol published the book which was almost certainly already in his mind in the Boston letter of 1865, and which would be the major scholarly production of his career: *American Literature, An Historical Sketch, 1620–1880.* Nichol had earlier published short studies of Byron and Burns, and he would later produce a brief study of Carlyle, but the study of American literature is easily the most important achievement of his research and scholarship. Publishing such a book on a subject so unfamiliar that, in an academic sense, it did not really exist, Nichol must have known that he was taking something of a gamble in terms of his own scholarly prestige. And there is some evidence suggesting that he recognized that in publishing this book he was exposing himself to attack. In November, 1882, he wrote to William Bell Scott in Newcastle alluding to his forthcoming publication:

I send you a first proof sheet . . . a month old, by which you will see I have not forgotten you. . . . The big book to which the sheet belongs will be out very shortly: but *please mention it to no one* till it is out. I have known a little vol. of mine applied for a year before for the purpose of attacking it.[13]

But Nichol never seems to have been reluctant to face up to opposition, and since at least the publication of his article on American literature in the *Encyclopaedia Britannica* in 1875, he had chosen to become the leading British authority on American writing. Again, Nichol's other main academic publications were, as noted above, on Scottish authors: Burns, Byron and Carlyle. Focusing thus on American and Scottish authors, perhaps the Glasgow professor of English Literature was already choosing to look beyond the English mainstream in literary study? In any event the motives that led a liberal progressive like John Nichol to write and publish his pioneering history of American literature were in the end probably more social and political than purely academic and scholarly.

So what kind of book is Nichol's *American Literature*? What approach to the study of literature does it reflect? From what standpoint does Nichol address the subject of the history of American literature? The short answer is that Nichol's approach is an historicist one: he believes that a text can only be understood and appreciated within its context. Thus *American Literature* is almost as much social and cultural history as literary history: politicians, orators, theologians, historians, are given almost as much prominence as poets and novelists. The work of individual writers is seen, interpreted, and assessed very much in terms of its social and political background. The American Civil War, for example, and all the moral and political debates that preceded it, are continually referred to. Nichol makes his approach explicit at the beginning of the book. He tells us he aims to discuss those authors 'who most conspicuously represent' the main periods and areas of America's literary history, but, significantly, he will 'illustrate their position' 'by reference to the history and politics of the time'.[14] This historicist approach extends to what Nichol sees as the continuing problem of Anglo-American cultural relations. English critics of America have always assumed the automatic superiority of the Old World over the New:

Few are able to divest themselves wholly of the influence of local standards. This is pre-eminently the case when the efforts of a comparatively young country are submitted to the judgments of an older country, strong in its prescriptive rights, and intolerant of changes, the drift of which it is unable or unwilling to appreciate. Our censors are apt to bear down on the writers of the New World with a sort of aristocratic hauteur. Englishmen are perpetually reminding Americans of their immaturity, scolding their innovations in one breath, their imitations in another . . .

The problem, Nichol argues, is at bottom one of ignorance: both Englishmen and Americans are 'ignorant of their mutual ignorance'. But his emphasis falls on English ignorance of America:

Untravelled Englishmen know much less of America as a whole – less of her geography, her history, her constitution, and of the lives of her great men – than Americans know of England.[15]

These are the kinds of view the *Edinburgh Review* had been articulating more than half a century earlier, and there are equally traditional echoes in Nichol's apologies for the limitations of America's literary achievements. In America, he suggests, practical activities have had to take precedence over cultural ones; the achievements of American culture exist in the future rather than the past; politics, commerce, material success have so far absorbed the American genius. These are all arguments with a history going back at least as far as the foundation of the new republic. In fact, at the end of the day, one has to say of Nichol's *American Literature* that, however amazingly innovative it is in one sense, in another, paradoxically, it was already out-of-date in 1882. Nichol's book is a celebration of the literary culture of New England in the 1830s, 40s and 50s – of the work of Emerson, Thoreau, Hawthorne, Longfellow, Bryant, Lowell. It is a celebration of that older America that in fact came to an end with the Civil War. Nichol sees the North's victory in the Civil War as a vindication of America's dedication to the principles and rights and freedoms the Founding Fathers enshrined in the Constitution. Though writing in the early 1880s, he does not see that American history has moved on – and moved on in ways that will further radically undermine the American dreams that the new republic once hoped to embody. Thus he finds little of value in the work of more recent writers such as Henry James, W. D. Howells, or – a true *bête noire* – Mark Twain.

In the long term, however, the methodology of Nichol's history of American literature would prove more important than his assessments of individual authors. His commitment to the historical approach to the study of literature remained unshakeable – for him literature and history were inseparable. Thus he believed that an Honours school in English could not be created at Glasgow until the necessary history courses had come into being. This in turn meant the establishment of a chair in History. Such a chair, finally created in 1889, was filled in 1893; but Nichol retired in 1889, and an Honours programme in English did not emerge until after the arrival of Nichol's successor in the English chair – the Shakespearean scholar, A. C. Bradley. However, Nichol's emphasis on the link between literature and history proved enduring; only in the 1950s did the Glasgow English Department drop the requirement that Honours students should take a course in British history.

Nichol then was a pioneer in the historicist study of American literature. He was equally a pioneer in two vastly important areas in the history of higher education in Britain: women's education and adult education. Throughout his career, Nichol did everything in his power to promote the cause of higher education for women – as early as the 1860s he was delivering a series of lectures in Glasgow, outside the university, aimed at a female audience, and his was undoubtedly a key role in creating the situation which led to the admission of women to Glasgow University in the 1890s. His commitment to the cause of what would now be called continuing or adult education was equally strong. From the 1860s on, he travelled extensively throughout England and Scotland lecturing on literary and philosophical subjects. Applauded as warmly in Dundee as in Penzance, he did as much as anyone to create what became later in the nineteenth century the University Extension movement. Nichol believed in education for all – and that all included women and working men.

Let us return, however, to the main focus of this essay. What role did Nichol play in bringing into being the formal academic study of American literature and history, and how can he be seen as a Scottish inventor of American Studies? Obviously Nichol's *American Literature, An Historical Sketch* is of central importance in this connection. What needs to be borne in mind is that, by 1882, not even within America itself had a comprehensive history of American literature appeared: Moses Coit Tyler's *History of American Literature 1607–1765* – to which Nichol acknowledges a debt – had appeared in 1878, but as its chronological span indicates, Tyler's history did not cover the literature of the new republic.

Nichol's history of American literature thus has a justifiable claim to be the first work of its kind in its field. But for a book to count it has to be used – read, studied, assimilated. The evidence here is more equivocal. Many of Nichol's works, including his studies of Byron and Carlyle in the English Men of Letters series, were published in America; the National Union Catalogue identifies frequent reprintings of these and other books by Nichol. But it lists only the original Edinburgh edition of *American Literature, An Historical Sketch*: are we to conclude that American publishers, confident of an assured American readership for studies of major British authors such as Byron and Caryle, took the view that there was no comparable market for a book-length study of America's own literature? The answer is almost certainly yes. A review of Nichol's volume in the Boston periodical *The Literary World* in fact cites both Adam and Charles Black in Edinburgh, and Scribner and Welford in New York, as publishers of the book.[16] But this is misleading.

Through the 1870s, Scribner had built a close relationship with the Edinburgh publishers, importing and binding the printed sheets of such works as the ninth edition of the *Encyclopaedia Britannica*. Even earlier, Scribner and Charles Welford had formed an importing subsidiary specifically for the purpose of bringing British published books to America.[17] Thus the Scribner and Welford Nichol was at best a New York bound version of the original Black edition: but at least the import meant that Nichol was easily available to interested American readers.

So what kind of notice was taken of Nichol's work in America? The *Literary World* reviewer finds in it many errors and inaccuracies, but 'as the work of a foreign critic' it 'deserves reading'; writing on Transcendentalism Nichol is 'in his element, as a Scotchman always is when dealing with philosophy'.[18] C. F. Richardson, of Dartmouth College, who was to publish his own *American Literature, 1607–1885* in 1887–88, writing on the criticism of American literature in the *Andover Review* in 1884, recognized the problem created by the close relationship between English and American literature, and argued that the foreign critic in particular required special qualifications:

The foreign critic of American literature should be thoroughly acquainted with both English and American political, social, and literary history; should perceive clearly that in England and America is a dominant and assimilating Saxon folk, working out a similar problem on similar lines; and yet should discriminate between variant conditions, aims, methods and results.[19]

Very much, one would have thought, what Nichol had attempted to do. But Richardson is not quite prepared to agree. 'No foreign historian of our literature', he writes, 'has shown himself possessed of all these qualifications. Professor Nichol has some of them, but his book is, after all, only an essay *toward* a history of American literature.'[20] However, when J. J. Halsey reviewed the first volume of Richardson's own history in *The Dial* of Chicago in 1887, he compared it somewhat unfavourably with Nichol's book – even if he was less than clear about Nichol's nationality:

Professor Nichol has upon the whole demonstrated that a fair-minded and earnest Englishman can come at the very heart of our literature.

'His book,' he continues, 'is the first criticism of that literature, and its rank is high.'[21]

Nichol's book, the available evidence suggests, created some ripples in America, but it seems not to have become a major focus for continuing critical or scholarly debate. Late-nineteenth-century and early-twentieth-century historians of American literature such as Henry A. Beers, Walter C. Bronson, Barrett Wendell and William P. Trent cite Nichol among their authorities – as do the editors of volume 1 of the *Cambridge History of American Literature* published in 1917. But the group of MLA scholars, who set about establishing the formal academic study of American literature within the American university system in the 1920s, make scant reference to Nichol. One suspects that the fact that he was a foreigner was a major problem. Fred Lewis Pattee, writing 'A Call for a Literary History' in the *American Mercury* for June 1924 refers to Nichol's 'now antiquated volume' but returns to it in the context of his discussion of what qualities are required of the American literary historian. Rather like Richardson writing forty years earlier, Pattee concedes that the foreign critic may possess the desirable detachment and impartiality, but will inevitably lack the necessary 'understanding of the American soul:'

The Scotch John Nichol's *American Literature*, the most detached history thus far published, falls fatally short at more than one vital point.[22]

What Pattee, like the other young scholars of his generation, was about was a kind of clearing of the ground: their joint aim was to re-establish the study of American literature on a new, modern, professional basis. Past efforts had to be set aside and a new beginning made.[23] But the problem of deciding how exactly the future study of American literature was to be pursued remained. What Arthur Hobson Quinn, W. B. Cairns, Fred Pattee, Percy H. Boynton, soon joined by Robert E. Spiller and Norman Foerster, decided was that American literature should be presented as an 'expression of national (historical) consciousness' and not as an 'aesthetic offshoot of English literature'.[24] Their view, that is, as Pattee, and therefore, one suspects, most of the others as well, must have known, was an exact reiteration of Nichol's view; their approach was Nichol's approach. Some years earlier the four-volume *Cambridge History of American Literature* had been published (1917–21). But while the *Cambridge History* asserted that as a survey of 'the life of the American people' it was more than 'a history of *belles lettres* alone' it nonetheless announced itself on its title-page as 'supplementary' to the *Cambridge History of English Literature*. This was not the view taken by the first generation of American professors of American literature: for them, just as for Nichol, American literature was distinct and separate, only to be understood within the specifics of the social, intellectual, political and cultural context of America itself.

American Studies, of course, as a subject in its own right, involves much more than the study of American literature. But Nichol's contribution to the invention of American Studies extends beyond his writing of the first history of American literature. I have already noted that the membership of Nichol's Old Mortality society at Oxford in the 1850s included the future statesman and scholar James Bryce. But Nichol's friendship with Bryce was of older date. Bryce became a student at Glasgow University in 1854, and soon came to know John Nichol, only a few years his senior. Given his future career, it is hard not to feel that knowing Nichol must have meant learning of – and perhaps beginning to share – his friend's enthusiasm for all things American. Certainly America seems to have been a shared interest for many members of the Old Mortality society at Oxford. Apart from Nichol himself, T. H. Green, another middle-class radical, was an active supporter of American democracy, and it was in the company of A. V. Dicey, one of Nichol's closest friends, that Bryce first visited the United States in 1870. After that visit, Dicey retained an abiding interest in America. In 1898, as one of England's most distinguished legal historians, he returned to Harvard where he delivered the Lowell lectures on comparative constitutions. And G. B. Hill, who had become a leading scholar of eighteenth-century English literature, visited Cambridge, Massachusetts, in 1893 and wrote a well-received account of Harvard College. However, among the Old Mortality group, it is the career of Bryce which is of the greatest significance. Bryce returned to America in 1881 and 1883, and in 1888 he published the first edition of his classic work *The American Commonwealth*. Revised and expanded editions appeared in 1889 and 1893–5, while the final version of 1910 is described by the DNB as 'to some extent a new book'. Like Nichol's *American Literature*, *The American Commonwealth* was a major pioneering work; but Bryce's searching and critical constitutional history of America was to have an impact far beyond anything achieved by Nichol's study. Particularly within America, *The American Commonwealth* acquired a reputation similar to that of Crèvecoeur's *Letters from an American Farmer* or De Tocqueville's *Democracy in America* and was read and studied with enthusiasm well into the twentieth century. Today its classic status would still be generally recognized. Bryce's book includes quite extended discussions of American culture, including its literature. His views are not identical to those of Nichol, as he tends to emphasize what American literature shares with English literature rather than what distinguishes the two; but he does agree that American literature, like, as he sees it, Scottish literature, has a kind of dual identity.

In the eighteenth century Glasgow and the Clyde were the main avenues for the export of Scottish influences of every kind initially to the American colonies and subsequently to revolutionary and post-revolutionary America. Hence it is wholly appropriate to find in the nineteenth-century Glasgow scholars John Nichol and James Bryce the original Scottish cultivators of the field that was to become American Studies. In the twentieth century their tradition was re-established by a succession of distinguished Americanists at the University of Glasgow: D. W. Brogan, Esmond Wright, Peter Parrish, William Brock, But it is Nichol and Bryce who deserve recognition as the Scottish pioneers of American Studies.

NOTES

1 See Andrew Hook, 'The Scottish Invention of the USA' in Mario Materassi and Maria Irene Ramalho de Sousa Santos (eds.), *The American Columbiad, 'Discovering' America, Inventing the United States* (Amsterdam: VU University Press, 1996), pp. 149–61.

2 See chapter 9, above.

3 For an extended account of Spalding and his *History*, see Alistair Tilson, 'Who Now Reads Spalding?,' *English Studies in Canada* (December 1991), 469–80.

4 William Spalding, *A History of English Literature* (Edinburgh: Oliver and Boyd, 1853), p. 409.

5 William Spalding, *The History of English Literature*, revised 14th edition (Edinburgh: Oliver and Boyd, 1877), p. 382.

6 See *The St Andrews University Calendar* (1875–76), p. 97 (Rhetoric and English Literature M A Pass Examination, November 1874).

7 Professor W. A. Knight, *Memoir of John Nichol* (Glasgow, James MacLehose, 1896), pp. 58, 121.

8 *Ibid.*, p. 114.

9 *Ibid.*, pp. 96–7.

10 *Ibid.*, p. 140.

11 *Ibid.*, pp. 151–2.

12 *Ibid.*, p. 276.

13 The italics in the letter are Nichol's own. The letter is part of the Troxell Collection in the Special Collections section of Princeton University Library.

14 John Nichol, *American Literature, An Historical Sketch, 1620–1880* (Edinburgh: A. & C. Black, 1882), p. vi.

15 *Ibid.*, pp. 2, 7, 12.

16 See *The Literary World* (Boston: 24 March 1883), p. 88. Unsigned review. *The American Catalogue, 1876–1884* records no American edition of Nichol's book.

17 See *Dictionary of Literary Biography*, vol. 49 (Detroit: Gale Research Co., 1986), pp. 412–14.

18 *The Literary World*, p. 88.

19 C. F. Richardson, 'The Perspective of American Literature,' *Andover Review* (November 1884), p. 480.

20 *Ibid.*, pp. 480–1.

21 J. J. Halsey, 'American Literature,' *The Dial* (February 1887), p. 244.

22 Pattee's article was reprinted in Norman Foerster (ed.), *The Reinterpretation of American Literature* (New York: Harcourt, Brace, 1928), pp. 3–22. See p. 6.

23 Is this why by 1935 Pattee appears to have erased Nichol from his memory? In the Preface to his *The First Century of American Literature 1770–1870* (New York and London: D. Appleton-Century, Co., 1935) he makes no reference to Nichol and describes C. F. Richardson as the 'maker of the first systematic presentation of American literary history' and 'a pioneer scholar'.

24 See Robert E. Spiller, 'Those Early Days: a Personal Memoir,' in *The Oblique Light: Studies in Literary History and Biography* (New York: Macmillan, 1968), p. 258.

CHAPTER 10

Scottish Rhetoric and the formation of literary studies in nineteenth-century England

Linda Ferreira-Buckley

'[I]n *Literis Anglicis*, Blair is the man.' So declared Stephen Potter in 1937 in *The Muse in Chains*, his playfully adroit account of literary studies in the British Isles. Although 'Kames and Campbell are of the greatest importance in the history of criticism', Hugh Blair 'was the kind that begets Movements, and enlists Followers.'[1] Today such claims are apt to be met with scepticism, but in the late eighteenth and early nineteenth centuries, the name of Hugh Blair and his fellow Enlightenment Scots had indeed been at the centre of discussions of literary studies in the English-speaking world.[2] Dwelling in Aberdeen, Glasgow, St Andrews and especially Edinburgh – the 'second Athens' or 'Athens of the North', as the southernmost Scottish city was called – these and other Scottish intellectuals formulated the theories and rules by which belletristic discourse would be composed and judged, disseminating them in university and public lectures and organizations, as well as in books and periodicals. In the last century and a half, however, their reputations have declined, their influence has been lamented, and their accomplishments rarely celebrated, while Englishmen are presumed to have invented institutional English Studies in England. In recent years, the Scots have been acknowledged by literary historians writing about the emergence of English studies, but these scholars too have failed to see the extent of the Scottish presence in England.[3] In this chapter, I shall argue that the Scots bear primary responsibility for institutionalizing English literature, first in eighteenth-century Scotland and subsequently in early Victorian England.

My argument is not only that the Scots, through their texts and educational establishments, shaped the institution of English Studies in England, but also that in doing so they drew upon classical rhetoric and transferred to vernacular literary studies offices formerly entrusted to rhetoric and her sister arts in the trivium, thus broadening the audience for ancient learning. This chapter focuses on early English courses in London's first two universities, University College and King's College. Scottish universities trained many of the first administrators and professors (of English and Rhetoric and of related subjects like Logic and Moral Philosophy); Scottish theorists like Blair, Campbell, Smith, David Masson and George Jardine provided the bases for the curriculums and lectures; and Scottish rhetorical treatises were used as class texts and set books, and were awarded as prize books.[4] The chapter closes by touching upon other vehicles by which Scottish belletristic pedagogy was disseminated in England, thereby encouraging less formal forums for literary study.

Many of the men who exercised a formidable influence over the development of English Studies had attended the High School of Edinburgh, whose rigorous classical course of study typified good Scottish secondary schools. Overseen by the Town Council, the High School – called the Tounis School to signify its civic affiliation – sought to prepare boys for university. A city-appointed committee recommended in 1709 that the curriculum emphasize classical rhetoric, counsel that was heeded as students were increasingly immersed in classical theory and practice. Students read a great deal of Latin prose and poetry, attending not only to style but ferreting out political and moral lessons as well. Students wrote abstracts and analyses of ancient and modern works, practised double translations, prosing and other standard stylistic exercises, all of which were preparatory to composing more original discourses. The most senior boys were entrusted with delivering orations to the academy, the culmination of a student's formal work. Extracurricular activities provided further opportunities to read, write and speak. Students were encouraged to avail themselves of the many texts, contemporary as well as classical, available in the school's library. Prior to the nineteenth century, boys studied English only by way of the classical languages. Over the eighteenth century the Town Council and faculty did not lose their faith that civic responsibilities were best met by those schooled in the classical tradition.

Scottish universities sought to build upon this foundation although not a few undergraduates arrived without a secure grounding in the ancient languages. The curriculum was classical, as students were educated in the trivium of Logic, Grammar, and Rhetoric, though not always under those appellations. Students gained proficiency in composing and analyzing Greek, Latin and English through a variety of grammatical exercises, including imitation, varying, paraphrasing, prosing and transposition.[5] The Scots were steeped in the classical tradition but also committed to reworking it to suit modern conditions. John Stevenson, Professor of Logic and Metaphysics at Edinburgh from 1730 to 1775, introduced Blair and others to the study of English literature during his long tenure at Edinburgh.[6] Alongside Homer's *Iliad*, Longinus's *On the Sublime*, and Aristotle's *Poetics* and other classics, he considered the work of such contemporaries as Addison, Dryden and Pope.[7] Prescriptions for correctness were introduced by rule and reinforced by literary example. It was for Stevenson's class that Blair wrote the essay, 'On the Beautiful', which was read in public on the close of the session. Blair himself treasured the composition throughout his life 'as the first earnest of his future fame', according to Lionel Thomas Berguer, one of his editors, and indeed it served as the genesis of his later work on taste and literature.[8]

Blair's concern with criticism and literature was hardly unique. The collection of prize-winning essays (some composed in Latin, some in English) written for Stevenson between 16 April 1737 and 27 April 1750 indicates the university's broad commitment to literary studies as a means of character development. What's more, students learned to associate eloquence of expression and the ability to derive pleasure from it as an indication of the Good. Although many of the essays treat classical subjects – the celebration of Greek and Roman letters was a commonplace – modern literary subjects are well represented as students wrote about the works of such authors as Milton, Cowley and Addison. They also expounded on such themes as style, friendship, conversation and taste. According to a student composition dated May 1740, taste is 'that Faculty of the Mind, which distinguishes all the most concealed Faults and nicest Perfections in Writing'. It is a discriminatory faculty, 'less the Effect of Genius than Judgment', hence one instilled by education and nurtured by exercise. The young author, David Clerk, observes 'Taste is now become the fashionable word in the fashionable world.' Taste indeed persisted as a popular topic at university, serving as the subject of long essays like Clerk's and earning frequent mention in essays on other topics as well.

Taste, delicacy, correctness, criticism, style, righteousness – indeed the entire constellation of concerns attendant on belletristic rhetoric – gained even wider currency in mid century with the advent of Blair's university course and publications. (We can take Blair as our lodestar, for not only was his work the most widely disseminated and most frequently cited, the belletristic theories of such other Scottish literati as Campbell, Kames and Smith accord with the major premises and broad outline of Blair's project, at least for our purposes.[9]) In these and other discourses Scottish theorists reformulated the classical rhetorical theory they studied at school and university in light of contemporary philosophy. (According to Lloyd Bitzer, Campbell's *Philosophy of Rhetoric* is a reaction to Hume's scepticism.) They counselled their students not to neglect classical theory – the necessary grounding of all literary study – but rather to advance it through scientific investigations since they believed, as Roger Emerson has written, that rationally-grounded knowledge could be found and used to improve the human condition.[10]

By slighting invention, eighteenth-century belletristic rhetoric shifted focus from production to reception. Blair's work, for instance, was designed for 'those who would improve their literary powers; and those who merely wish to improve their critical judgment'.[11] This shift, a response to the growing availability of print, encouraged the proliferation of literary criticism in the nineteenth century. And thus Blair's course offered 'a critical examination of the most distinguished species of composition both in prose and verse', for in following the French belletristic rhetoricians, Scottish rhetoric changed education significantly by positing that all discourse – whether oratory, history, poetry, or drama – stems from polite letters and belongs to rhetorical studies. In this view, 'Poetry indeed is properly no other than a particular mode or form of certain branches of oratory.' Eloquence, according to Campbell, is 'the grand art of communication, not of ideas only, but of sentiments, passions, dispositions, and purposes'.[12] The study of rhetoric and belles lettres was not limited to teaching one to persuade, then, but now also 'to enlighten the understanding, to please the imagination, to move the passions, or to influence the will'. Invoking Cicero and Quintilian, he adds that it is '[t]hat art or talent by which discourse is adapted to its end'.[13] Subsequent English discussions about the powers of literature devolve from claims made for belletristic rhetoric.

The Scottish literati deemed the English language worthy of serious, university-level study and claimed for the study of the finest vernacular literature benefits heretofore reserved for classical texts. (True, Renaissance rhetorics such as Abraham Fraunce's *Arcadian Rhetoric, or the Precepts of Rhetoric made Plain by Examples* (1584), Thomas Blount's *Academie of Eloquence* (1654), and George Puttenham's *Art of English Poesie* (1589) had drawn examples from the literature of English writers to illustrate the lesson at hand, but they had had little effect on the *institutional* study of language.[14]) Intellectual descendants of Francis Hutcheson, the literati believed, as Blair puts it, 'the exercise of taste is, in its native tendency, moral and purifying'. Moreover, they came to see taste as an act of cognition, as Barbara Warnick explains in *The Sixth Canon*.[15] In Blair's words:

There are indeed few good dispositions of any kind with which the improvement of taste is not more or less connected. A cultivated taste increases sensibility to all the tender and human passions, by giving them frequent exercise while it tends to weaken the more violent and fierce emotions.

> These polish'd arts have humaniz'd mankind,
> Soften'd the rude, and calm'd the boist'rous mind

The elevated sentiments and high examples which poetry, eloquence, and history, are often bringing under our view, naturally tend to nourish in our minds public spirit, the love of glory, contempt of external fortune, and the admiration of what is truly illustrious and great.[16]

With taste at its centre, instruction in rhetoric became not simply instruction in effective communication but a vehicle for the transmission of culture. The literati also called attention to the practical benefits accruing to those aspiring to professional and social advancement.

Throughout the eighteenth and the early nineteenth centuries, then, students at Scottish universities acquired knowledge of and came to value both classical and contemporary literatures, especially English literature. What's more, literary topics were often taken up by the myriad societies, clubs and publications that helped to sustain the fabric of polite society, knitting together the intellectual and social, town and gown.[17] Appreciative of this study and praising its formative influence, graduates of Scottish schools and universities went on to assume leadership roles in the north; others carried the Scottish influence southward. They brought with them the assumption that English language and literature were academically worthy and morally improving.

Wishing to emulate the Scottish universities at home and the German ones abroad, Glasgow poet Thomas Campbell proposed a London university in an open letter to Lord Henry Brougham in a February 1825 issue of *The Times*. England had not established a new university since the founding of Cambridge in the thirteenth century, and planners argued that Oxford and Cambridge, however celebrated, neglected the practical needs of the country; modern times required an institution designed to meet its challenges.[18] Commencing instruction in 1828, University College (or London University, as it was first called) was home to England's first post-secondary English Department.

Serving as President of University College for its first decades, Brougham was constant in his support of the English classes, which he conceived of as courses in critical literacy.[19] He wished to encourage the habit of wide reading (all the belles lettres would be included), for such reading was, in his view, a precondition of all national reform. Born and reared in Scotland, Brougham had attended Edinburgh High School and the University of Edinburgh, and considered the education in letters he had received there as a model. He excelled in the university's debating club and was an active participant in organizations like the Speculative Society, which often took up literary topics. (Brougham credited Edinburgh Juvenile Literary Society with teaching him oratory.[20]) The specific shape of the first English Literature courses can be traced to Scottish belletristic Rhetoric and were a marked contrast to the traditional offerings of Cambridge and Oxford, where Latin and Greek still monopolized the curriculum and examinations but had lost their connection with preparing students for public life. Graduates of the northern universities comprise a significant percentage of those founding and administering University College, significant because they brought to the enterprise assumptions about education that were more egalitarian and progressive than those of graduates of Oxford and Cambridge, whose commitments tended to be more traditional and conservative.[21]

Brougham's candidate, Thomas Dale, became the first Professor of English Language and Literature in England, where he offered two courses: 'Lectures on English Literature' and 'Principles and Practice of English Composition', whose tripartite division into the history of language, philosophy of language, and principles of speaking and writing was modelled on Hugh Blair's course. The Reverend Dale had studied the classics and divinity at Corpus Christi College, Cambridge, where he was awarded an MA. As was typical of the time, Dale's facility in the vernacular was learned by way of classical training, but when he taught students privately to supplement his income, he looked to Scotland for a philosophy of letters, drawing upon the work of Campbell, Kames and Blair. Dale's union of religion and literature, like Blair's, addressed moral rather than theological issues likely to offend his audience, achieving what Blair's biographer Robert Schmitz calls 'the eloquence of cultured moral comfort'.[22] Blair's literary theories and the examples he chose to illustrate them expressed a safe middle ground that suited well the temperament of an institution which aimed to be non-sectarian, yet sought to represent itself as ethically principled. The purposeful use of

literature to inculcate desirable virtues like goodness, loyalty, patriot-
ism and mental discipline – formerly the hallmark of Greek and Latin
programmes – is ascribed to the vernacular as well as to the classical.
The catholicity of belletristic rhetoric allowed it to be adopted and
adapted by the range of men who first taught English Literature.

The inaugural address of the English professorship, 'Course upon
the Principles and Practices of English Composition', reveals the philosophy that drove both the language and literature courses, the latter
beginning on January 1829 upon completion of the former, the language
course providing the underpinnings for any study of written texts. The
overall pattern and the particular topics followed Blair. Dale deplores
the ignorance of the vernacular that students in England, '[h]owever
conversant with studies that are strictly classical', often bring to university, public and professional life. The cause of such 'deficiency'? Dale
blasphemes: ' "Youths," it is erroneously argued, "must learn the ancient
or foreign languages from tutors, while an acquaintance with their own
is spontaneously and inevitably attained; – in this they require neither
instruction nor assistance – reading and observation will be found of
themselves sufficient to accomplish all." '[23] (Dale also disputes the claim
that English grammar shares essential features with that of Latin or
Greek, a theory whereby English is seen as degenerative of the classical
paradigm.) English literature merits, even requires, instruction.

[T]o what other cause, than the want of early attention to the perusal of
English authors and the practice of English composition, can we attribute the
familiar fact – that the classical student, when summoned to sustain his part in
the active intercourse of society, is so often found to speak in his own language
with hesitation, and to write with difficulty? Wherefore is he thus embarrassed
and perplexed, but because he feels that his powers of expression are altogether inadequate to embody in suitable form, the conceptions of his mind;
and that unless he will hoard his intellectual stores like the gold of a miser,
for his own selfish and solitary gratification, his only alternative is to occupy
a much lower place in public estimation, than to which he is justly entitled?[24]

To be sure, classical studies once schooled men in what were indisput-
ably the reigning languages of civic and scholarly discourse, a claim
that no longer held. The exigence for studying the vernacular literature is made by way of the shortcomings of students with only classical
training. Scholarly accomplishments do not release one from the moral
responsibility to contribute to the public good.

He goes on to justify the study of grammar and style as essential to
interpretation by citing George Campbell: ' "Grammar, in its general

principles", observes the author of that invaluable work, The Philosophy of Rhetoric, "has a close connection with the understanding".'[25] Students would then examine a variety of literary compositions, with the instructor 'explaining the various figures of speech, commencing with that first-born of fancy, Simile, and proceeding next to others of the same class, Metaphor, Personification, Allegory, and the rest; constantly illustrating the misemployment, as well as the proper and legitimate use of each, by appropriate examples, selected as far as practicable from the writers of established reputation'.[26] Excerpts from literary selections also comprise the last third of the course, with the instructor 'delineating the character, analysing the constituents, and exemplifying the employment of various styles'.[27]

'[T]o think with freedom and correctness' is 'immediately connected with,' indeed 'dependent on, the study of literature in general, and specifically of English literature'.[28] The term 'literature' here refers to all educated letters; he wishes to use them as rhetorical models to lay bare the 'construction of thought' therein. Literary theory is thus architechtonic, providing a framework by which to discipline a student's programme of reading. Dale is invoking the design of Scottish belletristic rhetoric. Students

will not be long in discovering, that regard and admiration are far from being exclusively due to the great masters of antiquity; that their own literature can boast of writers equally eminent in almost every department of composition; and that, if claims of a language on our attention are to be decided by the number, the variety, and excellence of the authors who have employed it, the English language may fearlessly challenge comparison with any other, living or dead.[29]

Professors of Greek and Latin, long used to their discipline reigning unchallenged, at least in academic circles, were unlikely to be won over by Dale's insistence that

if the Greek and Latin writers, owing to the superiority of their language over ours in variety, flexibility, and softness, have surpassed us in ease, grace, and elegance of diction; that advantage is fully counterbalanced by the animation, vigour, and energy of expression conspicuous in our own authors, and still more by a magnificence of conception in them altogether unequalled by the most valued relics of antiquity.[30]

From the very first lecture, then, the study of English would threaten entrenched interests, in this case those who preserved and perpetuated the classical tradition.[31]

Following the Scottish pattern, the Literature course per se began with an extensive review of the language lectures. After this review came a historical survey of English letters and two disquisitions of a more general nature: 'On the present State and Prospects of English literature' and 'The Connection between Literature and Morals'. Clearly, the approach and terminology bear Blair's imprint. When on the completion of the academic year students competed for university-wide academic honors, first prize for the best English essay was a 'Shakespeare, well bound' or 'Blair's *Lectures*'.[32]

The study of English language and literature threatened those who championed classical studies, for under pressure from the professors of Greek, Latin, and Mathematics, Dale resigned. Archival records suggest that objections suffered by the English professor came not from university administrators, politicians, or faculty at large, but rather from professors of Greek and Latin, who worried that their turf was being invaded (particularly objectionable was Dale's decision to include principles of translation); that student enrollment would decrease in more traditional courses as students opted for one they assumed would be less formidable; that the subject was not truly worthy of university-level study.

Dale's successor, Alexander Blair, a Scotsman with a degree from Glasgow who had been Thomas Campbell's earlier preference,[33] assumed the professorship of 'English Philology, Rhetoric, and English Literature', which he held from 1830 to 1836. As a graduate of Glasgow University, where he studied both logic and rhetoric under George Jardine, Alexander Blair instructed the junior class in the basics of rhetoric and the principles of English grammar and instructed the senior class in the principles of general rhetorical style. The 'principal object' of English Literature, he said, is 'to make the student acquainted with what has been written in the language, & a little to guide him in judging of it'. Twenty preparatory lectures outlined the history of the literature and language in the British Isles 'from the earliest to the present time: – giving general views of both, in connection with great political causes, the state of manners, etc.' such that '[S]triking illustrative extracts' drew connections among style, content, and historical context. He too used Hugh Blair's *Lectures on Rhetoric and Belles Lettres* as the class text.[34] As Franklin Court describes him, Blair 'was a budding philologist who envisioned English literature, much like his eighteenth-century namesake did, as primarily a vehicle for teaching taste'.[35] No trifling matter, taste contributed to the high seriousness with which letters were studied.

Just so, the 'Mathetes' letter he and John Wilson had sent to Coleridge's *Friend* called for a great teacher – 'an enlightened contemporary writer' – who would work through the vernacular to uplift society.[36] Another course, Blair promised, would more explicitly 'treat the principles of Composition'. After modeling rhetorical analysis, Alexander Blair would ask students to write original compositions, with pedagogical commitments learned from Jardine.[37]

Extant course materials and examinations suggest that Blair's successor, Henry Rogers, was also influenced by the connection of Scottish belletrism with moral philosophy, although philological and historical study was becoming more prevalent in the curriculum, in part because such approaches lent themselves more readily to examination and because prestige was beginning to be increasingly associated with research rather than with teaching. Motivated by what he feared were the obsolescent but still powerful institutions of Oxford and Cambridge, Rogers became a frequent contributor to the *Edinburgh Review*, whose attacks on the commitments of the ancient universities to classical studies and whose championing of the northern universities indicate the seriousness of this issue to British intellectuals. Scottish periodicals like the *Review* were eager to publish essays that derogated the uselessness of classical education as practised in England while arguing the advantages of Scottish approaches.

The commitment to Scottish belletristic studies continued with yet another Scottish professor of English at University College, London. David Masson had been educated at the Aberdeen Grammar School, at Marischal College and at Edinburgh University. He was Professor of Language and Literature at University College, London, from 1853 until 1865, at which time he returned to his beloved Scotland to become a professor of Rhetoric and English Literature at the University of Edinburgh, where he was to remain happily for the next thirty years. His magisterial productivity and appeal as a lecturer would do much to advance the cause of English Studies at University College. Under Masson's guidance, the junior and senior offerings in English thrived. The junior class was 'A Course on the History, Structure and Idiom of the English Language, and on the History of English Literature'. The senior class, taught according to the belletristic rhetorical model under which Masson was himself schooled as a young man in Scotland, was 'A systematic Course of Rhetoric, illustrated by critical Studies of the more remarkable English Authors'. The course had four units: 'I. Historical Literature. II. Expository or Didactic Literature. III. Eloquence and Oratorical Literature. IV. Poetry and the Literature of Prose Fiction'. The fee for the course, which included exercises in composition, was £3.[38] Masson's priorities, passions and procedures are manifest in his final course examinations, which indicate that his concerns altered little over his dozen years in London. The following represent the range.

Students enrolled in the senior rhetoric course in 1853–54 were asked eleven questions, including these:

1. State the general division of Literature into kinds or departments adopted in the arrangement of the Course; and explain the grounds of that division. Under which heads would you rank the following passages, intrinsically considered; and why? [passages of prose and poetry follow]

3. If you were to draw up an account of the social state of any country at any given period – say Portugal at the present time – where would you begin, and how would you proceed? Is there a general scheme or method useful as a mechanical help in such cases, to make up for the deficiency of literary art; and, indeed, instinctively adopted, more or less, by the best literary artists? State the principle of such a scheme; and refer, in connexion with it, to Mr. Macaulay's survey of the social state of England before the Revolution.

6. What did the ancient rhetoricians discuss under the head of 'Invention'; and what was the nature and use of the Topics in ancient Rhetoric?

8. Characterize the style of Burke's writings and speeches.

9. State Aristotle's theory of the nature of Poetry, and contrast it with that of Bacon. Test Aristotle's theory upon the following passage from Spenser. – [nine-line passage follows]

The twelve questions seniors were asked the following academic year included the following:

4. Name the more eminent of the Scottish metaphysical writers; and characterise briefly the expository style of each writer named.

10. What is the true theory of Verse in relation to Poetry? What is Wordsworth's theory on the subject? Apply these theories to the following passages: –

> (1) For Rhetoric – he could not ope
>   His mouth, but out there flew a trope.
>   And when he happened to break off
>   I' the middle of his speech, or cough,
>   He had hard words ready to show why,

> And tell what rules he did it by;
> Else when with greatest art he spoke,
> You'd think he talked like other folk. – Butler.

(2) The splendour falls on castle-walls,
>   And snowy summits old in story;
> The long light shakes across the lakes,
>   And the wild cataract leaps in glory.
> Blow, bugle, blow; set the wild echoes flying.
> Answer, echoes, answer – dying, dying, dying.
>   – Tennyson.

11. Name in chronological order, the chief English writers of prose-fiction; characterise Dickens and Thackeray; and state in what respects these two writers represent opposite tendencies in the present literature of prose-fiction.

Students enrolled in the junior course in 1853–54 took a two-part examination, the first in language and grammar, which queried students in tradition and current matters, including new philological knowledge; and the second in literature. Students were expected to demonstrate expertise in literature in response to these questions:

1. Divide the history of British literature into periods, as in the Course; and mention the most conspicuous names belonging to each period. Give more exactly the dates of Chaucer, Skelton, Spenser, Bacon, and Shakespeare.
3. What was the nature of Skelton's literary activity; and in what respect may he be taken as the literary representative of the period to which he belonged?
4. Paraphrase the following sentences from Bacon's Essay on *Friendship*, so as to evolve the full meaning of every clause. [Passage follows.]
5. From what poet do you judge the following lines to be taken; and in what respects is it characteristic of him? [nine-line passage follows]

And in 1854–55 the following were included on the literature examination:

2. Turn into prose the following passage from Hamlet, arranging the words so as to make the syntax and meaning more obvious: [sixteen-line excerpt follows.] Explain the phrases 'this side of our known world', 'law and heraldry', 'stood seized of', 'moiety competent', 'comart', and 'carriage of the article designed'.
3. In the following passage from the same play (addressed by Hamlet to his father's ghost), explain the phrases 'fools of nature', 'shake our

disposition', and 'reaches of our souls'; and state in what respect the whole passage, and, in particular, the first in the foregoing phrases, is to be regarded as characteristic of Shakespeare's habitual manner of thinking and feeling.

5. What general principle, applicable to the history of literature at all times and in all countries, may be deduced from an observation of the state of English literature between 1640 and 1660?

7. What were the characteristics and peculiarities of the dramatic literature of the Restoration?

8. Characterise Dryden's genius, and indicate generally the nature of his influence on English poetry.

Senior rhetoric exams were designed on the belletristic–classical model in which Masson was himself schooled, in which the term 'literary arts' refers to educated or literate texts generally. They studied oratory alongside texts written for the eye, as was common practice in literature classes. Masson queried students about types of writing on the assumption that innate qualities differentiated them. Students identified and discussed distinguishing characteristics of prose and poetic types, examining large concepts like genre as well as the smaller patterns of paragraphs, sentence, phrase and word. They were expected to analyse style, to identify tropes and to discuss their use and effect. Students defined rhetoric, discussed its canons, wrote about its key theorists and practitioners, both ancient and modern. Analysis prepared students to read their world: students were to read literature as living documents; a man's style reveals his character and a nation's letters its character. As did Blair, Masson attended more closely to analysis of discourse than to production on the assumption that skill in reading fostered skill in composition. The practice also reflects an increasingly print-based culture.

Many of the same concerns are manifest in the junior literature examination. Additionally, the junior class took up ethnology, the comparative, 'scientific' study of human beings, which required students to examine discourse to uncover the characteristic spirit or attitudes of a community's literary production, training that presumably contributed to their senior studies as well. Students were asked to translate archaic passages and render poetry into prose, exercises common in western rhetorical education. Masson's philological interests are Janus-faced, of course, pointing not only to the grammatical analysis characteristic of standard classical exercises and to Blair's close analysis of stylistic concerns like syntax and diction, but also to the German advances in linguistics that would come to dominate English studies by the end of the century. On the other hand, Masson's examinations register changes: he treats the historical data surrounding a text more systematically; he discusses prose fiction with more assurance; he seems eager for students to be acquainted with the whole sweep of literary history.

King's College, London, was established in 1831, the Anglican response to that 'Godless Institution of Gower Street', University College. Although two of its founders, H. J. Rose and Edward Copleston, would have preferred to have the classics dominate the curriculum to halt the utilitarianism they so despised, they conceded that like its rival institution, King's College depended upon a constituency intent upon studying modern subjects deemed 'useful'. The archives of King's College register the influence of Scottish belletristic rhetoric on English Studies, although the institution's affiliation with the Anglican Church allied it closely with Oxford and Cambridge, and hence less with the northern universities. In forming King's, the Council studied closely the curriculum and governance of leading universities on the continent, America and Scotland, where the appropriateness of studying English was non-controversial. The influence of Scottish rhetoric, of course, had long since monopolized the language curriculums of Yale, Columbia, Edinburgh and Glasgow, where English literature was taken up as part of the study in rhetoric, moral philosophy, humanities and occasionally logic and elocution. (At Edinburgh, the report notes, no one can attain the MA without taking the course in rhetoric and belles lettres.)

From its opening, both the university and school at King's College offered courses in English, designating them mandatory for full-time students, and an annual prize was awarded in the subject. While classical study continued to be revered, it could not help but be somewhat diminished in a curriculum of which modern subjects were also part. Proficiency in English and familiarity with its literature (whereby a student availed himself of benefits such study bestows) was an explicit part of the institutional mission. In an address on the opening of King's College School, the principal defended the rise of proprietary grammar schools and their more modern course of study, careful however to maintain that a 'sound classical education' like that offered by the public grammar schools is 'the best foundation upon which to erect the superstructure, not only of polite, but of practically useful knowledge'. He cautions, however, that 'such knowledge, however accurate and extensive, is but the means towards an end; and even the habit thus acquired will be useful only so far as it is brought to bear upon practical subjects'.[39] King's College takes as its mission 'furnishing [students] the means of discharging with credit the business of the world, while, at the same time, we store their minds with resources, which may afford intellectual amusement, and innocent pleasures during the hours of recreation; training them, in a word, in dependence on the Divine blessing, to become useful subjects of the state, and intelligent, honourable members of society'.[40]

Vernacular language and literature were bound up with the institutional mission of developing good, loyal and productive citizens. Because of its affiliation with England's educational establishment, King's College, unlike University College, never opposed the practices of the old schools, nor did it proclaim any admiration for Scottish practices. Nonetheless, King's College faculty were well aware of the curriculum in place at its rival institution. Dale's inaugural lecture was printed and made available, and his instructional plans were advertised; so too the secular university's practices were frequently before the public as they were alternately praised and pilloried in press and pamphlet.

Unable to secure a suitable candidate for the English professorship (the Charter mandated that all faculty members be Anglicans, the effect of which was to disqualify most graduates of Scottish universities), and short on operating funds, founders first entrusted the teaching of English literature and language to the professors of classics and mathematics, Joseph Anstice and T. G. Hall. Although founders were apparently unwilling to sanction the practice by official vote, Anstice lectured on English literature for an hour on Tuesdays, beginning with the formation of the English language before moving on to 'the general merits of the principal English authors, and the times in which they flourished'. He then presented to the class 'select portions of the works of the best English writers'.[41] These were complemented by Hall's history lectures. When Anstice died unexpectedly, the Council sought to make the vernacular language and literature a more substantial part of the curriculum.

The charge fell to Thomas Dale, who, beginning in 1835, taught 'English Literature and Composition'. Based in Hugh Blair's belletristic rhetoric, the curriculum replicated his offerings at University College. (Between professorships, Dale had privately schooled students in rhetoric and belles lettres.) Dale combined a course of lectures on the 'Origin and Formation of the English Language' with '"History of English

Literature",' 'illustrating the subject by appropriate specimens from the most eminent authors of each successive period'.[42] During the second term, he held forth on the history of the Middle Ages, 'noting especially the rise and progress of Literature, together with the causes that favoured the advancement of civil liberty, and the development and diffusion of religious light'. Dale endorses Blair's faith in the efficacious social and moral effects of belles lettres, though both he and Blair make clear that such study cannot substitute for religious instruction. Both insist on close textual analysis as key to textual understanding.

Excerpts from English literature illustrate the principles of proper style either in their observance or in the breech. Students were called upon to explain the nature of an error's marring a poetic or prose selection and to correct it. Arbiters of correctness were not above censure. At the close of the academic year the junior class took an English Language Examination, in which they were asked the following:

15. What are your objections to –
    1. The character of taste, when brought to its most perfect state. Blair.
    2. Nothing is more universal than the relish of beauty. Blair.
    3. It is argued the most extreme rarity. Hume.
    4. Delights of a much more inferior and unprofitable nature. Addison.
    5. No man had ever less friends and more enemies. OF TWO EVILS CHOOSE THE LEAST.
    State the causes of the errors, and correct them.[43]

Inspired by the message of the finest literature and trained to discern the appropriateness of its style (Blair insists the two are linked), students would come to recognize and shun the superficial attractiveness of false ornament that might tempt them to fall prey to vices made appealing.

On his retirement from King's College, Dale prepared two editions of Blair's *Lectures on Rhetoric and Belles Lettres*, which help to explain the philosophy that guides his own teaching. Although he compensates for what he considers Blair's deficiencies, attending especially to early vernacular literature to augment Blair's neoclassical selections, he wholeheartedly affirms Blair's approach. In his introduction to the Blair edition Dale observes in his discussion of Alfred:

It could not but occur to this penetrating and judicious prince that the obstacle most materially impeding the mental and therefore the moral improvement of his people, was the existence of one kind of literature for the educated classes, in other words, the ecclesiastics, and another for the uneducated, a term at that time almost synonymous and coextensive with the laity. He needed not to be taught the lesson by others which he was foremost to teach them, that whenever popular improvement is neglected, through the vanity or prejudice of a chosen few, the injustice that is done to the community will infallibly work out its own retribution, both in the degradation of the national mind, and the detriment of the public weal.[44]

Here again Dale insists that study of the vernacular language and literature is a means to virtue, public as well as private. He invokes Blair's promise that an education in vernacular letters was essential to a society struggling to right its political, social and moral order. English literature reflects the moral rectitude of its people, thus providing a beacon to righteous conduct. Throughout his teaching career, Dale pushed the Scottish plan.

Similar themes are taken up, but more ardently, by F. D. Maurice, who inherited the course. More so than at University College, English Studies at King's College benefited from the conviction that the vernacular language and literature were linked to national allegiance.[45] Maurice's ideas and practices (including close analysis of texts) would later secure a place for English Studies in two other institutions with which he had strong connections, Queen's College, London, and the Working Men's College.[46] Subsequently, Henry Morley served as an evening lecturer (his Unitarianism disqualified him from serving on the regular faculty), offering two courses, 'The Origin and Structure of the English Language, Illustrated by Our Literature from the Earliest Times to the Invention of Printing' and 'The Principles of Composition, Illustrated by the History of English Literary Composition from the Appearance of Sir Philip Sidney's "Defence of Poetry" to the Establishment of the Edinburgh Review'. Morley too combined language study with 'literary' analyses of very different types of texts. On Masson's departure for the University of Edinburgh, Morley assumed the English professorship at University College, London. Although University College and King's College maintained distinct identities, their exchange of faculty and curriculum ensured that they were mutually influential. At both London universities literature was studied in order to achieve a number of goals: excellence in using the vernacular, proficiency in composition, mastery of broad cultural discourse to inculcate national pride and cultural values, and enhancement of aesthetic appreciation *in the service of virtue.*

The appointments of other English professors at London universities confirm the Scottish influence on English education in vernacular letters. In letters of application, candidates graduated from Scottish universities detail their rhetorical training; not a few cite the influence of Blair, Campbell and Kames. In letters written on their behalf, recommenders under whom candidates had studied detail the pervasive influence of Scottish belletristism, an influence also seen on professors in the sciences and philosophy.[47] (It is worth noting too that works by Blair, Campbell, Kames and others – to which early English professors make reference – were available in the libraries of University College and King's College in order that students might pursue belletristic studies independently.) I do not mean to suggest that these courses drew slavishly upon Scottish precedents. Rather, these early English Studies courses were broadly based in belletristic rhetoric, whose principles and practices they variously drew upon, adapted, developed, sometimes disputed.

Other vehicles conveyed the Scottish influence on developing conceptions of 'English Literature': mechanics institutes, literary societies and books for secondary schools and home tutorials. Eighteenth-century Scottish texts were reprinted and revised. During the nineteenth century, Blair's *Lectures*, for instance, exerted considerable influence in Britain, going through twenty-six complete and fifty-two abridged editions. Victorians also adapted Scottish belletristic rhetoric to nineteenth-century needs in developing new books like Alexander Jamieson's *A Grammar of Rhetoric and Polite Literature; comprehending the principles of language and style, the elements of taste and criticism; with rules for the study of composition and eloquence.* Its influence also manifests itself in reading anthologies like Lindley Murray's *Introduction to the English Reader; or, a selection of pieces in prose and poetry; calculated to improve the younger class of learners, in reading; and to imbue their minds with love of virtue* (1799), which drew one-third of its selections from Blair's works and saw nearly three dozen British editions by 1865.[48] An American expatriate settled in London, Murray was devoted to Blair and to the Scottish Enlightenment ideals he embodied. He even drew the epigraph for his enormously popular *Grammar* from Blair's *Rhetoric*.

Such books were popular in establishments like the London Mechanics' Institute, founded in 1823, one of five hundred such establishments that were to populate England by 1850.[49] While many Mechanics'

Institutes failed, others flourished by delivering lectures to workingmen (most often skilled craftsmen, shopkeepers, and other professional and commercial people) or becoming more popular centres of culture. Some provided serious study in a variety of subjects, others sponsored more casual lectures, especially on 'literary' subjects, leading to charges that they produced dilettantes.[50] What did the workers hope to gain from such lectures? Chartist Thomas Cooper, himself an artisan, recalls in his autobiography the pleasures he derived from reading great works of literature and testifies to Scottish belletristic rhetoric's influence in shaping that experience: 'Blair's "Lectures on Rhetoric and Belles Lettres"' was another book that I analysed very closely and laboriously, being determined on acquiring a thorough judgment of style and excellence.'[51] Taking careful and extensive notes, Cooper read a range of literary texts, examining closely passages that he would commit to memory. Extraordinarily disciplined, he woke at three or four in the morning and worked at his studies until seven, at which time he would begin a long day of cobbling shoes. He read as he ate his afternoon meal, resumed his studies when work stopped at eight or nine in the evening, 'and, then, either read or walked about our little room and committed "Hamlet" to memory, or the rhymes of some modern poet, until compelled to go to bed from sheer exhaustion'.[52] Afterwards a schoolmaster and journalist, Cooper lectured evenings for a variety of organizations. He recalls that he

lectured on Milton, and repeated portions of the 'Paradise Lost', or on Shakespeare, and repeated 'Tam o' Shanter'; or I recited the history of England, and set the portraits of great Englishmen before young Chartists, who listened with great interest; . . . [I] made the young men acquainted, elementally, with the knowledge of the time.[53]

It was necessary not only to read widely but to assess that reading – to understand its merits and demerits, both linguistically and morally, the linguistic a window into the moral value of a text. Works like Blair's *Lectures* helped one learn such discrimination, for the approach was accessible and replete with literary excerpts that illustrated the principles under study.

Lectures on literary subjects were also popular among ladies who recognized style as cultural capital. In thirty-two years of teaching in Great Britain, William Banks, who had studied Greek, Logic, and English 'both grammatically and rhetorically' at Glasgow University, modelled his literary course on Blair's *Lectures on Rhetoric and Belles Lettres*.

His lecture series, which followed his *Discourses on Belles Lettres; or Polite Literature. Containing Observations on Genius, Taste, and Criticism; and a Critical Examination of the Most Eminent Authors in Every Department of British Literature*, did not vary significantly over the course of his career. (Banks promised that these lectures would be available to students by subscription.) After delivering this course of public lectures in Glasgow and Edinburgh for many years, he lectured for twelve years in the London area at 'distinguished Ladies' Schools', as well as for the families of gentlemen.[54] After covering fundamental principles like genius, taste and criticism, Banks turned to genres or types of writing, discussing essential features of types of discourse and requiring students to analyse the work of established writers. The underpinnings of his approach are those of belletristic rhetoric: that all polite letters, or educated discourse, share certain essential features and that in studying criticism – the principles of which apply to all textual productions – students strengthen their reasoning abilities and moral character. Banks's summary of his lessons on historical literature indicate the breadth of his approach:

Methods of preserving knowledge before the writing of history. – Origin of historical writing. – In what manner the facts that constitute history were first collected. – History of different kinds according to the nature of the events recorded; and according to the time included in the narrative. – Of the credibility of history. – Means of judging how far it it is worthy of belief. – First writer of history in English. – View of the progress of English history. – What ought to be the style of English history in general. – Critical examination of English historians, from the earliest to the present time. – Advantages of history; and order in which it ought to be read.

Such study was not just academic: criticism was central to education because it had power to shape individual lives and hence whole nations; conversely, 'Its existence as an art marks a degree of refinement in a nation, and great intellectual improvement in the individuals by whom it is practiced.'[55] As early as 1815 *The Times* noted the 'peripatetic philosophers, who give lectures for a guinea each course, in every village near London'.[56]

The discipline of English Literature, in many ways a Scottish creation, flourished in myriad forms, even as its detractors dismissed the study of vernacular belles lettres as trifling study for the subaltern. The belletristic school of rhetoric helped to shape the ideas of Victorian social prophets about education, literature and culture. Why did the lectures of Hugh Blair, who has long functioned as rhetoric's scapegoat, enjoy such a steady reception? Early educators read belletristic rhetoric more complexly than we do: they conceived of taste as an intellectual faculty that disciplined the mind as well as the heart and inculcated civic and personal virtue, points argued persuasively by Barbara Warnick and Sharon Crowley.[57] Blair, whom George Kennedy calls a modern Quintilian, considers Rhetoric and Belles Lettres as the centre of humanities education.[58] Blair's treatise – indeed the assumptions and promises of belletristic rhetoric – was attractive to these reformers, who set about developing a language curriculum grounded in the belief that the faculty of taste was inherent to some degree in all men but that education and social circumstance determined the extent to which that faculty would be developed. In reforming the curriculum – that is, in introducing the people to an English untainted by error and misuse and to the texts that embodied the knowledge and values 'Britain' held dear – educational reformers sought to transform the populace. Instruction in language and literature became not simply instruction in effective communication but a vehicle for the transmission of culture. Blair, as E. D. Hirsch has written, 'gathered and codified for the Scots materials that literate Englishmen had absorbed through the pores'. In an ironic turnabout, educators looked to Scottish belletristic rhetoric, as they pursued educational reforms in England.

Although Englishmen had periodically urged that English Literature be allowed a place in the Oxford and Cambridge curriculums, such proposals were firmly rejected until the end of the nineteenth century, by which time Scottish influences had established English Literature in the curriculums of England's new universities and colleges. Oxbridge's eventual acceptance of the vernacular into the curriculum was a belated act: convinced that such studies were permanent, many reasoned it behoved the two most ancient universities to assume leadership in vernacular studies.[59] As the fortunes of English Studies became secure in the university, 'Literature' became defined more narrowly and in the process lost sight of its historical ties to the rhetorical tradition. (One could argue that as the university became more engaged with research and less centred in pedagogy, its rhetorical past was deemed archaic and irrelevant.) Many Victorian educators, following Blair, make claims for the civilizing 'powers' of 'Literature', and 'Literature' – defined in ever more narrow terms – slowly displaces Rhetoric in the curriculum. Rhetorical theory was itself undergoing change: developments in British 'Rhetoric' were limited primarily to elocution and composition. And although such studies would be granted a place in

the post-secondary institutions until the century's end, rhetorical curricula were much diminished and rightly discredited.

Scottish belletristic rhetoricians brought together major currents
in European theory to better serve modern literary forms, redesigning
pedagogical practices in light of these theories. In so doing, they brought
to the new institutions a vernacular language curriculum that was
informed by classical rhetoric (at a time when the ancient schools were
struggling to reinvigorate a classical curriculum that had become moribund); they brought rhetorical theories that emphasized the growing
importance of print; they recognized the need to emphasize the analysis
as well as the production of discourse. In short, the Scots transformed
the study of language at home and in England.

NOTES

1 Stephen Potter, *The Muse in Chains* (London: Methuen, 1937), pp. 111–12.
   Potter, himself a graduate of Merton College, Oxford, wrote the book
   while a lecturer in English at Birkbeck College, London, itself descended
   from a mechanics institute. He traces the ancestry of the study of 'Eng.
   Lit.' through Scottish educators he dubs 'The Pioneers': Blair, Bain, Aytoun,
   Nichol, Minto, Masson and finally Saintsbury, who inherited Blair's chair
   and who praised Blair's survey of belles lettres as 'ingenious and correct'
   (p. 67).
2 See Douglas Ehninger and James Golden, 'The Intrinsic Sources of Blair's
   Popularity', *Southern Speech Journal* 21 (1955), 12–30; James Golden and
   Douglas Ehninger, 'The Extrinsic Sources of Blair's Popularity', *Southern
   Speech Journal* 22 (1956), 16–32.
   Among the admirers of Blair's *Lectures on Rhetoric and Belles Lettres* were
   David Hume, Thomas Reid, Ben Franklin, Thomas Jefferson and Char-
   lotte Bronte. Blair's reputation as a literary man derived not only from the
   Lectures and his critical works but also from his sermons, which secured the
   favor of George III, Schleiermacher, Jane Austen and Samuel Johnson,
   prompting the last to exclaim uncharacteristically, 'The Scotch write Eng-
   lish wonderfully well' (quoted in Golden and Ehninger 22). Golden and
   Ehninger attempt to ascertain the 'intrinsic' and 'extrinsic' sources of
   Blair's appeal.
3 See D. J. Palmer, *The Rise of English Studies* (London: Oxford University
   Press, 1965); Franklin E. Court, *Institutionalizing English Literature* (Stanford
   University Press, 1992); Robert Crawford, *Devolving English Literature* (Oxford: Clarendon Press, 1992). Palmer relegates the Scots to an appendix.
   My argument departs from that of Franklin Court, whose *Institutionalizing
   English Literature* also tends to diminish the Scottish role by overstating the
   differences between Scottish belletristic rhetoric and subsequent approaches
   to literature. Crawford's review of scholarship in *Devolving English Literature*

observes how scholars have let stand the assumption that 'the actual origins of the subject are in nineteenth-century England' (p. 12).

4 For their kind assistance I am grateful to the library and archival staffs of the University of Edinburgh; the Royal High School, Edinburgh; University College, London; King's College, London; the Education Museum, Leeds University.

5 Winifred Bryan Horner, *Nineteenth-Century Scottish Rhetoric* (Carbondale and Edwardsville: Southern Illinois University Press, 1993), p. 46.

6 Although the University of Edinburgh had forsaken the regenting model in favor of the professorial early in the eighteenth century, what was actually presented in a given course was determined by the professor's interests. Diverse disciplines dealt with the concerns of language and discourse. See Sir Alexander Grant, *The Story of the University of Edinburgh*, 2 vols. (London, 1884); Paul G. Bator, 'The Formation of the Regius Chair of Rhetoric and Belles Lettres at the University of Edinburgh', *Quarterly Journal of Speech* 75 (1989), 40–64.

7 Henry W. Meikle, 'The Chair of Rhetoric and Belles Lettres in the University of Edinburgh', *University of Edinburgh Journal* 13 (1944), 90; Robert M. Schmitz, *Hugh Blair* (New York: King's Crown Press, 1948), pp. 11–12.

8 Lionel Thomas Berguer (ed.), *Lectures on Rhetoric and Belles Lettres*, by Hugh Blair (London: T. and J. Allman, 1825).

9 To be sure, differences existed, often along regional lines, as Horner's *Nineteenth-Century Scottish Rhetoric*, which describes archival holdings of Scottish universities, demonstrates. See also Joan H. Pittock, 'Rhetoric and *Belles Lettres* in the North East', *Aberdeen and the Enlightenment*, ed. Jennifer J. Carter and Joan Pittock (Aberdeen University Press, 1987), pp. 276–81.

10 Roger L. Emerson, 'Science and the Origins and Concerns of the Scottish Enlightenment', *History of Science* 26 (1988), 338.

11 Herman Cohen, 'Hugh Blair's Theory of Taste', *Quarterly Journal of Speech* 44 (1958), 265–74.

12 George Campbell, *The Philosophy of Rhetoric*, ed. Lloyd F. Bitzer (Carbondale and Edwardsville: Southern Illinois University Press, 1963), p. lxxiii.

13 *Ibid.*, p. 1.

14 Less clear is the extracurricular role English literature played at the English universities. Adam Smith is said to have familiarized himself with English literature while at Oxford. During the seventeenth century students at Cambridge could opt to study vernacular texts like Robert Burton's *Anatomy of Melancholy* (1621), Thomas Fuller's *The Holy State and the Profane State* (1642), Sir Thomas Overbury's *Characters* (1614). Holdsworth's 'Directions for a Student in the Universitie,' which describes rules operative during the period in which Milton matriculated, states: 'Such as come to the University not with the intention to make Scholarship their profession, but only to gett such learning as may serve for delight and ornament and such as the want wherof would speake a defect in breeding rather then Scholarship, may instead of the harsher studies prescribed in the Callendar

read some of these or the like' (Harris Francis Fletcher, *The Intellectual Development of John Milton, Volume II, The Cambridge Period 1625–32* (Urbana: University of Illinois, 1962), vol. II, p. 647). The ancient universities did not encourage such study – indeed, frowned upon it – and never seriously debated incorporating English studies into formal studies until the end of the nineteenth century, with Oxford founding its Honours School of English Language and Literature in 1893.

15 See Barbara Warnick, *The Sixth Canon: Belletristic Rhetorical Theory and its French Antecedents* (Columbia: University of South Carolina Press, 1993), pp. 115, 117, 121.

16 Linda Ferreira-Buckley and S. Michael Halloran (eds.), *Hugh Blair's Lectures on Rhetoric and Belles Lettres. Edited with an Introduction and Critical Apparatus.* (Carbondale and Edwardsville: Southern University Press, in press), Lecture 1.

17 For a general discussion of these organizations see Davis Dunbar McElroy, *Scotland's Age of Improvement: A Survey of Eighteenth-Century Literary Clubs and and Society* (Pullman: Washington State University, 1969); and Richard Sher, *Church and University in the Scottish Enlightenment* (Princeton University Press, 1985). See H. Lewis Ulman, ed., *The Minutes of the Aberdeen Philosophical Society 1758–1773* (Aberdeen University Press, 1990), for documentation of cooperative inquiries into matters of discourse and language. Drafts of *Philosophy of Rhetoric* (1776), for example, evolved over the decades during which Campbell participated in the Aberdeen Philosophical Society, to which Campbell presented eighteen discourses on rhetoric, all of which were debated and critiqued (Ulman (ed.), *Minutes*, p. 26). Among the publications members penned while active at the society are James Beattie's *An Essay on the Nature and Immutability of Truth* (1770), James Dunbar's *Essays on the History of Mankind in Rude and Cultivated Ages* (1780), Alexander Gerard's *Essay on Genius* (1774), and Thomas Reid's *An Inquiry into the Human Mind, On the Principles of Common Sense* (1764).

18 *The London University Calendar for the Year MDCCCXXXI* (London: Thomas Davidson, for John Taylor, Bookseller and Publisher to the University), p. ii.

19 See Court, *Institutionalizing*, pp. 44–52.

20 Lord Henry Brougham, *The Life and Times of Lord Brougham* (London: 1871), I.3–6; II.262.

21 Five members of the first governing council and three of the first professors had been educated at the University of Edinburgh and were active in the city's debating and literary organizations; see Negley Harte and John North, *The World of UCL 1828–1990* (rev. edn London: University College London, 1990). Leonard Horner, who was charged with the college's daily management, was also educated at the High School of Edinburgh and the University of Edinburgh, where he and his brother Francis, a founder of the *Edinburgh Review*, became friends with Brougham. Another Scottish graduate, F. A. Cox, served as the school's first librarian and acted as secretary to the council.

22 Schmitz, *Hugh Blair*, p. 39.

23 Thomas Dale, 'An Introductory Lecture Delivered in the University of London, On Friday, October 24, 1828' (London: John Taylor, 1828), pp. 7–8.

24 *Ibid.*, pp. 9–10.

25 *Ibid.*, p. 15.

26 *Ibid.*, p. 27.

27 *Ibid.*, p. 28. Dale further describes the practice in a letter to the warden; see Thomas Dale to Leonard Horner, [-] April 1829, 'College Correspondence', University College, London.

28 *Ibid.*, p. 14.

29 *Ibid.*, p. 11.

30 *Ibid.*, p. 12.

31 The objections of Oxford and Cambridge contributed to the difficulties that plagued London's post-secondary establishments. With the force of tradition and parliamentary seats, the ancient universities prevented the new institution from acquiring the right to grant degrees, a disadvantage that London professors argued depressed enrollment. (Anand C. Chitnis, *The Scottish Enlightenment and Early Victorian English Society* (London: Croom Helm, 1986) documents other educational power struggles in his study of the influence of the Scottish Enlightenment in the medical, social and political thought and practices of early Victorian England.) Only with the establishment of the University of London, a degree-granting entity created in 1836 to maintain state control over education, were students able to acquire an officially recognized degree by passing examinations. The status and fortunes of English literary studies were bound up in such disputes, not least because what was at issue was the merit of the non-traditional disciplines.

32 Thomas Dale to Thomas Coates, Esq., 25 June 1829, 'College Correspondence', No. 1304, University College, London.

23 Court, *Institutionalizing*, p. 55.

34 H. Hale Bellot, *University College London, 1826–1926* (London: 1929), p. 113.

35 Court, *Institutionalizing*, pp. 55–6.

36 [Alexander Blair and John Wilson], 'Mathetes Letter', in *The Collected Works of Samuel Taylor Coleridge, The Friend* (ed.) Barbara Rooke (Princeton University Press, 1969), vol. II, p. 388. Wilson, a Scotsman who attended Glasgow and Oxford Universities, was a literary celebrant of Scotland and a frequent contributer to *Blackwood's Edinburgh Magazine*, sometimes under the pseudonym Christopher North. In 1820 he became the Professor of Moral Philosophy at Edinburgh.

37 Blair describes both courses in a letter seeking the Warden's approval, to which he appends a plan for the Senior class. Alexander Blair to Leonard Horner, 22 November 1827, University College, London.

38 *The University College, London, Calendar, for The Session 1854–55* (London: Walton and Maberly), p. 6.

39 *King's College Calendar 1834–35* (London), p. 11.

40 *Ibid.*, p. 12

41 *King's College Calendar 1833–34* (London), p. 14.

42 *King's College Calendar 1838–39* (London).

43 *King's College Calendar 1835–36* (London), p. 178.

44 Thomas Dale (ed.), *Lectures on Rhetoric and Belles Lettres by Hugh Blair, D.D. & F.R.S. ED.* (London: William Tegg, 1863), pp. xvii–xviii.

45 Alan Bacon, 'English Literature Becomes a University Subject: King's College, London as Pioneer', *Victorian Studies* 29 (1986), 606, 609.

46 *Ibid.*, p. 605.

47 Particularly relevant are the archival materials for 'Philosophy of Mind and Logic', taught by John Hoppus, from 1829 to 1866, which follow closely the work of Dugald Stewart, George Jardine and Adam Smith.

48 See Charles Monaghan, 'Lindley Murray and the Enlightenment', *Paradigm* 19 (1996), 3–26; Frances Austin, 'Lindley Murray: the English Textbooks,' *Paradigm* 19 (1996), 1–2.

49 See Thomas Kelly, *A History of Adult Education in Great Britain*, 3rd edn (Liverpool: Liverpool University Press, 1992), p. 147, n.1. Kelly notes that the 1851 *Census of Great Britain* records 1,017 'literary and scientific institutions' in England. Although such statistics are not wholly reliable, they point to vast sites of middle- and working-class education that have been explored only cursorily at best. Adults might study English literature at a variety of sites including libraries, reading rooms, book clubs, mutual improvement societies, workingmen's colleges, philosophical and literary societies, literary and scientific institutes, regular continuing lecture series or single lectures, informal study groups, and self study. Adults approached their reading with varying degrees of seriousness and commitment, with intentions ranging from the frivolous to the sublime.

50 James Hole, *An Essay on the History and Management of Literary, Scientific, and Mechanics' Institutes* (1853), pp. 27–32. This study determined that the number of scientific lectures offered continually decreased, while those on literary subjects increased to more than half the total. Also see Palmer, *Rise*, pp. 23 and ff.

51 Thomas Cooper, *The Life of Thomas Cooper* (London, 1872; 1877 edn cited), pp. 62–3.

52 *Ibid.*, p. 59.

53 *Ibid.*, p. 169.

54 William Banks to Council, Dr George Birkbeck, 29 January 1827, University College, London.

55 William Banks to Council, Dr George Birkbeck, 29 January 1827, Prospectus, University College, London.

56 *Times*, 9 November 1815.

57 See Sharon Crowley, 'Biting the Hand That Feeds Us: Nineteenth-Century Uses of the Pedagogy of Taste', *Rhetoric, Cultural Studies, and Literacy* (Hillsdale, OK: Lawrence Erlbaum, 1995), pp. 11–20; Barbara Warnick, *Sixth Canon*.

58 For a consideration of the particular ways in which Blair draws on Quintilian, see also S. Michael Halloran, 'Hugh Blair's Use of Quintilian and the Transformation of Rhetoric in the Eighteenth Century', *Rhetoric and Pedagogy: Its History, Philosophy, and Practice* (Mahwah, NJ: Lawrence Erlbaum Associates, 1995), pp. 183–95.

59 Potter, *Muse*, observes: 'It would have been reasonable to prophesy, when the great universities permitted entrance to English Literature, when they brought their machinery of teaching and their experience to bear on this great subject, on this art for which in the world England is most famous, that the Principles of that study would be evolved, that misconceptions would be cleared, that irrelevancies would be dismissed to the other Schools to which they belonged, that roots would be tended and superfluous growths pruned away: that the whole "Eng. Lit." attitude to the subject, especially, would be superseded entirely as being neither scientific nor humanist, as being popular in the worst sense of that word' (pp. 87–8). Not so, Potter concludes. With the entrance of Oxford and Cambridge came no *essential* changes in the teaching of literary studies. He sees them rather as part of an ancestral line reaching back to Scotland.

CHAPTER 11

'A centre at the edge': Scotland and the early teaching of Literature in Australia and New Zealand

Chris Worth

Recent investigations of the history of university teaching of 'English' in Australasia have focussed on demonstrating the extent to which it was part of an imperial system. Did not a towering figure in Literature at Sydney write in 1887 that his academic career was 'his main and conscious offering to the labours of empire'?[1] The curriculum and institutional practices of literary education are, Leigh Dale claims in her influential study, 'deployed in the interests of English cultural and political elites'; Andrew Milner identifies the Anglophile tradition in appointments to Australian university departments of English after 1945 as a continuation of the imperial commitment earlier in the century.[2] But many arguments constructed by post-colonial and cultural critics about literary studies in the settler nations of the South Pacific take for granted an uncomplicated notion of the *Englishness* of English. They also underestimate the dedication of teachers in the early years of the subject to equipping students to participate in but also to challenge a metropolitan culture that had, from the perspective of Sydney or Dunedin, to be conceived of in international terms or not at all. The ' "provincial" socio-economic ambition' which Crawford notes as being so characteristic of the eighteenth-century Scottish invention of 'English' Literature is as powerful in these southern Victorian cities as in Aberdeen or Glasgow.[3]

Taking account of the already ambivalent constructions of 'English Literature' by Scots described in the earlier chapters of this book generates a rather different genealogy for debates about national identity and provincial literary education. Moreover, whatever the painful elisions and silencing that went on as a consequence of the settler societies' self-creation in relation to Britain, the initial development of literary education in the southern colonies was marked by a robust validation of rhetorical composition and philosophic thought, as opposed to cultural refinement or national myth-making. No doubt the discipline

of English constructed ideas of tradition and Englishness which were
powerful hegemonic tools in Australia and New Zealand as in the
Empire generally. But the lingering rhetorical and philosophic traditions
identified earlier in this book, deployed in new circumstances, retain
also a kindness to literature's empowering role and contribute to energetic antipodean literary cultures, Anglophone but not English. This
chapter listens to the complexity of issues that are inscribed in English
teaching in cultures which define themselves by both their relationship
to the metropolitan centre and their difference from that centre.

The labourer for empire quoted above, for example, was Mungo
MacCullum, Professor of Modern Languages and Literature at the
University of Sydney from 1887 to 1920. A Glaswegian educated at
Glasgow University, he was deeply influenced by the Romantic monism
of Edward Caird.[4] As a Luke Fellow he studied at Berlin and Leipzig.
In 1879 he took this background to the University College of Wales,
Aberystwyth, as Professor of English Literature and History. In Australia
he gave a lifetime of service to Sydney University, eventually becoming Chancellor, long after his portmanteau appointment had been
fragmented into departments of English Language and Literature,
French, and German and Comparative Literature. It is an academic
success story, but has an eccentric orbit – around, not of, England. And
the justification for his work on English literature (on Shakespeare,
nineteenth-century poets and novelists, for example), was the existence
of a network of spaces in which the existence of cultural icons like
Shakespeare needed to be explained.[5] Echoing this nearly one hundred
years later, in his inaugural address as the first professor of English at
the new James Cook University of Townsville in 1978, H. P. Heseltine
argued that: 'no academic English department in Australia can expect
to make a significant contribution to the national (or international)
culture unless and until it is prepared to teach English as a foreign
literature'.[6] Familiar yet foreign, a mode of establishing continuity but
a proof of difference, a means of access to international status, yet a
demonstration of dependency, something that does not need translation but does need exegesis – these are conceptions of literature that
continuously perturb Australian and New Zealand notions of 'English'
studies as they do Scotland's. To see MacCullum as a malign tool of
Macaulay's heirs or Newbolt's predecessors is to underestimate the
extent to which he and others were replicating in the southern environment their own experience of accession to metropolitan culture as
Scots, and their own utilitarian *and* humanist sense of the value of

such accession, together with the consequent hesitancies and conflicts. Significantly, in 1923 MacCullum founded the local branch of Newbolt's English Association as the 'Australian English Association', with all that phrase's implicit paradoxes of nationhood. It reverted to being the 'English Association – Sydney Branch' only after MacCullum's death.

Heseltine's title for his inaugural address, which in turn gives me mine, is: *'A Centre at the Edge': On Professing English in Townsville*. This is a paradigmatic image of the anxieties of positioning inevitable in an imagined community like Australia, where self-fashioning revolves around relationships to larger, more powerful and yet distant cultural centres. Heseltine's address reveals to Dale the continuing influence, even within a nationalist Australian agenda (Heseltine has been one of half-dozen key figures in establishing *Australian* Literature studies in Australian universities), of 'Englandism' – the same 'Englandism' visible at Sydney University's foundation or in the enthusiastic participation of MacCullum, Wallace, Murdoch, Strong and other figures from Australian English Studies in the patriotic fervour of the First World War. Such a view is of course part of a contemporary suspicion of the instrumentality of university teaching of English Literature in a colonial system.[7] But Australasian literary teaching has often been undervalued by such powerful myth-making. So David Lodge playfully creates an image of an alien Arnoldian cultural tradition marooned on the shores of sybaritic hedonism: Rodney Wainwright at the University of North Queensland wrestling unsuccessfully to complete his conference paper on 'The Function of Criticism' amid the luxuriant vegetable growth and equally luxuriant sexual displays in his classes on 'Theories of Literature from Coleridge to Barthes'.[8] Dale's is another forceful image: English professors arriving to impose colonial myths, inculcating ideas of English literary superiority on a naive Australian population. But the issue is not so simple in a situation in which the appropriate metaphor for literary pedagogy is 'centrally on the edge', always contingent and contested.[9] An alternate image might be that of another Glasgow graduate, John Macmillan Brown at Canterbury University College. Working up to sixteen hours a day, encouraging engagement with literature across New Zealand through his publications (and at the same time making a small fortune from the sensible investment of his fees), Brown created an idea of English Literature that was colonial in the sense that it endeavoured to connect his students in the *ad hoc* accommodation of Canterbury College with a powerful cultural centre, yet was also determinedly democratic in its identification of the sources of vitality in society. He claimed, for example, in his 1894 lecture notes on the 'Era of Expansion', a particular role for the educated peasantry of Scotland: 'The new audience of literature was ready in the Lowlands of Scotland long before it was getting underway in England . . . The appreciation of literature had become an instinct among the peasantry.' While taught in school 'to look upon English as the proper medium of prose and of more sustained poetic efforts', the Scots had retained their interest in the ballad, local stories and popular lyrics, and so could both produce and appreciate a poet like Burns, who, argues Brown in a sustained and impressive account, 'brings out better than any poet of the last century the depth of the revolutionary current in Britain'.[10] The notion of an educated peasantry may seem an overly romantic one. But in New Zealand in the nineteenth century, where it was very easy to feel at the edge of the world, the connection with Scotland's education system had some point. Brown evokes the image perhaps in part in relation to his own destiny and personal history (son of a ship- master, a scholarship boy throughout his education), but in part also in the belief that 'English', as a language, as a rhetoric, and as a literary experience with cultural and ethical utility, opened up a space for change and progress in a settler nation dominated by economic necessity and conservative concepts of nationhood. In his writings Brown is as enthusiastic about the British Empire as MacCullum, as assured about the manifest destiny of properly trained people from British stock, as blind to the violently exploitative society which sustained settler life at the expense of indigenous inhabitants and their cultures. But already written into his conception of literary education is the perception that it might be a means of accession to the core of a new imagined community which would *not* be England.

From the beginning the position of 'English' Studies in Australia and New Zealand was determined contingently by larger educational debates. The establishment of university education took place between 1850 and 1920 as part of the evolution of colonial and then national identities, against and within multiply intersecting discursive fields and cultural conflicts. The conflicting models proposed for university educa- tion reflected the rapidly shifting dynamics of power and cultural energy within the colonies, provinces and countries as they grew and struggled to find an identity. In each of these debates the role of Scottish ideas or precedents was prominent. And arguments about tertiary education were anticipated by similar debates about secondary education. It is worth noting briefly how much the belief in the teaching of English

and English literature had become part of the rhetoric of educationalists with a Scottish background by the early nineteenth century. For
example, John Dunmore Lang, who had helped set up a very successful network of primary and secondary schools in New South Wales on
the Scottish pattern, deeply influenced notions of tertiary education in
the colony, to the considerable disquiet of the dominant Anglicans. His
1831 Australian College was intended 'to afford a course of education somewhat similar to what is given in the . . . classes of the Scottish
universities'.[11] In Melbourne Alexander Morrison challenged the classicism of the city's private schools by making Scotch College into the
image of Elgin Academy. He separated the teaching of English from
classical studies and in 1860 was the first in Australia to introduce the
study of English literature into the curriculum.[12] In both cases the widely
imitated success of the school led to suggestions that it might be the seed
of a Scottish-style Presbyterian university; a similar pattern occurred in
New Zealand in the 1850s. But, in contrast to the Canadian case
discussed above by F. E. Court, no antipodean university was established as a denominational foundation.

Religious and social heterogeneity undermined all sides' attempts to
make the model of an Australian university a religious, learned or
aristocratic one. Instead denominational colleges, closely linked with
school systems and religiously inclined benefactors, were established
parallel to teaching universities. The influence of one Scot may have
been decisive in this respect. Many of the writers in mid century who
joined in the debate about universities appear to have read William
Hamilton on university reform in the *Edinburgh Review*.[13] The extent of
his influence on the concept of a university, large in Australia and New
Zealand in comparison with, say, Arnold's or Newman's, would be
worth investigating in much more detail than can be done here. In
part he was important to proponents of university education because
what he wrote allowed them to argue their case against those (and
there were many in the infant colonies) who simply thought that there
was no room for such luxuries. He defended the 'perfectibility' of the
Oxford model with its high status and tradition, yet he accepted its
desperate need of reform; this justified colonial imitators in asking for
something more practical from their own universities. Hamilton can
be said to have identified to nineteenth-century Australia and New
Zealand an institutional location for, among other subjects, the utilitarian rhetoric of Scottish 'English' that Ian Duncan discusses. He was also
a powerful influence in the successful resistance to religious collegiate

models and to the dispersal of the teaching function away from the central body.

The arguments about the appropriate model for university organization were fierce. Stressful debates took place in Sydney, Melbourne and New Zealand: should the fledgling universities act only as a degree-validating bodies or be teaching establishments? The dominant models were (unreformed) Oxford, where colleges coached students towards university set examinations and a life in the learned professions (the gentlemanly model); the University of London and the 1845 Queen's University of Ireland, demonized as 'godless universities' by some, praised by others for being degree-awarding rather than teaching bodies and hence requiring little in the way of public support (a model attractive to those who were suspicious of gentility and culture on principle); and lastly the Scottish universities, which had less status than Oxbridge, but whose actual practices were clearly more appropriate to the colonial situation than were the others, especially since they could be imagined as supplying the deficiencies of secondary education (almost every Australian and New Zealand academic in the nineteenth century lamented the need to bring students up to tertiary level, part of normal Scottish practice). Not until the 1910s, when Auckland, Western Australia and Queensland were being founded, were American and continental models considered. By 1858, when religious certification was removed as a requirement for graduation at Sydney, Hamilton's idea of a central secular teaching university had triumphed.[14]

The defeat of the London model at Sydney after the arrival of the first professors had considerable effect, on the development of other Australian universities, and indirectly on the development of the teaching of English.[15] Departments were more likely within this structure to reflect the interests of their dominant members of staff, often stimulating productive conflict between different university departments' views. For example, the sense of difference between the Sydney and Melbourne departments of the 1940s generated energetic debate, while Leavisisms flourished in various forms at Melbourne in the 1960s in contrast with the growth of Australian Studies at Sydney and Queensland.[16] Perhaps Rodney Wainwright represents the Australian experience of English not so much in his painful incapacity as in his concerns with the *place* of criticism. No one aware of the debates in Australian universities in the 1950s or 1960s would have found it particularly surprising to read that English as a subject was 'ideological' and contingent.[17] In New Zealand, where tertiary education was established a few years later than in Australia (but astonishingly early given the size of its European population), provincial politics caused the creation of a national validating university which controlled the conferment of degrees, the examination of candidates and eventually the curriculum of the constituent colleges (the University of Otago in Dunedin, Canterbury and Auckland University Colleges and Victoria University College in Wellington).[18] This unwieldy central control collapsed only in the 1960s. Final examination papers were, moreover, set and marked in Britain, until 1940 in some cases. It may well be one reason why literary debate in New Zealand was less intense in the first half of the twentieth century than in Australia.

The 1850 foundation of the University of Sydney was a declaration of maturity by New South Wales. But it was also a claim of continuity with a tradition. To many this tradition was represented by Oxbridge and could most easily be secured by the appointment of Oxbridge 'men'. Foundation chairs at Sydney in Classics and Mathematics were made from Oxford and Cambridge respectively, as the legislature of the colony had demanded, although Scots were appointed in sciences.[19] The opening address by the Provost and first professor of classics, Rev. John Woolley (chosen over Arthur Clough, then Professor of English at University College London), has reinforced the post-colonial claim that the object was to ensure continuity with the university 'of King Alfred'.[20] Even so, the first Vice-Provost, Sir Charles Nicolson (an Edinburgh doctor by training), in envisaging the provision of lectureships in Literature, quoted from Hamilton's articles and drew attention to the 'humbler, but scarcely less useful, institutions of Scotland'.[21] In hot competition with Sydney, the University of Melbourne was incorporated in 1853. Surprisingly, given the Scottish influence in nineteenth-century Victoria, few of the early professors were Scots. In neither case was English part of the founding curriculum. The experience of the University of London in this regard seems to have been almost entirely overlooked; English Studies develops instead by a series of splits in the responsibilities of the professoriate.

As long as Oxford classics professors like Woolley and his successor, Charles Badham, or the polymathic Irishman Hearn at Melbourne, had 'Literature' as their domain, few students came into contact with 'English'. But MacCullum's appointment, described above, was a revolution. He had a wide literary and rhetorical education, professional training in literary research, and possessed a philosophy that was belletrist in the Scottish sense. He was not, in modern terms, an adventurous thinker

about texts, but his passionate belief that literary study was an appropriate academic endeavour and a contribution to national development
ensured that he not only nurtured the discipline as Sydney University
expanded in the 1890s, but also, through his extramural lecturing,
involvement with literary societies, and patronage of Australian writing, tied the university to the emergence of an Australian literary culture.
Despite the sneers directed by the *Bulletin* generation of Australian
writers against Oxbridge mimicry, Australian (and New Zealand)
universities had a major influence on the emergence of local writing
and readerships. MacCullum was no writer himself, but he had the
great poet Christopher Brennan as a colleague, and one of his gifted
pupils, John le Gay Brereton, eventually became the first Professor of
English Literature at Sydney. Moreover, the successful journal *Southerly*,
supported by MacCullum, gave Sydney writers a sense of publishing
in some sort of continuity with British literature, while increasing their
own nationalist confidence.[22] At Adelaide, where the teaching of English was established from the university's foundation in 1874, the first
Hughes Professor of English Literature and Mental and Moral Philosophy had been a Fife Presbyterian minister, John Davidson (St
Andrews and Edinburgh). He taught successfully until his death in 1881,
'in constant demand outside the university as a popular lecturer'.[23]
When the characteristically Scottish joint responsibility of English and
Philosophy was divided, the chair of English was intended for a South
Australian poet, Charles Jury. And in Western Australia (founded 1913)
the essayist Walter Murdoch, Australian himself, but with many Scottish
connections, was appointed founding professor. His department was
actively involved in the community and in attempting to understand
what the nature of Australian literature would be.

The failure to appoint Murdoch to the new Chair of English Language and Literature at Melbourne in 1911 has been seen as part of a
'cultural cringe'. It might be better to recognize it as a confirmation of
the increasing professionalism of the discipline and the university's
determination to retain contact with the strongest professional stream
in the subject, following informed debate on Council about the future
of the teaching of English. Should English have an aesthetic and critical
direction, or be linguistic, with the stress on 'derivations and structure'?[24]
Really there was no contest – the critical triumphed because of the
evident value, in the local circumstances, of learning which could be
argued to form thinking, rather than mimic the 'knowledge for its own

sake' of classical philology. And 'critical' still had Scottish associations. Although the successful rival to Murdoch, R. S. Wallace, was a graduate of Oxford, he was at the time of his appointment one of Grierson's best lecturers at Aberdeen (specializing in the history of English literature, Old and Middle English, English and Scottish literature). But the very success of Scottish educationalists in establishing the discipline of English in England in the nineteenth century ensured that such professional appointments to Australian English departments in the twentieth century were almost always of Oxford- and Cambridge-trained (if locally born) candidates. In 1894 when the University of Tasmania was established, with a Chair of Classics and English, the appointment went to a Cambridge graduate. Once the responsibilities of the Adelaide Professor were split into English and Philosophy, English there became a bastion of Oxonians. In Sydney the preference was for local graduates who then went to Oxford to complete a second BA or a further degree. Whether at Queensland, Western Australia, Tasmania, Adelaide, Sydney, or Melbourne, twentieth-century English teaching was soon dominated by a mixture of Oxford or Cambridge appointments from overseas or by Australians with Oxbridge degrees.[25] Dale and Milner point out how consistently from 1920 onwards Australian English departments appeal to Oxbridge for validation of their accession to international status. Exceptions could even find that their students had these expectations. Take the appointment of G. H. Cowling at Melbourne in 1927: he came from Leeds, which might be thought a model for the colonial universities, yet a student of the time noted that he was looked down on by many undergraduates because he did carry with him the prestige of Oxbridge.[26] While the 'eccentric' creation of English as a discipline in the colonies could be best envisaged by those who had come to the subject outwith Oxford and Cambridge, the accession of Australia to 'English' was inevitably if paradoxically also part of an Anglocentric turn, familiar from the eighteenth-century Scottish rhetorical and belletrist tradition, one which involved instituting at the centre of study of the discipline a notion of cultural centrality for 'Englishness', a notion, to use Leavis's words, that

English literature, magnificent and matchless in diversity and range, and so full and profound in its registration of changing life, gives us a continuity that is not yet dead. There is no other; no other access to anything approaching a full continuity of mind, spirit and sensibility . . .

These phrases are quoted by Heseltine in his account of why English became such an influential subject in the 1930s in England and in Australia by the 1940s (he puts a date on it: the 1941 appointment of the Cambridge-trained Allan Edwards at Western Australia).[27] This is a second coming of English. As Leavisite appointments (especially at Melbourne and briefly at Sydney) transformed the subject, the need to develop a critical account of an equivalent *Australian* tradition became even stronger in nationalistic Australian circles. Traditional attitudes to English were rapidly becoming ever more alien to the majority of the students, who shared, if less articulately, Les Murray's caustic viewpoint:

> Literate Australia was British, or babu at best,
> Before Vietnam and the American conquest
> career had overwhelmed learning most deeply back then:
> a major in English made one a minor Englishman
> and woe betide those who stepped off the duckboards of that.[28]

In general English teaching in Australian universities had been established too late to generate an 'Australian English' as conspicuously Scottish as Linda Ferreira-Buckley demonstrates in the present volume that 'London' English was. The next oppositional move for many of the departments mentioned above was to take the form of appointing locally trained Australians – and then to teach Australian literature. Even so, there were occasional reminders of what might have been. Professor Sam Goldberg, one of the 'Leavisites' at Melbourne in the 1950s and 1960s, once made a surprised comment about I. S. Maxwell, another popular and influential professor of English at Melbourne (Australian-born, but a postgraduate at Oxford). Goldberg recalled that in the 1940s Maxwell had just arrived from Sydney where he had been lecturing in the English department. At Melbourne the mode of English had been an 'Oxford type of English':

Maxwell introduced something that I think was very important – a stress on the 'critical', and by that he meant something that, curiously enough, derived, I think, from the Scottish rhetorical school. He was very fond of Blair and Kames and people like that, and it wasn't until many years later that I realised what the strengths of that tradition are.[29]

Scottish literary studies are once again a shadow presence within 'English Literature'.

In New Zealand the teaching of literature had a more obvious Scottish flavour, especially in the Presbyterian settlement of Dunedin.

G. E. Thompson notes that the idea of a university there was 'born in Scotland, and came to the colony with the first settlers'.[30] When the University of Otago was being conceived in 1868–71 the role of English was doubly ensured: a professor to teach English was considered by the proponents of the non-denominational university to be a key early appointment, and the Presbytery of Otago and Southland, who had a grant available to support teaching at the university, agreed that they would themselves provide for the establishment of a chair in English literature.[31] Even George Sale, the founding professor of Classics and English, a Cambridge graduate, saw a role for English larger than many of his peers, noting that the subjects he taught were part of a liberal education 'which in England is open to a few, in Scotland, I believe to many; but which here ought to be open to all'.[32] (Had Sale not accepted Andrew Hutchinson of Stirling High School would have been appointed.) Early in 1880 a chair of English Language and Literature, Political Economy and Constitutional History was established. On the recommendation of a committee headed by David Masson, a young Cambridge graduate called John Mainwaring Brown was appointed. His inaugural lecture demonstrates the extent to which Scottish notions of the democratic role of university teaching, for example as described by George Davie, continued at this stage to flow through to the colonies.[33] Brown argued for the importance of the study of English language, but decried the dry teaching of grammar. Instead he emphasized the role of comparative philology, and above all of literature, language in use, concluding that 'The great end of literary studies . . . Is the culture of the feelings.'[34] He placed emphasis on the possibility of moral education but also on the role of literary culture in the creation of a democratic civilized society (pointing to the example of Bain and Spencer as skilled analysts and Minto on style), concluding with a peroration: 'To contemplate literature as a part of the growth of society, is the final work of the student.' A brilliant and influential teacher, Mainwaring Brown disappeared while walking in the South Island in 1888, to be followed by a succession of Scottish-trained men whose involvement in the support of the distinctive nature of Dunedin's culture was considerable – Thomas Gilray (MA Edinburgh) joined Halkett-Brown (MA Aberdeen) in 1890, Herbert Ramsay (MA St Andrews) took over in 1921 and stayed until 1950 (to be followed by J. Y. T. Grieg, the Hume scholar).[35] Their influence on curriculum was limited both by the University of New Zealand's centralizing bureaucracy and by the examinations conducted from England; curricula,

questions and marking were essentially controlled overseas. Nevertheless literary pedagogy at Otago was part of the cementing of Dunedin's
perception of itself as an Edinburgh in the South, as the natural des-
tination for the bright school-leavers of both North and South Islands.
Happy to take on the role of educating the nation (a role redeemed
even after the establishment of other colleges by the canny creation of
a good medical school), Dunedin provided an admittedly provincial, but
nevertheless engaged, educational context for academic development
and for the kind of intellectual dissent of the kind in which James Baxter,
perhaps New Zealand's greatest poet (and grandson of John Macmillan
Brown), specialized while living in the city. Although further research
is needed to demonstrate how the university interacted with the shifting
cultural milieu of Dunedin, as a university town (and Aberdeen might
be a better parallel than Edinburgh) it clearly generated a usefully
contested environment for writers and artists.[36]

Meanwhile in Wellington, where the Caledonian Society had already
established 'university classes' in literature 'without any public assistance
whatever', two of the four founding professors in 1899 had impeccable
Scottish backgrounds – Rankine Brown (Classics – St Andrews, Worces-
ter College, Glasgow), and the professor of English and Mental Science,
Hugh Mackenzie, a Highlander educated in Aberdeen and St Andrews.[37] Mackenzie was not one of the new professional critics, rather he
was an amateur of literature, content to enthuse his students with his
reading, to expound on Matthew Arnold and poetry as a criticism of
life, to use Sweet and Skeat as the core of courses on English language.
Astonishingly he taught at Wellington from his arrival until his retirement in 1936 when Ian Gordon arrived from Edinburgh, another of
'Grierson's young men'.[38] It seems appropriate that Gordon should
have played a key role in the gradual dismantling of the external
examination system and the University of New Zealand.[39] While only
Gordon seems to have taught Scottish text-based courses in the 1950s
and 1960s, given the tradition of Scots involvement in higher education
in the country, especially in Otago, it is not surprising to find that the
teaching of Scottish literature has been more prominent and had a larger
cultural role in New Zealand than in Australia.[40]

While Otago was and remains the most distinctively Scottish of
the colonial settlements in New Zealand, the Scottish role in English
teaching was most important in the dominantly Anglican province of
Canterbury. Indeed, by appointing John Macmillan Brown as Professor
of Classics, History, English Language and Literature and Political

Economy in 1874, Canterbury established the most important genealogical link between the world of Scottish literary traditions which are the subject of this book and the South Pacific. Macmillan Brown's early career was one of continuing success, first at Edinburgh, where he became an ardent Carlylean, then at Glasgow, where he came under the influence of Caird (like MacCullum) and John Nichol, newly appointed as Professor of English Literature: 'It was Nichol who stirred my inner man and made me literary instead of mathematical in my ambitions', he recalled.[41] Following their footsteps, he won the Snell Exhibition at Balliol. After a couple of miscellaneous jobs according to his own account he indicated to Caird that he was ready to take a 'post in the colonies', preferably in New Zealand (he'd apparently already been offered places in India and Canada).[42] Jowett was on the selection committee, as was Blackie, and the result was a foregone conclusion. Notoriously, however, the Agent-General of New Zealand, Lord Lyttleton, called Brown into his office in London, and told him that he did not approve of his nomination as 'You cannot write Greek verse.' The reply, 'God help me, what would be the good of Greek verse for pioneers in a new colony?' indicates how clear Brown was about the potential for educational good his chosen field of English had.[43] Clearly the confidence with which he understood his vocation can be linked to an emerging belief in the destiny of English to mimic for an 'Anglo-Saxon' community the role of Greek and/or Latin as the language of world domination. (As F. E. Court points out in his account of Masson and Nichol, this colonialist 'English' notion of 'English' is itself generated in part by these influential *Scottish* teachers.[44])

Once in Christchurch Brown set about organizing the college, establishing its relations with the local population, and negotiating the ideas of university education held by his political masters. He worked extraordinary hours to give his students the kind of detailed teaching he thought they needed. Neither urbane Oxford nor the lecture halls of Edinburgh and Glasgow quite explain his pedagogy. It may have been the memory of Caird, who required his students to compose regular essays, then went through them individually, that suggested Brown's intense teaching methods. In all his courses he extended his criticism inwards towards composition and outwards towards issues of ethics, social responsibility and personal development, the lessons of the moral philosophy courses in Scotland never forgotten. All accounts of Brown by his colleagues and pupils draw attention to the energy with which he developed a conception of literature's importance to modern society

– not through a vague notion of the preservation of cultural values, but through an engagement with questions about writing. At one level this was astonishingly practical. He identified, for example, the teaching of 'the art of writing English' as his chief aim, drawing his model from Nichol's English Literature classes at Glasgow and stressing the practical and professional utility of the skills he taught.[45] He recognized the importance of journalism too, commenting once that 'journalism has taken the place that the church used to have'.[46] In his memoirs he looked back on the period when he was working for the Geological Survey in Scotland:

It is one of the features of Scottish Lowland life that has made its people so successful out in the world, this love of the literary side of English. It has drawn large numbers of Scottish youth into journalism in England, and especially in London. With their philosophical bent they have often become leader writers.[47]

Some of Brown's published lectures, like the course on Carlyle, are impassioned paraphrases of ideas, calling powerfully for continuing social critique.[48] Others, like the *Manual of Literature*, consist principally of historical and cultural material, although even these are informed by a remarkably clear vision of the social situation of literature, as in his comments on Scottish literary conditions quoted earlier. The Scottish example is crucial to his notion of a discipline of English that will engage fully with an emerging society. All through his pamphlet *Modern Education* this is manifest as a concern with the positive influence literary training might have on the creation of the settler nation. Many of his views now seem highly contentious, but in practice Brown took a liberal view of, for example, the suitability of a university education for women. Canterbury (like Otago) admitted women to degrees from the beginning, and although their claim to have graduated the first women in the British empire is wrong, certainly students such as Helen Cannon (the first woman to gain an honours degree) and Anne Bolton (both Canterbury 1880) owed something to Brown's help. Helen Cannon became headmistress of Christchurch Girl's High School and Brown's wife.[49]

How much can Brown's achievement be seen as an experiment with a more democratic notion of English? – not a replacement for the fading glory of the classics, not training for a clerisy devoted to the ennoblement or moral improvement of the nation, but a practical part of civic education in the new civilization of the settler world? Teaching huge classes, popularizing his lectures by allowing them to be widely reprinted, consciously speaking to women as well as men, there is an argument that despite his Social Darwinism, it was his Scottish background that motivated his image of teaching. He retained the belief that the cultural enlightenment of the subject would encourage society to interact on rational and democratic grounds.[50] By connecting English as a discipline to a tradition of rhetorical education, teachers like Macmillan Brown challenge contemporary accounts of the formation of English studies as happening 'in a context of political and cultural colonialism, and of the teaching of a high culture which was specifically that of the English ruling class'.[51] The role of early academic teachers of English Literature in Australia and New Zealand has a more complex relationship with the rhetoric of imperialism than is usually imagined. When MacCullum claimed that 'English literature' had a central place in the department of Modern Languages at Sydney, 'not necessarily because it is the best but because it is our own and incorporates the national ideal . . .', he expressed a common view.[52] But his claim immediately also invokes the self-contradictory nexus of assumptions and expectations that is inscribed in all literary teaching in non-metropolitan Anglophone cultures.

Accounts of modern literary studies have to acknowledge their international and multi-stranded origins. Literature and language in Australia and New Zealand continue to be shaped by a complex set of relations to fatherlands, mother tongues, cultural identities and post-colonial anxieties. These are places where the settler is still met by the indigene, where the recently-arrived are as numerous and as influential as the long-resident, where national allegiances are multiple, and where the dominant language is a *lingua franca* whose claims to be distinctively Australian can be challenged as much by the English in Perth as by Greeks in Melbourne, Maoris in Napier or Chinese in Auckland. In a world where the dominance of mass communication threatens to reduce the study of literature to an ever-decreasing minority pleasure, literary studies in Australia and (to a lesser extent) in New Zealand are rapidly metamorphosing into, for instance, cultural, post-colonial, or feminist studies, approached through perspectives that are comparativist, multicultural, gendered, self-aware. Scotland in the eighteenth century was the proving ground for a rhetorical approach to literature and language that attempted to make these the meeting place for a synthetic 'British' citizen. Australasia is one of the places in which a new rhetoric of criticism is currently being most urgently sought, a rhetoric which will recognize the multiplicity of local origins, the multiplicity of linguistic competencies, and the multiplicity of cultural experiences which together combine to make the multicultural citizen in the era of post-colonialism. As part of this process comes also an urgent need to recognize the complex interweaving of strands in the history of the subject of English literary teaching. For the fashioning of 'English' continues to be one of those contested fields in which to simplify history is to silence difference.

NOTES

1 Quoted W. Milgate, 'The Language and Literature Tradition', in *One Hundred Years of the Faculty of Arts* (Sydney: Angus and Robertson, 1952), p. 47.
2 Leigh Dale, 'Whose English – Who's English? Teaching Literature in Australia', *Meanjin* 51 (1992), 393–409; Andrew Milner, 'The "English" Ideology: Literary Criticism in England and Australia', *Thesis Eleven* 12 (1985), 110–29. See also Leigh Dale's extensive research in '"Courting Captivity": the Teaching of English Literature and the Inculcation of Englishness in Australian Universities' (PhD thesis, University of Queensland, 1992) – to appear revised in 1997 as *The English Men: Professing Literature in Australian Universities*.
3 *Devolving English Literature* (Oxford: Clarendon Press, 1992), p. 43.
4 See George Elder Davie, *The Democratic Intellect: Scotland and Her Universities in the Nineteenth Century* (Edinburgh University Press, 1961), pp. 328–35.
5 *Southerly* (1944). Special issue in memory of Mungo MacCullum.
6 Harry P. Heseltine, *'A Centre at the Edge': On Professing English in Townsville* (Townsville: James Cook University of North Queensland, 1978), p. 18.
7 See J. A. Mangan, ed., *Benefits Bestowed? Education and British Imperialism* (Manchester University Press, 1988); Gauri Visnawathan, *Masks of Conquest: Literary Study and British Rule in India* (New York: Columbia University Press, 1989); Brian Doyle, *English and Englishness* (London: Routledge, 1989).
8 David Lodge, *Small Worlds: An Academic Romance* (Harmondsworth: Penguin, 1985).
9 See Franklin E. Court, *Institutionalizing English Literature: The Culture and Politics of Literary Study, 1750–1900* (Stanford University Press, 1992), p. 165.
10 John Macmillan Brown, *Manual of English Literature: Era of Expansion, 1750–1850: Its Characteristics and Influences, and the Poetry of its Period of Preparation, 1750–1800* (Christchurch: Whitcombe & Tombs, 1894), p. 241.
11 Clifford Turney, Ursula Bygott and Peter Chippendale, *Australia's First: A History of the University of Sydney*, volume 1, *1850–1939* (Sydney: University of Sydney in association with Hale & Iremonger, 1991), p. 23.
12 *Australian Dictionary of Biography* (Melbourne: Melbourne University Press, 1966–), 'Morrison, Alexander'.
13 The most relevant essays are 'On the State of the English Universities, with More Especial Reference to Oxford' (*Edinburgh Review* 53 (June 1831), 384–427) and 'On the Right of Dissenters to Admission into the English Universities' (*Edinburgh Review* 60 (Oct. 1834), 202–30). Their collection in

book form in 1852 probably stimulated the interest in Hamilton's ideas in the 1850s.

14 Turney, Bygott and Chippendale, *Australia's First*, p. 91.

15 Turney, Bygott and Chippendale describe at length the complex politics as Woolley and his peers at Sydney wrested control of academic matters from politicians, *Australia's First*, pp. 61–91.

16 See on these rivalries John Docker, *Australian Cultural Elites* (Sydney: Angus and Robertson, 1974) and *In a Critical Condition: Reading Australian Literature* (Ringwood, Victoria: Penguin, 1984), as well as Milner, 'The "English" Ideology', and Dale, '"Courting Captivity"' and 'Whose English?'.

17 Court, *Institutionalizing English Literature*, p. 14.

18 See J. C. Beaglehole, *The University of New Zealand: An Historical Study* (Auckland: Whitcombe & Tombs for the New Zealand Council for Educational Research, 1937) and Hugh Parton, *The University of New Zealand* (Auckland: Auckland University Press and Oxford University Press for the University Grants Committee, New Zealand, 1979).

19 For a general account of the role of Scots in tertiary education in Australia, particularly significant in medicine and natural sciences, see Malcolm D. Prentis, *The Scots in Australia: A Study of New South Wales, Victoria and Queensland, 1788–1900* (Sydney University Press, 1983) and *The Scottish in Australia* (Melbourne: AE Press, 1987).

20 H. E. Barff, *A Short Historical Account of the University of Sydney* (Sydney: Angus & Robertson, 1902), p. 30.

21 *Ibid.*, p. 22.

22 See Docker, *Australian Cultural Elites*, chapter 7.

23 *Australian Dictionary of Biography*, 'Davidson, John'.

24 Ernest Scott, *A History of the University of Melbourne* (Melbourne: Melbourne University Press in association with Oxford University Press, 1936), p. 189.

25 See Dale's '"Courting Captivity"' for a complete list of appointments in English to Australian university chairs. See also the following institutional histories: Fred Alexander, *Campus at Crawley: A Narrative and Critical Appreciation of the First Fifty Years of the University of Western Australia* (Melbourne: F. W. Cheshire for the University of Western Australia Press, 1963); W. G. K. Duncan and R. A. Leonard *The University of Adelaide 1874–1974* (Adelaide: Rigby, 1973); Malcolm I. Thomis, *A Place of Light & Learning: The University of Queensland's First Seventy-Five Years* (St Lucia: University of Queensland Press, 1985).

26 Geoff Hutton, in Hume Dow (ed.), *More Memories of Melbourne University: Undergraduate Life in the Years since 1919* (Hawthorn, Vic.: Hutchinson of Australia, 1985), p. 29.

27 Heseltine, 'A Centre at the Edge', p. 11.

28 Les A. Murray, *Selected Poems: The Vernacular Republic* (Sydney: Angus & Robertson, 1976), p. 116; also quoted by Heseltine, 'A Centre at the Edge', p. 13.

29 Interview with Richard Freadman, in Richard Freadman (ed.), *Literature, Criticism and the Universities: Interviews with Leonie Kramer, S. L. Goldberg &*

Howard Felperin (Nedlands: Centre for Studies in Australian Literature, Department of English, University of Western Australia, 1983), p. 7.

30 G. E. Thompson, *A History of the University of Otago (1869–1919)* (Dunedin: n.p., [1919]), p. 12.

31 See Thompson, *History of the University of Otago* and W. P. Morrell, *The University of Otago: A Centennial History* (Dunedin: University of Otago Press, 1969).

32 Morrell, *University of Otago*, p. 38.

33 Davie, *The Democratic Intellect*, pp. 3–25.

34 J. Mainwaring Brown, *Inaugural Lecture: Delivered in the University Library, May lst, 1882* (Dunedin: University of Otago, [1882]), p. 11.

35 Morrell, *University of Otago*, p. 174.

36 See Erik Olssen, *A History of Otago* (Dunedin: John McIndoe, 1984), pp. 197–205. On Baxter, Frank McKay, *The Life of James K. Baxter* (Auckland: Oxford University Press, 1990).

37 J. C. Beaglehole, *Victoria University College: An Essay towards a History* (Wellington: New Zealand University Press, 1949).

38 *Ibid.*, p. 220.

39 See his 'Administration in the University' in *The University & the Community: Essays in Honour of Thomas Alexander Hunter* (Wellington: Victoria University College, 1946), pp. 267–81.

40 Alan Riach and Marshall Walker at Waikato are leading figures in Scottish Literature in New Zealand; in Australia Graham Tulloch teaches Scottish literature classes at Flinders. A number of other academics in universities scattered over both countries include Scottish authors and topics in their work. See Alan Riach's articles, 'Scottish Studies in New Zealand', *Scottish Literary Journal* 18 (1991), 63–69 and 'Scottish Studies in Australia: an interim report', *Scottish Literary Journal* 20 (1993), 49–61.

41 John Macmillan Brown, *The Memoirs of John Macmillan Brown* (Christchurch: Whitcombe & Tombs for the University of Canterbury, 1974), p. 25.

42 *Ibid.*, p. 73.

43 *Ibid.*, p. 75.

44 Court, *Institutionalizing English Literature*, pp. 123–41.

45 Brown, *Memoirs*, pp. 92–3.

46 Brown, *Modern Education*, p. 13.

47 Brown, *Memoirs*, pp. 71–2.

48 John Macmillan Brown, *Carlyle's 'Sartor Resartus': A Study* (Christchurch: Whitcombe & Tombs, n.d.).

49 W. J. Gardner writes about the first women graduates in New Zealand and Australia in *Colonial Cap and Gown: Studies in the Mid-Victorian Universities of Australasia* (Christchurch: University of Canterbury, 1979), pp. 68–111.

50 *Ibid.*, p. 64.

51 John Frow, 'The Social Production of Knowledge and the Discipline of English', *Meanjin* 49 (1990), 358–9.

52 Quoted in Turney, Bygott and Chippendale, *Australia's First*, p. 274.

CHAPTER 12

Scottish Literature and English Studies

Robert Crawford

Informed by the preceding chapters, this concluding essay reflects on aspects of the developing relationship between Scottish Literature and English Studies in the nineteenth and twentieth centuries. As we have seen in earlier chapters of this book the fact that the university study of English literary texts developed in eighteenth-century Scotland helped to condition its anxious emphasis on Anglocentric propriety in literary standards. This went hand in hand with the championing of native writing which could be seen as meeting those standards, and the lamenting over or repression of other kinds of native writing which did not. This meant that, as happened in some of the areas to which the subject was exported, the university study of English went against the grain of aspects of the native culture. Setting the Belles Lettres lectures of William Barron against a non-university text published in the same decade such as David Irvine's *Lives of the Scottish Poets* (1810) we are aware that while Irvine (as George Davie pointed out) celebrates the line of Scots vernacular poetry that runs from Allan Ramsay through Robert Fergusson to Burns, Barron elegizes or ignores this work.[1] Later Scottish university teachers of Rhetoric and Belles Lettres inherited the attitudes and curricular patterns of their predecessors. Even when they tried to modify these, as they did through a growing attention to Scottish literature, their perceptions remain shaped by an institutional history which inhibits the perception of Scottish Literature as a distinct subject for study and leads normally to the atomistic consideration of Scottish works only as far as they can be related to the English tradition, or seen in terms of British Literature. This problem, similar to one encountered in colonial and postcolonial territories, has been exacerbated and complicated in Scotland by the long, Anglocentric history of Rhetoric and Belles Lettres in the universities, and by Scotland's dual status as a nation subject to considerable internal colonialism within Britain (especially in the area of literary studies), at the same time as being a colonizing force within the British Empire from Nova Scotia to Dunedin.

These characteristics are apparent in the work of such nineteenth-century teachers as William Spalding at St Andrews, whose *History of English Literature* devotes a regretful half page to Burns, linking him to William Cowper (afforded two pages) and seeing him as 'a Scottish peasant' who 'has given to the literature of the Anglo-Saxon race some of its most precious jewels'.[2] This language of imperial tribute is indicative of Spalding's attitude towards the literature of his native Scotland, and grows from the precedents established by his eighteenth-century predecessors. Burns in Spalding's *History* ends a chapter, is isolated from a sense of the traditions that produced him, and appears as a short obligatory deviation from the mainstream narrative. How far the subject of 'English Literature' was simply a renaming of 'Rhetoric and Belles Lettres' which continued the approach and anxieties of its earlier incarnation is clear from the work of William Edmondstoune Aytoun, who took over the Chair of Rhetoric and Belles Lettres at Edinburgh when Spalding left it to go to St Andrews. It was Aytoun who, concerned that the title of his chair seemed vague, suggested in 1858 that it should be renamed either 'English Language and Literature' or 'English Literature and Composition'.[3] He told the 1858 Royal Commissioners,

What I do teach is, 1st, Vernacular Composition, comprehending the varieties and niceties of style, with a thorough explanation of the structure of the English Language. 2ndly the leading rules for spoken discourse; being, in fact, an analysis of the art of Public speaking. This branch includes an explanation of the principles of elocution; a subject which I regard as of vast importance to students, the majority of whom are utterly ignorant of the elegancies of speech. 3rdly I deliver a series of lectures upon the spirit of ancient and mediaeval literature; showing the different phases of literary progression and development. And, 4thly, I give a sketch of British literature, from its dawn to the close of the last century, distinguishing and characterizing each epoch, and showing the influence which external events have exercised upon its form and its tone.[4]

Here, at the very moment when the English-speaking world's first Chair of Rhetoric and Belles Lettres becomes one of English Language and Literature, we hear clearly the accents of the eighteenth-century Scottish university teachers, with their emphasis on correctness of speech and writing, 'purifying' the expression of their students; we see the clear emphasis on the teaching of literary composition as well as on critical and historical scholarship; we see the movement from the classical world to that of English literature and we see the Scottish emphasis on what is 'British'. Though there are notable new developments (such as the attention paid to medieval literature, including *Beowulf*), the shape of the subject as its nomenclature changes is very recognizably that established by the previous century's university teachers of Rhetoric and Belles Lettres.

Aytoun's attitude to Scottish literature is complex. He writes of the need to treat the term 'Rhetoric' in 'its catholic sense, as the art of composition . . . in entire accordance with the genius, usages and powers of our Saxon speech', and when he deals with a student's need to have 'a competent knowledge of the literature of his own country', it is English Literature that Aytoun means.[5] Nevertheless, Aytoun (like Blair before him) was an admirer of Ossian, and unlike Blair he was also an enthusiast for the Scottish ballads, of which he produced an edition, and on which he gave public lectures. In his modern study of Aytoun (most of whose lectures survive in manuscript), Erik Frykman sees Blair's *Lectures* as a significant model, but he also notes a certain Scottish nationalistic tone that can enter Aytoun's voice. Including praise for Burns, Scott, and the ballads in his lectures, he is nonetheless aware of a culture of hierarchical embarrassment about Scots-language work which has been generated within the academic milieu of which he is part:

I have not hesitated to make an experiment not usually attempted in our universities, and to bring before your notice, as in some respects poetical models, the native and untutored poetry of our own country. I have become quite accustomed to the smile of derision which curls on the classical lips at the bare mention of such a subject, and the scorn with which our Doric is regarded.[6]

Aytoun is caught in a not untypical double-bind. A member of the Scottish Rights Association, which articulated certain Scottish constitutional grievances, though it stopped short of calling for the reinstatement of a Scottish Parliament, and the author of poems in English on Scottish patriotic themes, Aytoun is also confusingly entangled in the Anglocentric thrust of his subject. So he calls '*The Thistle and the Rose*' [sic] by the medieval Scots poet William Dunbar that poet's greatest poem not least because of what Aytoun most peculiarly terms its 'pure English dialect'. His worry about 'an absence of refinement' in medieval Scottish writing shows him to be a professor of English still entrapped in that cultural self-censuring so familiar among Scottish professors of Belles Lettres, and so often exported by their disciples.[7] Certainly, Aytoun does not articulate any full history or theory of Scottish literature,

though he is prepared to pay more attention to it than were his predecessors. Occasionally, in public lectures, Aytoun went further than
he did in the classroom, attempting to articulate a sense of cultural
difference in Scottish writing which gave it a 'national' quality. By this
he seems to have meant an ability to appeal to a 'mixed audience'
which united the Scottish nation in a way that cut across barriers such
as that of class. For him English poets wrote more for an upper-class
audience and lacked real popular appeal, 'But take Burns, and Scott,
and Hogg, and Motherwell, and Allan Cunningham, with their predecessors David Lyndsay and Allan Ramsay and Robert Fergusson,
– these are adored of the people.'[8] Whether or not one accepts this
point as it stands, it can be linked to a sense of a more democratic
culture which has been felt and continues to be felt to characterize
Scottish culture and institutions, including the universities, when set
against the more exclusive traditions of English public schools, Oxford
and Cambridge. There are signs of awareness in Aytoun's work that
the subject he professes is coming under increasing pressure from
those aspects of his native culture which, historically, that subject has
repressed. Aytoun's career shows English Literature as a university subject becoming more clearly a site of negotiation between English and
native, non-English voices.

As preacher, lecturer, teacher of composition, editor, and moulder
of writers, Blair had played a full part in the literary and cultural life
of his time. It is worth reminding readers of Aytoun's work as a poet,
novelist and short-story writer, because these should be seen as informing (and occasionally contradicting) his position as an academic.
Aytoun's poetry was successful in his own day and survived into the
twentieth century in the Oxford Poets series; his short stories and
verses were reprinted in Edinburgh as recently as 1964.[9] Aytoun not
only lectured on ballads; he wrote them. His work in composition was
strongly underpinned by an interest in creative writing. He engaged in
current literary controversies, attacking the Spasmodic School, and
(despite telling the 1858 Commissioners that his lectures ended with
the eighteenth century) he taught his students about recent and contemporary writing, admiring in particular the work of Tennyson and
Elizabeth Barrett Browning.[10]

In combining creative work, including the composition of pieces
with a Scottish patriotic tone, with a university career as a professor
of Belles Lettres/English, Aytoun was not alone. At Glasgow University Aytoun's contemporary Professor Robert Buchanan, an admirer

of the Scottish eighteenth-century rhetorician George Campbell, whose *Philosophy of Rhetoric* was prescribed for the Glasgow students until the later nineteenth century and for Edinburgh students as late as 1910, wrote patriotic historical dramas with titles like *Wallace* (1856).[11] At St Andrews Aytoun's former student, Professor John Veitch, successor to William Spalding as Professor of Logic, Rhetoric, and Metaphysics in 1864, was a prolific poet in English and Scots. Veitch moved later to another chair at Glasgow and wrote a book on the *History and Poetry of the Scottish Border* (1878). John Nichol, Veitch's unsuccessful rival for the St Andrews chair, later became the first professor at Glasgow to have the words 'English Literature' attached to his professorship. Nichol too was a publishing poet and dramatist, friend of Swinburne and mentor of Spasmodic poets and (later) John Davidson. This linkage between the encouragement of approved literary talent, the practice of writing, and the university teaching of Literature continued to be strong in nineteenth-century Scottish universities as it had been in those of the eighteenth when Blair encouraged and championed the work of James Macpherson. In Aytoun's class entitled 'Rhetoric and Belles Lettres (English Language and Literature)' prizes were 'awarded for composition in prose and verse, and for accomplishment in elocution'.[12] Nichol's popular textbook *English Composition* (1879) was a manual not only of prose, but of verse composition. Though the bulk of students' work took the form of essays supplemented by oral and written examinations, the aim of the subject, as made clear in the titles of such works as Alexander Bain's widely used *English Composition and Rhetoric* (1866), was composition as well as critical endeavour, and the subject was one of which verse as well as prose was part. Though the emphasis in the teaching of composition remained on an Anglocentric correctness akin to that which had alienated such earlier Scots poets as Robert Fergusson, these later university Scottish teachers of the reading and writing of English Literature were increasingly aware of the delicate cultural balance of their position. At St Andrews University not only do occasional Scottish texts appear on the syllabus, but the heading 'English and Scottish Literature' begins to appear in the later nineteenth century.[13] Though even this heading is unusual, at the various Scottish universities teachers began to speak and write about Scottish literature in a manner rather less directly apologetic than that of their eighteenth-century predecessors. However, the way in which those predecessors had developed the subject, and the expansion of that subject far beyond the Scottish universities continued to generate pressures on native

Scottish reading and writing. In this regard the Scottish situation anticipates and parallels some of what would happen in North American, Indian and Australasian universities.

Andrew Hook has written in an earlier chapter of this book about Nichol as a pioneer of the study of American literature; interestingly, one of Nichol's earlier publications was *A Sketch of the Early History of Scottish Poetry* (1871), though his own poetry was written exclusively in English. Nichol also wrote a study of Carlyle and articles on Dunbar and Lindsay for T. H. Ward's large anthology *The English Poets*, but Scottish Literature was scarcely the focus of his university teaching. Indeed the Composition course which Nichol developed at Glasgow is closely tied to ideas of English propriety and acknowledges 'obligations to the older writers – as Lord Kames, Blair, Campbell, and Barron on style'.[14] Like these 'older writers' Nichol emphasizes the virtues of perspicuity and 'Purity in the Use of Words', reminding students that 'The words used in good English composition must be classic English words. Every violation of this rule is a **Barbarism**.' He goes on to list 'The use of provincial or slang words or expressions' as one of 'the most frequent sources of Barbarism', yet interestingly he soon begins to backtrack in a way that is again indicative of a sense of native cultures resisting such regulation, and is certainly at odds with the emphasis of many of his predecessors:

Provincial or even Slang Words and Phrases are sometimes tolerable in conversation, where the least objectionable are a useful check on formality. When employed dramatically they may be especially appropriate, as in the Irish and Welsh of Shakespeare, the Scotch of Scott, and the cockney dialect of Dickens. The natural language of a writer is always the best – *e.g.*, the Scotch dialect of Burns. But the forced assumption of a dialect is an affectation to be carefully avoided.

Slang terms must be used in writing, if at all, with great discretion; they should rarely find a place in serious compositions. Americanisms, as 'Britisher', 'Skedaddle', and the peculiar use of 'Clever', 'Calculate', 'Guess', 'Reckon', &c., with the mongrel speech adopted by some humorists, are only admissible in satirical pictures of American manners.[15]

For some, such strictures, like the admonitions of the eighteenth-century university teachers, will seem mere pedantic professorial fussiness; yet the widespread circulation of such rules among generations of student auditors and readers of academic textbooks, reinforced by the position of authority of the universities within nineteenth-century society, means that we should take seriously even small shifts of emphasis within this system of cultural authority. For Nichol, the linguistic position is more complex than it was for such teachers as Blair and Witherspoon who simply banned Scoticisms or Americanisms. While Nichol retains an Anglocentric emphasis, he is increasingly aware of pressures from British and American native, non-Addisonian cultures which he is willing to tolerate, providing, like the Scots language used in Scott's novels, they can be controlled and contained within a dominant, Anglocentric framework. It is significant that the poetry of the man widely regarded as Scotland's national bard, Burns, does not appear as a set text at Glasgow in the nineteenth century, though by 1900 there appears a paper whose title 'English Imaginative Literature from the death of Burns to Byron' manages both to exclude Burns from the syllabus and to imply that he is English.[16] John Nichol is another of the mid-nineteenth-century teachers of English in whose work we can see a pressure for the emergence of fuller consideration for native cultural difference in language and literature; yet Nichol's consideration of Scottish literature remains limited; despite certain Scottish pressures, the title of his subject governs his excursions into his own or other non-English cultures. As his Glasgow inaugural lecture makes clear, he saw literature as bonded to history which, for him, meant the history of Britain, and he saw the Honours degree in English as requiring at least one paper in British History.[17] The Glasgow Honours degree in 'English (Language, Literature, and British History)' in the early twentieth-century maintained this pattern.[18]

While some commentators have linked the growth of English Studies at Oxford University to imperial expansion, in looking at the longer history of the subject in the Scottish universities, we can see that this is simply an outgrowth from the connection between university English, Britishness and colonialism which has its origins north of the border. This emphasis on 'Britishness' harks back to the eighteenth-century origins of the subject when university teachers were training Scottish students in how to succeed in the increasingly unified British state and so gain access to the rewards available in Britain and her formerly English colonies. In various ways these connections are plain in the work of nineteenth-century Scottish English departments. In the 'old model' English Preliminary Examination in English at St Andrews as late as 1896 students had to answer a paper which asked not only such questions as 'How does Shakespeare contrast the behaviour of the French leaders with that of the English on the eve of the Battle of Agincourt?' but also a series of questions on history and geography which concentrated on Britain and her empire.[19] If Aytoun was telling

his mid-nineteenth-century Edinburgh students that studying Rhetoric
could 'open to you the doors of fame and fortune', in a way that recalls
some of William Barron's exhortations, the subject of English Literature was normally less openly presented as suited for students' material
advancement, but it did remain tied to the maintenance and development of a national, Scoto-British ethos.[20] If there are links between the
development of the subject in the Scottish and English universities in
the later nineteenth century, there are also differences, not least the
Scottish concern with Britishness rather than mere Englishness, and the
often subterranean sense of a Scottish inflection. True to the eighteenth-
century Scottish belletrists' wariness about exhibiting clear markers
of cultural difference, Edinburgh's Professor David Masson thought
that Scottish distinctiveness should not be exhibited but internalized.[21]
At Edinburgh in 1866, Masson's rather defensive inaugural lecture on
'The State of Learning in Scotland' took issue with Matthew Arnold's
pro-European attack on English 'provincialism', introducing a distancing Scottish note and arguing instead that attention to national origins
was crucial and that the greatest works of literature frequently had a
local root. Masson emphasized the desirability of links between literary
men and the local community, stressing also the interconnectedness of
literature and national history. He was aware that there might be fledgling poets among his students, but he spoke to them in terms of Milton's
example rather than that of Burns. Conscious of a certain Scottish
inferiorism, Masson argues the case for more linguistic scholarship that
takes to do 'with our own English, in which we have nearly all yet to
do; and with the Celtic languages, which we have shamefully neglected,
though they belong chiefly to our own islands', yet his own clear
emphasis is on 'British Literature' and 'English Literature'.[22] It is with
one of Masson's students, however, that the germs of a theory of
Scottish literature emerge, one which, when developed by the poet
Hugh MacDiarmid, leads to the thorough questioning of Anglocentric
standards in Scottish literature and, eventually, in the university teaching of English in Scotland. Since this represents the most thorough
shift towards cultural liberation from the more oppressive aspects of
the subject of English as developed in Scotland's universities, it is the
course of this shift and its consequences, rather than the general growth
of the subject in Scotland to which I shall devote the rest of this chapter, though I shall conclude by relating what has happened to English
in Scotland to the global development of the university subject and to
aspects of its potential future.

G. Gregory Smith (1865–1932) was a distinguished student under Masson at Edinburgh, and became his assistant there. Trained in English at Edinburgh, then history at Balliol College, Oxford, Gregory Smith was sympathetic to Masson's emphasis on the link between the historical and literary, as well as on the importance of local culture; he became editor of the Scottish Texts Society from 1899–1906, after which he edited the work of Henryson. An 1892 Ordinance had recognized English (Language, Literature and British History) as an Honours Examination Group, and Smith played a considerable part in the redesigning of the Edinburgh English course, linking it firmly to national (British) history. However, when the major English critic George Saintsbury arrived in Edinburgh to succeed Masson in 1895 he too had a strong influence on the young Scottish teacher. Saintsbury was a committed European in his criticism and he commissioned Gregory Smith to contribute a volume on *The Transition Period* (i.e., the fifteenth century) to his multivolume series 'Periods of European Literature' which had as its series epigraph the Arnoldian words, 'The criticism which alone can much help us for the future is a criticism which regards Europe as being, for intellectual and spiritual purposes, one great confederation, bound to a joint action and working to a common result.'[23] Such sentiments underpin T. S. Eliot's 'mind of Europe', a phrase found in an essay ('Tradition and the Individual Talent') which is shaped, as is Eliot's view of Scottish Literature, by his response to the work of Gregory Smith. Smith stands at the intellectual intersection not just of academia and the making of literature, but precisely at the intersection of a rather nationalistic, Scoto-British, anti-Arnoldian current flowing from his teacher Masson and concentrated on writing from England, and a broader, pan-European, pro-Arnold current associated with Smith's great friend and mentor, Saintsbury, over thirty volumes of whose work were in Smith's personal library.[24] His position makes Gregory Smith importantly emblematic in the history of literary studies, and peculiarly crucial both for Scottish writing and the university study of English in Scotland and beyond, so much so that in 1932 his obituarist in *The Times* wrote that 'Scottish literature owes more to Gregory Smith than to any contemporary'.[25]

Gregory Smith was appointed to the Chair of English Literature at Queen's College (later Queen's University), Belfast, in 1905, retiring in 1930. In Northern Ireland he seems to have been something of a Scottish cultural imperialist, paying far more attention to the literature of Scotland than to that of the island he lived in, yet he impressed his

colleagues with something of the breadth of vision encouraged in him
by Saintsbury: 'He had an extraordinarily wide range of knowledge
about other literatures, and could see our own in perspective.'[26] The
importance of the work which Smith built towards in this period is
that for the first time it provided something that could do duty as a
theory of Scottish literature which would release the study and practice
of that subject from the constraints under which it had laboured ever
since the beginnings of English literary study in the Scottish universities.
Before leaving Edinburgh, Gregory Smith had read the proofs of law
lecturer J. Hepburn Millar's *Literary History of Scotland*, which Saintsbury
called 'the first really good and really literary history' of the topic,
adding that 'Scottish Literature ought to be the subject of much greater
"acquaintance" than it enjoys; more particularly (if one may say so
without offence) on the northern side of the Tweed.'[27] It is ironic and
revealing that as a tactful Englishman Saintsbury (who failed in his
efforts to obtain money for a lectureship in Scottish Literature) could
advance the cause of Scottish Literature as a general subject area in
a way that Scottish-born university teachers of English in Scotland,
curbed in part by a sense of native cultural inferiorism that had become
part of the culture of university English, were slow to do.[28] Other late
nineteenth- and early twentieth-century works of Scottish literary history
can be clustered round Millar's, though, to show that, while its development was at first scattered, there was growing institutional interest
in Scottish Literature. One of the chief of these works was *Three Centuries
of Scottish Literature* (1893), a selective history, sympathetic towards Scots
vernacular work, written by Hugh Walker, the Scottish Professor of
English in St David's College, Lampeter, who produced his study with
the encouragement and editorial assistance of Henry Jones, Professor
of Logic, Rhetoric and Metaphysics at St Andrews.[29]

At least as important, however, is the growing *popular* pressure for
the official and substantial recognition of Scottish Literature within academia. This popular pressure involved the powerful Burns Federation,
and led to extended public debate in the early years of the twentieth
century, recorded in such patriotic intellectual magazines as *Scotia*.[30]
By 1910 the third edition of T. F. Henderson's 1898 *Scottish Vernacular
Literature* makes mention of the 'Great Scottish Historical Exhibition'
which was being held to raise money for a professorship at Glasgow
University which would 'conjoin Scottish literature with Scottish history'.[31] This was the 'Scottish Exhibition of History, Art and Industry'
staged in Kelvingrove Park in 1911 as a celebration of native culture

which to some degree countered the global, international focus of the Glasgow International Exhibitions of 1888 and 1901. In the 1911 exhibition literary materials, books and manuscripts were shown alongside a panoply of great and small historical materials – from a full-size 'Typical Scottish Town Hall' to Flora Macdonald's slipper.[32] In mass exhibition culture of the period, as in university English Studies, strains between internationalism and nationalism are visible, and the 1911 exhibition demonstrated the widespread public enthusiasm for the development of the study of Scottish culture at a time when the Liberal Government's vital Scottish MPs were committed to devolution for Scotland and to Irish Home Rule. The linking of history to literature so strong in the teaching of English in the Scottish universities, conditioned the debate about an emerging subject of Scottish Literature. Argument went on as to whether money should be raised for a chair of Scottish History, with literature as a mere adjunct of historical study, or whether Scottish Literature might be seen as 'worthy of perusal for its own sake'.[33] This is the first time that the emphasis on linking national history to national literature in a university has clearly recognized in curricular terms that in a Scottish context this means that the native history and the native literature are those of the Scottish nation. The issues being discussed here parallel discussions about literature's connections with non-English national identity abroad – in Ireland, the United States, and (later) Australia, for instance. In the event the money raised from the 1911 Glasgow exhibition was insufficient to fund a chair immediately, but two series of public lectures were established: one in Scottish History, one in Scottish Literature. It was via public lectures that the subject of Belles Lettres had eventually entered the eighteenth-century Scottish universities, and, in the twentieth century, Scottish Literature as a demarcated subject would take the same route. In 1912 it was the series of public lectures on Scottish Literature which the Principal of Glasgow University, Sir Donald MacAlister, invited G. Gregory Smith to deliver.

Gregory Smith accepted the invitation to give these public lectures 'with very great pleasure'.[34] This was surprising since he hardly ever gave public lectures, and had in Belfast a reputation for being aloof, even reclusive, but his uncharacteristic willingness to straddle the academic and public arenas was to have important consequences. He chose for the title of his 1913 lectures a general one – 'Scottish Literature' – and his style in them reflects a wish to address a public as well as a university audience.[35] Their publication delayed by the First World

War, Smith's lectures did not appear in book form in *Scottish Literature: Character and Influence* until 1919 when they attracted the attention of T. S. Eliot, whose reaction in 'Was There a Scottish Literature' reactivates the older attitude of seeing Scottish Literature not as a subject in its own right but as a flickering gathering of individual works and moments in comparison with the continuous tradition of English literature.[36] Eliot's scepticism set the tone to be taken by such later Scottish critics as Edwin Muir, but Smith's work also attracted the attention of Hugh MacDiarmid, and gave that poet not only the title of his first book, *Annals of the Five Senses* (1923), but also supplied him with 'the Caledonian antisyzygy' – a whole Scottish aesthetic of contrariness and clashing opposites which Smith developed out of nineteenth-century Scottish romanticism (especially Stevensonian romanticism).[37] This aesthetic has remained throughout the twentieth century the basis of theorizing about Scottish literature from MacDiarmid to Kurt Wittig and Karl Miller, though it has recently been complicated by the advocates of a Scottish Bakhtinian standpoint, including Christopher Bittenbender, Roderick Watson and the present writer.[38] Where perceptions of Scottish literature in the later nineteenth century had been shaped both by the heritage of Belles Lettres in Scotland and by the pressures felt in Arnold's *On the Study of Celtic Literature* and his awkward, limiting view of Burns, Gregory Smith gets rid of the freezing of Celtic literature in a misty attitude:

... we should be loath to surrender the opinion that opposites and contrasts in an individual or literature are, more often than not, original and constitutional in that individual or literature, and that neither of the contraries may be imposed from without. To separate the contrasts in character, as Scott, with the licence of the novelist of his age, has done in his chapters on Saxon and Norman, or Arnold in his Essay, is to place the obverse of a coin in one bag and the reverse in another.[39]

Gregory Smith lets Scottish literature be viewed as emotionally and culturally complex, full of mixing contraries because, he argues, 'Scottish literature is more medieval in habit than criticism has suspected ... It takes some people more time than they can spare to see the absolute propriety of a gargoyle's grinning at the elbow of a kneeling saint.'[40] MacDiarmid saw the absolute propriety of that image, and pinched it for his poem *A Drunk Man Looks at the Thistle* (1926). Building on the anti-Arnoldian arguments of the St Andrews academic J. C. Shairp and taking issue with Arnold's introduction to the Oxonian T. H. Ward's *The English Poets*, Smith argues that Burns is not 'provincial' in any pejorative sense; instead, he celebrates Burns's 'transcendent realism'. Smith stresses the importance of *literary* history for Scottish culture, mentioning Hepburn Millar's work, and warns against the danger of valuing Scottish writing just for its patriotic historical associations. To do the latter, he cautions, is to cut Scottish work off from wider standards of literary judgment and to 'risk that a national literature will be rescheduled as an ancient monument, and be no more than a pleasure-spot for tourist readers in search of the picturesque'.[41] In short, Smith, the student of Masson, is sensitive to the local and historical in seeing Scotland's own literature as her 'national literature', but at the same time as an admirer of Saintsbury he wants to maintain a wider Anglophone and European perspective which can be called on by the reader and writer when appropriate. Again, connections with the issues discussed by Chris Worth in the preceding chapter of the present volume are evident. Gregory Smith is no ghettoizer, and suggests that if Scotland 'dream of a renaissance,' she must move beyond her 'hoarier tradition of kail and potatoes', i.e. the 'Kailyard' writing of Barrie, Ian Maclaren and S. R. Crockett which was then popular.[42] Though MacDiarmid was not always in accord with Gregory Smith's project (the two differed on the use of Scots, for example), the academic had produced what the poet called 'the first text-book I would like to put in the hands of any young Scot likely to play a part in bringing about a National Renaissance'.[43] In producing this work, and without necessarily aiming to do so, Gregory Smith became the first university teacher of English to effect the liberation of Scottish literature in academia from its subordination to Anglocentric norms, and he contributed to the powerful interaction of academia and Scottish writers in developing the new literary movement which was to be crucial in the articulation of a modern Scottish literary identity. Though, like Burns, MacDiarmid was not a university product, he can be seen using the work of Gregory Smith (and even Saintsbury) in developing his 1923 'Theory of Scots Letters' and his later articles 'Towards a Creative Scottish Criticism'.[44] MacDiarmid seizes on Gregory Smith's cautious, often belletristic work, and gives it an aggressive swagger which propels it into modernist debates. Thanks to Gregory Smith, MacDiarmid is able to shift the centre of gravity of literary production and literary studies in Scotland so that there begins in the early twentieth century a gradual movement even in the Scottish universities to accord full recognition to Scottish Literature as a branch of study, allowing it access to the privileges and penalties of institutional power two centuries after Adam Smith, Blair, Watson, and others had sought to eradicate the very markers of cultural difference which Gregory Smith and MacDiarmid were keen to identify, celebrate and even redeploy.

Given the way in which today the international English language remains strongly but vestigially linked to England, and across the English-speaking world from Australasia to Canada we see literature and the teaching of Literature frequently involving a wish to assert native voices and traditions in the face of Anglocentric norms, the works of Gregory Smith and MacDiarmid, in addition to their importance within Scotland, are widely emblematic. MacDiarmid's fierce fighting for Scottish Literature in some ways anticipates the more moderate arguments in 1950s Australia, for instance, which led to poets and academics arguing about the relative status of Australian and English Literature in the pages of *Meanjin* in such essays as A. D. Hope's 'Australian Literature and the Universities'.[45] Yet the nature of the long history of English teaching in Scotland's universities has meant that while around the world there has been a proliferation of such university departments and subject areas as Australian Literature, Caribbean Literature and Canadian Literature, powerful institutional support (as distinct from individual passion) for the teaching of Scottish Literature emerged remarkably late. Though it is arguable that the subject name 'English' has become embarrassing in many contexts, and that it is good for Scottish Literature to be taught alongside other literatures, even if the overall department is still called 'English', it is worth pointing out that even now there remains in Scotland itself only one small separate department of Scottish Literature (set up at Glasgow University in the 1970s); only since the 1980s have there been chairs devoted to Scottish Literature at any of the Scottish universities, and there is now *one* established chair in the subject; interdisciplinary centres devoted to the study of Scottish culture in the round are an even more recent development. This is not to say that enterprising individual academics in the Scottish universities have not been publishing on and teaching Scottish Literature for a longer time, but institutional and organizational recognition have been slow in coming. At times it may have been easier for teachers of Scottish Literature to pursue their careers abroad in countries such as America, Canada, and New Zealand, whose own colonial history and Scottish inheritance were more sympathetic to the way in which internal colonialism was bound up with the teaching of vernacular literature in the Scotland which also enjoyed more than its share of the British imperial project. If the origins of the teaching of English in the Scottish universities are imperial and political, geared to the maintaining and strengthening of the British constitution, then it would be naive in the extreme to think that in Scotland or elsewhere the subject has ceased to be political. Certainly the most distinctive work produced in modern Scottish university English departments has tended to go against the Anglocentric institutional legacy of the subject in Scotland and align itself with political projects aimed at securing the right of the people in Scotland to control their own affairs. So, for instance, the work of Cairns Craig at Edinburgh University has resulted not only in his editing of the only modern multivolume *History of Scottish Literature* (1987–88), but also his editing for the Edinburgh publisher Polygon of the 'Determinations' series of volumes which deal with matters of Scottish cultural and political independence. At St Andrews University the work of Douglas Dunn in his poetry, criticism and in the editing of such anthologies as *The Faber Book of Twentieth-Century Scottish Poetry* (1992), which brings together work in English, Scots and Gaelic, and the *Oxford Book of Scottish Short Stories* (1995) demonstrates across a broad field a commitment to Scottish cultural and political self-determination that is not smallminded. Parallel work by Roderick Watson, now Professor of Scottish Literature at Stirling, has resulted not only in his one-volume history *The Literature of Scotland* (1984) which was the first such book emanating from a university to see the Scottish literary tradition as a continuous one which includes work in Scots and Gaelic as well as English, but also in his milestone anthology, *The Poetry of Scotland* (1995), the first fullscale anthology of Scottish poetry to contain work in these three languages. These projects follow the seminal, but smaller-scale lead given by Hugh MacDiarmid, whose 1940 anthology *The Golden Treasury of Scottish Poetry* pioneered a newly reintegrated view of Scottish literature which saw it as written in several languages. Though there have been earlier surges of academic work on Scottish literature, and many earlier clamourings for Scottish self-rule, it is surely no accident that these above-noted works of the 1980s and 1990s, like the poetry and prose of the present writer in *A Scottish Assembly* (1990), *Devolving English Literature* (1992) and elsewhere, were being produced at a time when devolution and the restoration of a Scottish parliament was a clear possibility to be struggled for. The British general election of 1997 saw the landslide victory of a British Labour government committed to devolution for Scotland, and saw Scotland returning to Westminster only Members of Parliament whose parties were committed to

a Parliament in Edinburgh (a proposal fiercely opposed by the 1980s
and 1990s governments of Margaret Thatcher and John Major, whose
Conservative Party lost all its Scottish seats in the 1997 general election). Such writing within contemporary Scottish academia is as clearly
political as was the eighteenth-century development of university English Studies, but is geared to complicating and often reversing the
Anglocentric emphasis built into the subject of vernacular literary study
in Scotland where the university subject of English remains a highly
political one with a contested native inflection. What needs to be
sounded is not a pugnacious Wee Scotlandism, but a note of confident
Scottish internationalism. It is to be hoped also that a wider international understanding of the history of the university subject of English,
and of the legacy of the subject in Scotland, will heighten awareness
of the current position of Scottish Literature which remains too often
either ignored or lumped in with 'English', its cultural inflections and
position airbrushed away in syllabuses across five continents. That
position is beginning to change with the foundation of Scottish Studies
centres in Europe, North America and Australasia, and with the internationalization of Scottish literary studies. This internationalization,
and the wider understanding of Scotland's position in (and repression
by) the development of university English may help criticism of Scottish Literature escape from a continuing danger of ghettoization. Only
through dissemination of their ideas via international publishing houses
and through a much wider dialogue with other areas of literature and
literary studies can Scottish literary academics improve the position of
the study of Scottish Literature within the university subject of English
which their predecessors did so much to create.

Despite many similarities with literary-political debates in other
nations, there are also ways in which the cultural and political situation
in Scotland has left the study of Scottish Literature in a significantly
different condition from that of literary studies in many other parts of
the world. The drive to identify and maintain concepts of tradition that
underpin a cultural identity (which, lacking its own political institutions, feels flickeringly endangered) has led to a resurgence of interest
in literary and institutional history, of which this volume is part. Efforts
at reconstruction and construction rather than deconstruction dominate the recent study of Scottish Literature. The most welcome theoretical presences are much less those of Derrida and poststructuralism
than those of firstly Bakhtin, whose contention that 'one's own language
is never a single language' has a strong resonance in Scotland, and

whose theories of carnival and dialogue are widely applicable there; and, secondly, feminism, the lateness of whose flowering in Scottish literary studies may be explained, emblematically at least, by a final reference to Gregory Smith.[46] For, having seen in an earlier chapter of this book how issues of gender were pertinent to university literary studies from at least the days of Greenfield, we are obliged to note that the admission of women as students, even graduating students in late nineteenth-century Scottish universities did not lead to the sort of sea-change brought about by the campaigns of the suffragettes in the wider public arena. Gregory Smith's time in Belfast and Saintsbury's in Edinburgh are of note today not least for the men's attitude towards one of their most talented students, Helen Waddell, later to win fame as a translator and as a writer on medieval literary culture. In their flirtatious meetings and correspondence, Gregory Smith, Saintsbury and the student Waddell play out an elaborate dance in which Saintsbury imagines Waddell in erotic poses, and sends her his fantasies about their spending the night together.[47] More carefully and coolly flirtatious, Gregory Smith encouraged Waddell's work, but Waddell became aware that he was 'dead against the appointment of women' to academic posts.[48] The unpublished novel which Waddell co-authored imagines her as Gregory Smith's wife, yet sees him as an oppressive presence.[49] Its feminist awareness and suffragette sympathies are at the opposite end of the spectrum from Gregory Smith's attitudes and published work. His *Scottish Literature* has no place for Susan Ferrier, Margaret Oliphant, or Violet Jacob. Out of five hundred references in the index, only one is to a Scottish woman as an author. All this is iconically important, and matters not least because Gregory Smith's academic construction of Scottishness and a Scottish tradition in literature reinforced MacDiarmid's tendency to undervalue Scottish women's writing. Together poet and academic helped construct the vision of Scottish literature that has prevailed until very recently inside and outside universities – a view of Scottish literature as a male preserve. This makes recent work on gender in Scottish writing and on the history of Scottish women's writing especially welcome, and may caution modern academics lest in unpicking the Scottish invention of university English we end up liberated from simple Anglocentrism but in thrall to other equally or more oppressive prejudicial limitations.

Yet part of the work of making ourselves conscious of the earlier history and development of university English is neither simply to reposition Scottish Literature in the curriculum nor to unravel disciplinary history until we stand simply surrounded by a tangle of discarded rubbish. Rather it may be that an understanding of the subject's genesis alerts us to certain persisting characteristics and to the strengthening and comprehension of configurations and tensions within the subject of 'English' at present. For one thing, it is clear that throughout its history there has been uncertainty about where the boundaries of the subject lie. Teacher after teacher has fought shy of establishing too minutely defined boundaries at the same time as attempting to outline and develop the subject within the university. So it was that Aytoun wanted the subject's title changed from 'Rhetoric and Belles Lettres' to 'English Language and Literature'. Yet this concern about the fluid or uncertain nature of the subject may have maintained its importance. George Davie has argued that teachers such as Spalding, Aytoun and Masson maintained a strong interest in Rhetoric and that Aytoun was turning that subject into 'the theory of literature' in a more modern sense.[50] Certainly the nineteenth-century Scottish university English courses maintained a strong emphasis on the principles of criticism, and the term 'literary theory' was used in the curriculum early this century.[51] In this way we can connect Robert Watson's emphasis on 'Rules which are common to all the different kinds of Discourse' to much more modern developments in semiotics, rhetoric and literary theory.[52] Yet I wish to end on a note that attends to another distinctively Scottish turn in the subject, one which may give historical backing to contemporary developments in English.

The term 'Belles Lettres' is now normally used pejoratively, but for the early university teachers of English in Scotland it signalled an interest in aesthetic composition which led Blair to help mould the work of such internationally important writers as Macpherson and Burns. It marked a sometimes foolish, but sometimes positive, and always active interest in contemporary literary production. It is commonly suggested that the teaching of contemporary literature and the teaching of creative writing are newfangled and controversial phenomena. Viewed against the background of Oxbridge syllabuses, this may be so, but it is clear that from the beginnings of Rhetoric and Belles Lettres in the Scottish universities, the reading and writing of contemporary literature was bound up with the subject. We see this emphasis persisting in the mid nineteenth century when such figures as Aytoun, Buchanan, Veitch and Nichol were practising writers as well as teachers of criticism and composition. Such examples may be seen as giving strong historical backing to the teaching of creative writing as a longstanding, integral part of the subject of English. In Scotland, the presence of writers within English departments has a long and strong, if not always a continuous history. Norman MacCaig's years as Reader in Poetry at Stirling University enriched the lives and works of many students. In the years after World War II Edwin Morgan worked within the Department of English Literature at Glasgow, becoming a titular professor there and exercising considerable influence over many among the younger generation of Scottish poets. Morgan's colleague the critic and poet Professor Philip Hobsbaum, whose remarkable work as a literary catalyst in London and in Belfast heralded his arrival in Glasgow, has shown both an unusual interest in the development of the early university teaching of English in the Scottish university and a marked ability to build bridges between his work as an academic and his organization of writers groups involving such authors as James Kelman, Liz Lochhead and Tom Leonard, all of whose writings involve tensions between vernacular and 'standard English' which have been at the heart of writing and reading in Scotland for centuries.[53] At the same time, the head of the young Department of Scottish Literature at Glasgow University, and an energetic campaigner for Scottish Literature within the universities was another poet, Alexander Scott. Though these poet-professors are now retired (Scott died in 1989), and though for all or most of their careers they did not formally teach creative writing, their portfolio of activities reflects a too often ignored aspect of the earlier university traditions of English. In the early 1990s at St Andrews Douglas Dunn and the present writer established the first degree in creative writing in a Scottish university. This may be seen as a revitalizing of an earlier tradition within the university subject of English in Scottish universities where creation and criticism were closely aligned and where the same person might be both poet and teacher. The modern development of creative writing in Scottish academia might also be viewed as a belated formal catching up with the subject which has for many years been part of the American university curriculum and which is increasingly taught in English and other universities. What is significant about the growth of creative writing in the modern British university sector is that it is normally conducted not in separate departments but within the department of English. It may be that too often teachers of creative writing, like teachers of composition in some American universities, are treated as peripheral to the core of the subject. If we look at the long history of university English, we can see this as a recent and peculiar phenomenon. I hope that not only modern developments in literary theory which blur distinctions between the reader and the writer, but also a fuller understanding of the history of English as a subject within the universities may see a positive revaluing of the place of all acts of writing within the curriculum.[54] It is unlikely, indeed undesirable that all suspicions and mutual envies between those who work in academia and writers at work in the wider community will cease; it is also unlikely that university teaching will lead directly to the production of the best writers; but the ongoing expansion of creative writing within the world-wide university subject of English is likely to lead at least to a greater imaginative inwardness with the composition of literature, and one that is more in tune than many people realize with the long-term history of the university subject of English.

NOTES

1 George Davie, *The Democratic Intellect*, 2nd edn (Edinburgh University Press, 1964), p. 212.
2 William Spalding, *The History of English Literature* (Edinburgh: Oliver & Boyd, 1853), p. 359.
3 Erik Frykman, *W. E. Aytoun, Pioneer Professor of English at Edinburgh* (University of Gothenburg, 1963), p. 27.
4 *Ibid.*, pp. 28–9.
5 *Ibid.*, pp. 28–9.
6 *Ibid.*, p. 45.
7 *Ibid.*, p. 46.
8 *Ibid.*, p. 45.
9 William Edmondstoune Aytoun, *Poems* (Oxford University Press, 1920); W. E. Aytoun, *Stories and Verses*, ed. W. L. Renwick (Edinburgh University Press, 1964).
10 Frykman, *W. E. Aytoun*, p. 44.
11 Philip Hobsbaum, 'A Guid Chepe Mercat of Languages: The Origins of English Teaching at Glasgow University', *College Courant* 71 (1983), 11; *Edinburgh University Calendar 1910–11*, p. 98.
12 *Edinburgh University Calendar 1859–60*, pp. 27–8.
13 *St Andrews University Calendar 1897–98*, p. 163.
14 J. Nichol and W. S. McCormick, *Questions and Exercises in English Composition* (London: Macmillan, 1893), p. 6.
15 John Nichol, *English Composition* (London: Macmillan, 1879), pp. 33–5.
16 *Glasgow University Calendar 1900–1*, p. 69.
17 John Nichol, *Inaugural Lecture to the Class of English Language and Literature in the University of Glasgow* (Glasgow: MacLehose, 1862); Hobsbaum, 'A Guid Chepe Mercat', p. 13.
18 *Glasgow University Calendar 1902–3*, p. 537.
19 *St Andrews University Calendar 1896–97*, pp. 311–12.

20 Frykman, *W. E. Aytoun*, p. 26.
21 On this and its consequences see George Davie, *The Crisis of the Democratic Intellect* (Edinburgh: Polygon, 1986), pp. 41–5.
22 David Masson, *The State of Learning in Scotland, A Lecture* (Edinburgh: Edmonston & Douglas, 1866), pp. 21 and 26.
23 G. Gregory Smith, *The Transition Period* (Edinburgh: Blackwood, 1900), p. [ii].
24 *A Catalogue of Books . . . including the Library of the late Prof. G. Gregory Smith* (London: Hodgson & Co., 1932), pp. 41 and 44 (a copy of this is in Queen's University Library, Belfast).
25 Unsigned obituary for Professor Gregory Smith, *The Times*, 5 March 1932. Unless otherwise indicated, information on Gregory Smith's life and career comes from the file of obituaries for him in Queen's University Library, Belfast. I am grateful to Michael Smallman and Christopher Bittenbender for supplying me with copies of this material.
26 'Death of Famous Scholar' (unsigned article), *Northern Whig*, 5 March 1932 (in Gregory Smith's obituary file, Queen's University Library).
27 J. H. Millar, *A Literary History of Scotland* (London: Unwin, 1903), p. viii; George Saintsbury, *The Memorial Volume: A New Collection of his Essays and Papers*, ed. A. M. Clark, A. Muir and J. W. Oliver (London: Methuen, 1945), pp. 212–13.
28 George Saintsbury quoted in 'A Scottish History Chair for Glasgow University' (unsigned article), *Scotia* 1 (1907), 239.
29 Hugh Walker, *Three Centuries of Scottish Literature*, 2 vols. (Glasgow: Maclehose, 1893), vol. I, p. viii.
30 'A Scottish History Chair for Glasgow University' (unsigned article), *Scotia* 1 (1907), 234–48.
31 T. F. Henderson, *Scottish Vernacular Literature*, 3rd edn (Edinburgh: Grant, 1910), p. ix.
32 Perilla and Juliet Kinchin, *Glasgow's Great Exhibitions* (Bicester: White Cockade, 1988), pp. 95–125.
33 Henderson, *Scottish Vernacular Literature*, p. ix.
34 G. Gregory Smith to Sir Donald MacAlister, 14 July 1912, University Correspondence, Glasgow University Archives.
35 Information about the title chosen by Smith is supplied by Ms Lesley Richmond of Glasgow University Archives in a personal communication to the present writer, 10 March 1995.
36 G. Gregory Smith, *Scottish Literature: Character and Influence (London: Macmillan, 1919)*; T. S. Eliot, 'Was There a Scottish Literature?', *Athenaeum* (No. 4657), 1 August 1919, pp. 680–1; see Robert Crawford, *Devolving English Literature* (Oxford: Clarendon Press, 1992), pp. 250–9.
37 Smith, *Scottish Literature*, p. 4.
38 Hugh MacDiarmid, *Selected Prose*, ed. A. Riach (Manchester: Carcanet, 1992); Kurt Wittig, *The Scottish Tradition in Literature* (Edinburgh: Oliver & Boyd, 1958); Karl Miller, *Doubles* (Oxford: Oxford University Press, 1987);

Christopher Bittenbender, 'Beyond the Antisyzygy: Bakhtin and Some Modern Scottish Writers', Ph. D thesis, St Andrews University 1996; Roderick Watson, 'Dialogics of "Voice" and "Place": Literature in Scots and English from 1700' in P. H. Scott, ed., *Scotland: A Concise Cultural History* (Edinburgh: Mainstream, 1993); Robert Crawford, *Identifying Poets: Self and Territory in Twentieth-Century Poetry* (Edinburgh University Press, 1993); Robert Crawford, 'Bakhtin and Scotlands', *Scotlands* 1 (1994), 45–55.

39 Smith, *Scottish Literature*, p. 33.

40 *Ibid.*, p. 35.

41 *Ibid.*, pp. 42–5, 58 and 61.

42 *Ibid*, p. 51.

43 Hugh MacDiarmid, *Contemporary Scottish Studies*, ed. Alan Riach (Manchester: Carcanet, 1995), p. 64.

44 MacDiarmid, *Selected Prose*, pp. 16–33; C. M. Grieve (i.e., Hugh MacDiarmid), 'Towards a Creative Scottish Criticism', *Scottish Educational Journal* (1925), 450–1, 485–6, 508–9.

45 A. D. Hope, 'Australian Literature and the Universities', *Meanjin*, 2 (1954), 165–9.

46 M. M. Bakhtin, *The Dialogic Imagination: Four Essays*, ed. Michael Holquist, trans. Caryl Emerson and Michael Holquist (Austin, Texas: University of Texas Press, 1981), p. 66.

47 D. Felicitas Corrigan, *Helen Waddell, A Biography* (London: Gollancz, 1990), pp. 112–13.

48 *Ibid.*, p. 134.

49 Helen Waddell and Maude Violet Clarke, *Discipline: A Collaboration*. A copy of the typescript is in Belfast in Queen's University Library Helen Waddell Collection (MS 18/21).

50 Davie, *The Democratic Intellect*, p. 352, note 4.

51 At St Andrews, e.g., the older class on 'Principles of Criticism' has become (Hegelian) 'Literary Theory' by 1911 (*St Andrews University Calendar 1911–12*, p. 294).

52 Robert Watson, *A Treatise on Rhetorick*, p. 1a, St Andrews University Muniments, MS PN173.W1.

53 Hobsbaum, 'A Guid Chepe Mercat', pp. 10–17.

54 This topic is further discussed by Douglas Dunn and the present writer in Robert Crawford, ed., *Launch-site for English Studies: Three Centuries of Literary Studies at the University of St Andrews* (St Andrews: Verse, 1997).

Index